GIL SCOTT-HERON

GIL SCOTT-HERON

Pieces of a Man

MARCUS BARAM

ST. MARTIN'S PRESS NEW YORK

www.stmartins.com

Designed by Steven Seighman

Library of Congress Cataloging-in-Publication Data

Baram, Marcus.
    Gil Scott-Heron : pieces of a man / Marcus Baram. —1st ed.
        p. cm.
    ISBN 978-1-250-01278-4 (hardcover)
    ISBN 978-1-250-01279-1 (e-book)
  1. Scott-Heron, Gil, 1949–2011.   2. Soul musicians—United States—
Biography.   3. African American musicians—Biography.   4. African American
poets—20th century—Biography.   5. Poets, American—20th century—
Biography.   I. Title.
    ML420.S433B37 2014
    782.421643092—dc23
    [B]

                                                                        2014026384

St. Martin's Press books may be purchased for educational, business, or promotional use. For information on bulk purchases, please contact Macmillan Corporate and Premium Sales Department at 1-800-221-7945, extension 5442, or write specialmarkets@macmillan.com.

First Edition: November 2014

10 9 8 7 6 5 4 3 2 1

To Liza and Roscoe

CONTENTS

Photo by Chuck Stewart

GIL SCOTT-HERON

INTRODUCTION

The crowd of four hundred people, squeezed in front of the stage, whispered in nervous anticipation. The Sounds of Brazil, a small nightclub in downtown Manhattan, is known for showcasing world music from salsa and samba to bhangra and bossa nova. But on this night, the audience wasn't there to dance or to indulge their eclectic tastes. On September 13, 2007, a clear and balmy night, they were there to await the return of a long-missing artist, a creative genius who had reemerged into the light after a dark journey.

And he was late. While the minutes ticked, rumors ricocheted around the space. "Man, I heard he nearly died up in there." "Maybe he did and we'll just get a ghost up onstage tonight." "If the ghost shows up—you know how Gil is." "Maybe he took the money they gave him and smoked it up." "I heard he's working on a new album." "No, for real? He's back? It's been so long. I've been dying to hear some new Gil."

Somebody shushed the crowd, voices broke off in mid-sentence, and people turned their heads to look down below stage right. There, a tall, dark figure in a dark cap moved through the crowd with an unmistakable presence—a jacket hanging on a skeleton, the figure barely shuffling along the floor but with a characteristically smooth stride. After mounting the steps, Gil Scott-Heron was handed a microphone and stepped to the front of the stage. He stood straight, though he leaned to his left. His sunken cheeks were framed by a scruffy white beard, and a few wisps of gray hair stuck out above his ears. He teetered on his feet and seemed on the verge of falling over but he kept standing. Eyes brightening, he opened his mouth in a gentle smile.

"Good evening." His distinctive baritone broke the silence. "Glad to be anywhere." Some members of the audience shouted, "We love you!" He bobbed back and forth, his shadow bouncing along behind him on the back wall of the club. "For those of you who bet that I wouldn't make it here tonight, you lose!"

The warm applause was more than just a greeting for a favorite son, whose annual pre–Martin Luther King Jr. Day concerts every January were eagerly anticipated by his fans. This was a special night because it marked Gil's first concert since his release from prison five months earlier in May. He was paroled after serving almost a year in prison for violating a plea deal on a drug possession charge.

Gil had been battling drug addiction for more than two decades, releasing only one album since 1982 and often canceling concerts at the last minute, so his fans realized this was a special moment. It wasn't just the usual miracle that he was onstage, competently tapping out the chords to "Home Is Where the Hatred Is" on his trusty Fender Rhodes. Amid frequent rumors of his demise due to a fatal illness or old age or an overdose, and widespread fears that he wouldn't survive prison in his frail condition, here he was again, singing lyrics that were haunting in their self-referential poignancy:

> You keep saying, kick it, quit it, kick it, quit it
> God, but did you ever try
> To turn your sick soul inside out
> So that the world, so that the world
> Can watch you die

The moment lingered, the power of that image on everyone's mind: a haunted soul baring his innermost pain and yearnings, almost like a ghost back from the dead to describe his death rattle to a rapt audience. But Gil wasn't playing along with the morbid mood. He smiled his crooked smile, winking at the audience and talking. Talking and jiving and rapping and joking and philosophizing like in the old days. He talked about an upcoming new album and a soon-to-be-released memoir, assuring his fans that the spirits were still guiding him and smiling on him. Sure, he was weaker and slower, but he was still Gil, the revolutionary prophet, griot, and stand-up comic who was always one step ahead of the rest of us.

With a touch of humor, Gil gently reminded the audience to take off Martin Luther King Jr. Day, describing the importance of the decade-long effort he helped lead to honor the civil rights icon. "My grandma used to always say, 'If you don't stand for something, you'll fall for anything.'" He took that lesson to heart, and it imbued his lyrics with a power and a sense of justice that few had matched over the last few decades. "Amen," shouted a woman standing by the stage, nodding her head and clapping her hands. With that, Gil was back, even if it was only for a little while.

I.

CAN'T GO HOME AGAIN

On April 1, 1949, a cold, drizzling day, at Chicago's Provident Hospital, one of the first black hospitals in the country, Gilbert Scott-Heron was born to Bobbie Scott and Gillie St. Elmo Heron. She was a librarian with a wicked wit and a creative yearning who grew up in the small town of Jackson, Tennessee. He was a professional soccer player with a charming smile and a competitive streak who was born in Jamaica.

Bobbie's story evokes the journey of many African Americans in the Deep South. She was born in Jackson, a sleepy river town in western Tennessee, to Lillie Hamilton Scott and Robert William Scott, the second of their four children.

Bobbie, tall and graceful, was quietly observant and studious, with a sharp wit. She went to Lane College—a black school created in Jackson in 1882 for former slaves—where she flexed her literary skills. Assistant editor in chief of the school yearbook, she took classes in anthropology, history, linguistics, and international studies and graduated with a 4.9 grade point average. At age twenty-one, like millions of southern blacks who moved up north to take well-paying jobs and to escape the racism of the South, Bobbie headed north. In Chicago she moved in with her aunt Annabelle McKissack, a seamstress, and Annabelle's husband, James, a chauffeur.

On a night in 1947, just a few months after she had moved to Chicago, Bobbie met Gillie St. Elmo Heron at the Windy City Bowling Lanes. Gillie cut a stylish figure, favoring the high-waisted pants popular at the time and dancing to big band hits like Louis Jordan's "Is You Is or Isn't You Ain't My Baby?" At six feet tall, with a copper complexion, brownish-red hair, and hazel eyes, he was quite a ladies' man in the clubs.

He was impressed with Bobbie's slim figure, her razor-sharp wit, and her nonchalance about what he did for a living. It's not clear if she recognized his name at that moment, but she soon learned about his fame as the first African American to play professional soccer in the United States.

Gillie's journey to Chicago was a different migration from Bobbie's. He was born in Jamaica to a well-known family that traced its roots back to Scotland. Heron's lineage had its share of drama and tragedy familiar to many Caribbean people of African descent. His great-great-grandfather Alexander Heron left Wigtownshire in Scotland in 1790 for Jamaica to get rich in the slave trade. Three years later, he had a little land and owned a few slaves. By 1797, he had bought six hundred more acres and many more slaves on numerous coffee plantations, including Shooter's Hill and Cane Valley. The Scots were notoriously brutal slave owners, and better at making money in the trade than the English. Even after slavery was outlawed on the island and across the British Empire in 1834, the Herons employed hundreds of former slaves in near-slavery conditions.

The Herons could live up to the worst stereotypes of decadent slave owners, capable both of importing opera singers from Europe for private performances and of brutalizing blacks in sadistic ways. Alexander Heron's son, Alexander Woodburn Heron, who was known as the Captain, had two sons who shot down thirsty black farmers in separate incidents during a severe drought in 1897. As biographer Leslie Gordon Goffe relates, Walter Vivian Heron shot a man in the face, and shot and "disabled for life" another for drinking from his cattle pond. At the Shooter's Hill plantation, Herbert Hugh Heron, Walter's brother, confronted some black farmers taking water in buckets from the pond, but he was chased away. He came back the next day with a shotgun and shot one of the men, says family historian Richard Mitchell. The shooting was so shocking and cruel that it reverberated around the small island. Even the plantation owner's newspaper, the *Gleaner*, expressed outrage at the incidents, opining that it was "a pity there are men living whose ears are deaf to the cries of their fellow men in distress."

The Captain's first-born son, Charles Gilbert Heron, was cast out because he was a bastard child of his father's dalliance with a fifteen-year-old seamstress. Charles found work as a shopkeeper and fathered seventeen children with six different women, including a black woman named Kate, who was Gillie's grandmother. She raised Gillie's father, Walter Gilbert Heron, on her own, since Charles had left for Panama, where he had many other children and eventually died of yellow fever.

Walter Gilbert Heron wasn't much of a father, either. He sired children by several different women though he was married and spending money on horse racing and drinking. "He was a failure," says Mitchell. "His father was probably one of the richest people on the island and he lived off of that legacy." Eventually, his wife Lucille took their kids, including twelve-year-old Gillie, and left Walter in 1939, heading for the States, where she had relatives living in Cleveland.

Even at an early age, Gillie stood out for his athleticism. While still in junior high school, he once out-sprinted Henry McKinley, who later won Jamaica's first gold medal at the 1948 Olympics, in the 400-meter dash. In addition to running track in high school in Cleveland, Gillie was a talented boxer, making it to the semifinals of the Golden Gloves middleweight competition. But it was soccer that brought him fame and trouble. When he was only nine, he scored twenty-two goals in a twelve-game season, and then in high school he scored twenty-seven to lead his team into the league championship. During the Second World War, he served with the Royal Canadian Air Force, but always found time for sports. While stationed in London, he wrote letters home eagerly describing how he taught athletics and managed to find time to play soccer and baseball.

When Gillie returned to the States, he went to Detroit and joined tens of thousands of other young men working in the automobile plants. He took a job with the Hudson Motor Company, making forty-five dollars a week as a stock selector in a factory. But every day, he watched the clock, eagerly anticipating the closing whistle, when he could rush out to the soccer field and play in an amateur league. In 1945, he scored forty-four goals for Venetia, a team in the Detroit District Soccer League, and started to attract attention. When John MacInness, the manager of the Detroit Wolverines, a professional team, spotted him playing, he was impressed, calling Gillie "smart, just like a cat." On June 7, 1946, a year before Jackie Robinson made history and broke the color barrier in baseball with the Brooklyn Dodgers, Gillie did it in professional soccer when he was signed by the Detroit Wolverines. And he soon delivered, scoring three goals in his first game, against the Chicago Vikings.

Armed with a giant smile, a great sense of humor, fast legs, and a stubborn determination, Gillie took the professional soccer world by storm. The sport, though overshadowed by baseball and football, was experiencing a renaissance in the 1940s and '50s, with teams sprouting across the country from Pittsburgh to Portland. And the North American Soccer League was eagerly snatching up talented players, despite the fact that the sport was not nearly as common in high school and college athletics as it later became. The intense competition led teams to take risks that would shake up the segregated world of professional sports.

On a team full of white players, Heron made his debut with the Wolverines at Chicago's Comiskey Park in the first soccer game played under electric lights, scoring twice and impressing the hometown fans. But though he performed well, he started encountering the deep racism that dogged him throughout his professional career. While the faces of white players graced billboards all over the city, the ads never featured Heron, who was the top scorer in the league, with sixteen goals. He was also paid less than every other white player on the team. By the end of the season, however, the team had declared bankruptcy, and Heron was sold to the Chicago Maroons in 1947.

In Chicago, the audience was bigger and the stage was more prominent, but he still wasn't in the top tier when it came to getting paid. He was paid only thirty dollars a game when he came to Chicago, just five dollars more than he'd made in Detroit. In contrast, the Maroons' star, Pete Matevich, one of the highest-paid players in the world, was earning one hundred dollars a game. But to Heron, it was a paycheck, and he was getting paid to do something he loved.

Just as Jackie Robinson was spiked by racist white players on opposing baseball teams, Gillie was often kicked and pushed and bullied by opposing players. Even in Chicago, the overwhelmingly white hometown crowd would sometimes jeer and taunt him, calling him "blackie" and "nigger." Unlike

Jackie Robinson, Heron didn't silently endure the punishment. He fought back and resisted every slight. In a game against Hansa, a German-American team, Gillie struck a halfback who had kicked him up and down the field for much of the game. He was ejected for brawling and suspended. Once, when officials ignored some opposing players' foul play, Gillie kicked the ball over a fence into Lake Michigan, notes biographer Goffe.

His feats on the field, slighted by the white press, were celebrated in African American newspapers and magazines, such as the *Amsterdam News* and the *Chicago Defender*. In July 1947, Gil was featured in an *Ebony* magazine profile. Called the "Babe Ruth of Soccer," Gillie struck a heroic pose, clutching a soccer ball in his right hand and looking sharp in a Detroit Wolverines jersey. Described as a "muscular, handsome 24-year-old," he was rated the top offensive player in the North American League. The *Ebony* writer breathlessly compared his sixteen goals in the previous season to hitting two home runs per game in eight consecutive games. In the coming season, the journalist wrote, Heron "will be watched by the fans much as baseball rooters keep an eye on home-run king Hank Greenberg."

Watching Gillie from the stands was Bobbie, his steady girlfriend by then, who glowed with pride but endlessly worried that he would be targeted by racist soccer fans. After games, she would look him in the eye and tell him to watch his temper, reminding him that black athletes in her hometown of Jackson were not allowed to play against whites. Gillie would smile, hold up his clenched fists, and tell her that she had nothing to worry about.

Bobbie became pregnant in the summer of 1948, and the couple married on August 20. She was twenty-two, and he was twenty-six. Though the trip was too long and expensive for her to attend the ceremony, Bobbie's mother, Lillie, gave her blessing to the union. But Gillie's mother, Lucille, was never happy with the relationship, upset that her caramel-skinned son had chosen a darker-skinned wife rather than marrying "out of color" (to a lighter-skinned or white wife), as some Jamaicans preferred.

Though the couple looks happy in some photographs during that period, they started bickering soon after moving in together. Gillie liked to go out late and party with friends. When he came home long after midnight, Bobbie would be waiting for him with a mouthful of sharp words, seething with anger. But Gillie didn't change his behavior. In fact, he expected her to be at home, cooking their meals and taking care of the baby while he lived the life he wanted. Their arguments grew more intense, and Gillie became violent on a few occasions, Bobbie would later tell their son. That was the last straw for Bobbie, and she started thinking about a life on her own.

Gillie's performance on the field was also suffering: he played poorly for Chicago Sparta, a team he joined in 1948 after playing for the Maroons, and he was not invited to participate in the U.S. Olympic soccer team trials. Though he scored the game-winner in his last match for the team on November 6, he was dropped by Sparta.

Out of work, off the front pages, and in a miserable marriage, Gillie was frustrated and ready for a change. He and Bobbie split up, though the circumstances have been much debated among family members. Gil (known as "Scotty") was raised to believe that his father abandoned the family, heading back to Detroit and leaving Bobbie alone with their baby. But some of the Herons have insisted that it was the opposite—unable to overcome their differences, Bobbie took Gil with her and left her husband. In his memoir, Gil sided with his mother but he painted a more flattering picture, claiming that his father left a year later, after he was offered a lucrative contract to play for one of the world's greatest soccer teams, the Scottish powerhouse Celtic. He did play for Celtic, but not before he had first moved back to Detroit, to the crowded Heron family home on Kenilworth Street. For two years, he played for the local amateur team, the Corinthians, with three of his brothers, Poley, Cecil, and Gerald, supplementing his income by working at the Hudson Motor Company painting cars for sixty dollars a week. It seemed that his life as a professional athlete was over, until he was given a second chance. When Chelsea toured the United States in 1951, one of the team's scouts heard about Gillie's exploits on the field, went to a Corinthians game, and was impressed with his performance. That summer, Gillie was invited to take part in a public tryout at Celtic Park in Glasgow, Scotland.

In July 1951, Gillie took a train to Montreal and departed aboard the SS *Columbia* for England with the third-class ticket that Celtic had sent him. Upon his arrival, he quickly realized how much bigger a stage he had stepped on, watching Celtic play Aberdeen before a crowd of one hundred thousand at Hampden Park. In his debut performance against Morton, Gillie won the game "almost singlehandedly," 2–0. He was quickly dubbed "Black Flash" and "Black Arrow" by fans and British sports reporters. Newspapers around the world, from the *Chicago Tribune* and the *New York Times* to papers in Canada and Australia, noted his debut. Black newspapers in the United States were bursting with pride, sometimes to the point of hyperbole—the *Amsterdam News* crowed that a million people had shown up to watch Gillie's debut when it was more like forty thousand. Gillie reveled in the attention, buying snazzy suits at the finest stores in Glasgow and posing for pictures in various trendy nightclubs.

Far from home, living the high life and playing on one of the top soccer teams in the world, Gillie wasn't ready to return to Detroit or to go back to his family. He didn't see his son again for almost twenty-five years.

2.

SCOTTY, WHY YOU RUN SO FAST?

Back in Chicago, it was a stressful time for Bobbie. A librarian surviving on a small salary, she could not afford child care for Scotty. After weeks of anguished conversations, it was decided that she would send Scotty to live with her mother, Lillie, until she got herself back on her feet.

So, on a frigid night in December 1950, when he was just a year and a half old, Scotty took the train from Chicago with his grandmother back to Jackson. Lillie, fifty, her long black hair always swept up in a hairnet and with a large mole near her lip, stood just over five feet tall but she blazed with self-confidence.

The daughter of a sharecropper, Lillie Hamilton had grown up poor in the rural cotton-growing area known as the Heart of Dixie, in northwestern Alabama, cheek by jowl with Tennessee and Mississippi. Lillie's grandmother had been a slave, and her daughter Ella, Lillie's mother, was probably the product of a rape at the hands of a white man. By 1900, Ella and her husband, James Hamilton, were working as sharecroppers outside Russellville and living in a log cabin, barely making ends meet. Ella's four children were eager to escape and make a better life for themselves. When she was still a teenager, Lillie took the bus north to Jackson. It was a segregated town, but the black neighborhood in southern Jackson was relatively self-sufficient, and it was possible to carve out a lower-middle-class life there.

In 1919, when Lillie was eighteen, she married Robert Scott, a tall, strong insurance broker who was well respected in the community, and they raised their family with a stern but loving touch, stressing the importance of education.

During the crash of 1929, Robert lost much of his money, went blind less than ten years later, and eventually became so mentally unstable that he had to be committed to a psychiatric hospital. He had died of syphilis just two years prior to Lillie's bringing Scotty back to Jackson on that train. Though fiercely independent, Lillie had been heartbroken by his death, and her grandson Scotty lifted her spirits.

When baby Scotty showed up in Jackson, a sleepy river town in western Tennessee, the community welcomed him as one of its own, "like the prince of the neighborhood, who knew everyone and was cared for by all." Surrounded by farms and graced with a folksy southern charm, the town and its people left an indelible impression on him. Amid the dogwoods and poplars, Scotty grew up a real country boy, walking barefoot in the unpaved streets, playing baseball with older boys and flirting with their sisters. He adored his grandmother Lillie, and later in life he considered Jackson the only home he ever really knew and loved. It was the place where he grew up, started writing, first heard music, learned to play piano, and realized the courage of his convictions. It was the town where it all began.

They lived in a two-story house with a little backyard on South Cumberland Street in South Jackson, the black part of town. The neighborhood was full of family, real and imagined, from aunts and uncles to multiple cousins and close friends. At dusk, Lillie would sit on the front porch and catch up on the latest gossip with Aunt Sissy and Cousin Lessie and Uncle Robert. The little boy, short and scrawny with a toothy smile, would play ball with neighborhood kids, run errands for Lillie, and sit through the services at Berean Baptist Church around the corner from the house. In the backyard, he and Lillie planted tomatoes, spring onions, and cabbages; roses and a pomegranate bush graced the front yard. It must have been so clear to him: a loving home, a close-knit community, good knockabout friends, lying on the front porch sipping Kool-Aid.

Once a bustling black neighborhood, South Jackson had seen most of its young adults join the Great Migration north to work in the factories or find other opportunities in Chicago, New York, and other urban areas. That left a "hole in the middle," as Gil later noted, a gap between the older and younger generations. As a result, the past was always present in the form of older neighbors and relatives during his childhood, and he was constantly being reminded of local history and his own proud heritage. Though his grandfather had passed away, his reputation loomed large. Wherever Scotty went in town, folks would call him "Bob Scott's boy" and nod their approval, recounting the time that "Steel Arm Bob" once bested Negro Leagues legend Satchel Paige, 1–0, in a baseball game played in Jackson in the 1920s.

Lillie, raising Scotty just as she had her own children, prepared him for the future, teaching him to read and count in the center room of her house and instilling in him a lifelong respect for education and knowledge. Every night, they would read the Bible together before he went to bed. On his fifth birthday, she walked him over to St. Joseph's Elementary School, the same Catholic school his mom had attended in the 1930s. The school, a dilapidated three-story brick edifice on Tanyard Street, intimidated him with its mystery and size, and he once recalled the school's "shadowy-cloaked hallways filled with an eternity of God-fearing intimidation for young Black kids like me imprisoned there." The religious rituals and Catholic order also turned him off—the kids were required to attend Mass every morning before classes and to study the catechism. "At morning mass, it was standing, sitting, kneeling, wheeling, dealing, silent, on prompts from occasional mumbling from the altar. Phooey!"

But he got a good enough education there to be able to skip a grade in public school after the St. Joseph's school building was condemned by the city. His new school, South Jackson, was the black elementary school in a strictly segregated town. Everything was separate in Jackson—there were black parks and white parks, a black Little League and a white Little League, and even separate county fairs, the first week for whites and the second week for blacks. This was all new to Scotty, and it was an eye-opener. His neighborhood was self-contained. "We lived our lives and they lived their lives. We had our own neighborhood grocery stores, black doctors and dentists, our own local college," remembers fellow student Portia Hegmon. But that community was nurturing in a way that distinguished it from the urban mayhem of cities up north. "We were all poor but nobody knew how poor they were because everybody was doing the same," said Gil. "I had no idea how poor I was until I had to compare myself to other people who took that seriously. Up here, up North, they took that much more seriously."

Scotty was keenly aware of the divide, but South Jackson was his home, and he lived like any overstimulated kid in any town in America in the 1950s. His massive baseball card collection and his knowledge of dirty jokes were the envy of his friends, he required a dozen stitches after a particularly fierce slide into third base in a sandlot game, and he loved to scarf down hamburgers and hot dogs at Savage's Grill. Scotty played football and basketball, playing most positions, but he never played his father's sport, soccer, which was practically unknown in Jackson. And he had a reputation for a mastery of marbles and jacks.

In the second grade at South Jackson Elementary School, he made his musical debut, singing "Jamaica Farewell," by Harry Belafonte, during a talent show, somehow fitting for the boy whose father had left the island to come to the States. During another talent show, he dressed up Calypso style and sang "Besame Mucho," to the surprise of his fellow students, who had never heard a black person speak Spanish. "He wasn't walking the beat or the path that the rest of us walked," says childhood friend John Odom. "But kids liked him." His sense of humor, good-natured spirit, and charisma made him popular with the other kids. "He could have talked his way out of anything he wanted," remembers Hegmon. "There were a few times he would get in trouble for something and he'd always get away with it."

Along with buddy Gillard Glover, Scotty loved to serenade girls in school. To impress the prettiest girl in class, Wanda, he flipped the chorus in Ritchie Valens's "Donna" to "Oh, Wanda." The singing was fun, but it wasn't the music as much as a tool for flirtation. He and three other friends formed their own little fraternity, called the Imperials. They donned blue blazers and gray slacks and had their own membership cards. Scotty wrote the group's hymn:

Imperials, we cherish thee, we'll always think of you tenderly
Imperials, Imperials, you're the one we love

Thoughts of you in our hearts will stay
We'll always salute the blue and the grey . . . Imperials . . .

Around that time, in one of those moments that single-handedly changes
the course of a life—and the recollection of which became a standard line
in almost any interview with Gil—Lillie got a piano for him. When the
funeral parlor next door closed and was throwing out furniture, she asked
the junkmen what they were going to do with an old upright piano. For six
dollars, they sold it to her and moved it into her home through a side door.
Thus began Gil's real music education. At that piano, Lillie taught eight-
year-old Gil a few simple chords and notes. Soon enough, she was writing
arrangements for gospel songs for him to play for her Thursday night sewing circle when the women came over and sat in the living room. At church,
he sneaked over to play the piano when he wasn't cracking jokes to other
kids in the choir: "Did you ever read the book *Africa*, by I Sure M. Black?"
The rest of the time, "he was a blur, running wherever he went in these
brown lace-up shoes," remembers friend Walter Pedro Newburn.

Later, he started taking piano lessons for twenty-five cents a week with
Anona Tyler, a prim and proper woman in her sixties. Tyler was a hoarder;
her house was full of neatly stacked newspapers and boxes, and dozens of
cats that would roam the halls while she gave her lessons. Gil and the other
kids would all sit outside on Tyler's porch until their turn came for their
half-hour lesson. While most of the kids hated taking lessons, Gil loved it,
remembers fellow piano student Portia Hegmon. "He was the only one who
was that good," she recalls. "He had an innate talent that we didn't have
and he would spend more time practicing because he wanted to."

Gil went home after his lessons and experimented with chords on that
old upright, trying out different rhythms and attempting to mimic some of
the blues songs he heard on the radio. On his grandmother's shortwave radio, she would play the uplifting hymns of gospel music. But every once in
a while, he sneaked a listen to WDIA, out of Memphis, to hear doo-wop, or
the latest rhythm and blues by the Orioles and the Ink Spots, or blues by
Jimmy Witherspoon and Lightnin' Hopkins. When his aunts and uncles
from Chicago or New York came through town, they would bring the new-

est records by Thelonious Monk and Miles Davis, further widening his exposure to music. Gil also developed a lifelong taste for popular culture, though he was one of the last kids in the neighborhood to watch TV. He made up for lost time, though, eagerly watching popular cartoons such as *Top Cat* and *Rocky and Bullwinkle*.

Gil was good in school; though his study habits were poor, he was an A student through the sixth grade. He was keenly aware of the family pressure to excel at his studies—his mother had been a superlative student through high school and college, and Lillie often talked to him about his aunt Gloria, who had graduated from college with honors and was teaching English overseas, sending postcards and gifts to the house on South Cumberland Street from Indonesia and Egypt. When neighbors commented on Gil's intelligence, Lillie would quip, "He may be smart alright but he can't tie his shoes."

It was a loving home, and Gil adored his grandmother. But he knew that something was missing in his life. Most of his friends, such as Odom, had a mother and a father, who would help their children with homework and cheer for them at baseball games. Gil just had Lillie. He never heard from his father, whose name was rarely mentioned by Lillie or her friends. And his mother was more like an aunt to him, occasionally stopping in Jackson for visits. In the middle of the night, Gil would wake up and feel alone. He wondered why his parents didn't want him. What had he done wrong? He never came up with an adequate answer, but that feeling of abandonment gnawed at him. And it made him even more grateful that he had Lillie. Though she could be tough, sometimes rapping his knuckles when he misbehaved, at least she was there for him.

One of the gifts Lillie gave him was a love of reading. Lying on the floor in Lillie's library full of books, he read Agatha Christie stories and his favorite Batman comic books, which he voraciously collected. "One of my clearest memories is walking into his room and thinking, 'Jesus Christ!' There were magazines, comic books, and books piled from the floor to the ceiling. It was like a maze," remembers Carenna Ransom, his cousin on his mother's side. Gil also liked to thumb through the *Chicago Defender*, one of many African American newspapers, which landed every week on Lillie's doorstep delivering news about the budding civil rights movement as it spread through the South in the 1950s. The *Defender* featured Langston Hughes's popular "Jesse B. Semple" series, stories about an Everyman living in Harlem who dispenses nuggets of commonsense wisdom. "I loved the Simple Stories [*sic*] because the least educated, least appreciated people came out on top," explained Gil.

Perhaps taking inspiration from Hughes and Christie, ten-year-old Gil started scribbling two- to three-page pulp detective stories full of murders and intricate plot twists in a special notebook that he lugged back and forth from South Jackson Elementary School. Odom says that Scotty had a special gift for writing fiction, complete stories with a sense of dramatic timing and complex protagonists. He also had a distinctive writing style when it came to putting pen to paper. "While writing, he held his pencil in an odd way, with the calloused knuckle of his right thumb down on the paper and the pencil being held between his fore and middle fingers." Years later, another physical oddity, his arched back, inspired the nickname Spiderman among friends.

The community in Jackson helped fuel and nurture his budding creativity. The new bookkeeper at Lane College, Albert Porter, and his wife had become friendly with the family, giving Gil and Lillie rides to church services and helping out with babysitting. Porter, who was educated and a bibliophile, lent the boy his Smith-Corona typewriter, on which Gil would tap out his stories, savoring the *ka-chunk* sound at the end of a line.

Over time, Porter became a father figure to Gil in many ways. He saw the boy struggling to make sense of the world around him and yearning to express himself in words. And the educated bookkeeper helped open Gil's eyes to injustice in the world, often talking to him about the budding civil rights movement and the brutality experienced by poor blacks in the Deep South. When Lillie wanted to see what was left of her family in Russellville, Alabama, Porter drove her and Gil in his own car. The experience was a rude awakening to the misery of life in America for many rural blacks. Her coal-mining brothers—Lynch had developed lung cancer and lost his mind, and Flynn ended up working in a graveyard for pocket change—were dead. And her remaining brother, Morgan, was eking out a meager existence as a sharecropper, just like his father and millions of other southern blacks for whom not much had really changed since the Emancipation Proclamation.

Lillie felt lucky to have escaped poverty and achieved a working-class life in Jackson, and she made sure that her grandson didn't take for granted the opportunities available to him. Gil was learning about black pride, too, hearing about prominent African Americans who overcame racism and adversity to excel. His grandmother told him stories about Marcus Garvey and W. E. B. Du Bois, civil rights pioneers who preached self-determination for the black community. One summer, Gil took the train to Chicago to stay with his mother, who was living in the middle-class Woodlawn neighborhood, where he was exposed to a growing black professional class.

While blacks up north were making more money and sometimes advancing to the top of their professions, down south things seemed to be regressing. Back on the front porch in Jackson, Gil remembers hearing graphic accounts of the brutality of the racist South. Lillie discussed with her friends the murder of Emmett Till, a fourteen-year-old boy killed for allegedly whistling at a white woman in Mississippi, and of Mack Parker, a truck driver lynched by a white mob after being accused of raping a white woman. With a stern face, gently shaking her head, Lillie would whisper, "God bless them."

Gil always expressed pride in Lillie's feisty reputation. When whites strode ahead of her in line at an uptown store, she would hold out her money and loudly proclaim, "I was here before them." Though blacks couldn't ask for credit in stores, she would insist on it, and she had no problem complaining about unequal treatment. Once, she approached the white ticket seller at the bus station in Corinth, Mississippi, and denounced the filthy condition of the black waiting room. In Jackson, she worked as a laundress out of her home, sometimes doing the police chief's clothes, and she doggedly pushed him to address the problem of segregation. "She was an issues woman, looking at things in terms of what's fair and not fair," said Gil.

3.

BROKEN AND THEN UNBROKEN

During the decade that Gil spent growing up in Jackson, the sleepy segregated town was going through its own transformation. The civil rights struggles bubbled under the surface, slowly simmering and spilling over into violence by the end of the 1950s. And the changes were constantly being observed and monitored, and sometimes encouraged, by Lillie and other relatives during their porch discussions, while Gil lay on the floor listening. In 1954, newly elected Tennessee governor Frank Clement vowed "never" to integrate the schools. Soon, civil rights activists started engaging in nonviolent protests and registering voters at the Highlander Folk School, in nearby Monteagle.

It was two steps forward and one step back for the civil rights movement for the rest of the decade. A year after racists dynamited an integrated school in Nashville, Martin Luther King Jr. sent one of his trusted aides, James Lawson, to the city to train college students and set up an affiliate of his Southern Christian Leadership Conference. The next front in the civil rights struggle was an epic feud in western Tennessee over voting rights that required the interference of the federal government. After an all-white jury in 1959 convicted a local black farmer of killing a sheriff's deputy when they raided his farm, blacks in Tennessee were motivated to register to vote so that they could serve on juries. But the counties of Fayette and

Haywood refused to let blacks vote in the Democratic primary in August 1959, and the federal government soon sued Fayette's Democratic Party Committee, the first lawsuit of its kind filed under the Civil Rights Act of 1957. The fact that Washington was enforcing the landmark act encouraged local activists in Tennessee, who had been waiting for just that type of signal to start taking to the streets and protesting segregation.

Nashville desegregated its public facilities on May 10, 1960, in the face of large demonstrations, but things didn't improve in Jackson, or in Fayette County as a whole. When white landowners threw black sharecroppers off their land and kicked them out of their homes because the blacks were trying to vote, the blacks were forced to live in tent cities with dirt floors on donated land. In Jackson, students at Bobbie's alma mater, the all-black women's college Lane, asked Albert Porter to help them organize demonstrations. In retaliation, a local white man pulled a gun on Porter and threatened his family. But Porter took up the task anyway, organizing the picketing of buses and sit-downs at the lunch counters at the stores Woolworth and McLellan, the first such protests in town. "We did it because we had to do it if we ever wanted to be treated with respect," says Porter.

The rallies didn't go over very well: whites poured hot coffee on the lunch counter demonstrators and cursed out young blacks picketing the buses. When Gil's neighborhood pal, twelve-year-old John Odom, walked downtown with a picket sign, he was called a nigger. But Odom remembers the self-sustaining skills of the black community in Jackson. "Segregation was oppressive, it was bothersome, it was a pall that hung over everything. It was an ever-present problem, but at the same time people had to live their lives on a daily basis. Within the confines of the black community, we were happy and had great friendships."

On October 13, 1960, six students at Lane were arrested for challenging segregated seating on buses. Soon, a white man was arrested for shooting a rifle into one of the dormitories at the school. The next month, the Jackson police jailed 144 blacks, many of them Lane students, who were marching in support of voting rights in the county, and blacks started boycotting downtown businesses. The quick chain of events in Jackson and around the county got results. Memphis began desegregating its schools, and black customers were allowed to eat at the lunch counter at the Greyhound bus terminal in Jackson. And when the newly elected president, John F. Kennedy, was asked at a nationally televised press conference about the tent cities in Fayette County, he stated his vigorous commitment to "making sure that every American is given the right to cast his vote without prejudice to his rights as a citizen."

Amid this escalating series of events, Gil and Lillie's life together remained relatively the same, until the morning of November 7, 1960. It was a Monday, and Gil had gotten up early to make breakfast, frying bacon and eggs in a skillet. Across the hall, he saw Lillie lying in her bed, but he kept quiet, wanting to let her sleep. But after he dropped the frying pan once and called out her name and she didn't budge, he knew something was wrong. When he touched her wrist, he found that "she was as cold as ice and so stiff with rigor mortis that I could barely lift her arm." Lillie had died in her sleep.

Hysterical, the twelve-year-old called a neighbor, whose son dropped the phone upon hearing Gil's screams of pain and confusion. "He was traumatized," remembers Porter. "I called his mother, and she was shocked. She knew her mother was ill but not that sick. Scotty stayed with us that night and we tried to make him feel at home."

Gil remembers the intensity and surrealism of the funeral on that cloudy morning: grown men bent in half, sobbing in front of his grandmother's casket. His aunt Gloria came back from Bangkok, along with Aunt Sam Ella and Uncle William from the Bronx. His mother, Bobbie, arrived from Puerto Rico, where she had taken a teaching job. It seemed as if half of South Jackson was at Berean Baptist that day, with Lillie's church friends giving remarks and singing in the choir and Porter helping carry her coffin.

The overpowering emotion of these adults shook Gil and scared him, and he feared that he would be blown away by a grief so powerful that he would never recover. So he shed no tears on that day, though his heart was broken.

Lillie's death left him "with a permanent psychological scar . . . I was essentially an orphan, maybe because I loved her so much or knew her so well." Her memory guided him throughout his life, through to the very last days.

Nearly every story or anecdote he told in interviews throughout his career related to Lillie. In addition to the memorable story about her buying the piano from the funeral parlor, he liked to say that she instilled in him his strong sense of justice and his social conscience. He long attributed his activism to the lessons he learned from his grandmother. He later wrote a poem, "On Coming from a Broken Home," which poignantly captures his feelings about her and his childhood in Jackson.

Lillie always made him feel loved, even as his temporary stay with her became permanent, raising him like one of her own children. Her presence verged on the supernatural to young Gil, who wrote that she "raised everyone she touched just a little bit higher and all around her there was a natural sense, as though she sensed what the stars say and what the birds say."

Broken and then unbroken. Lillie's death changed everything. Soon, Bobbie Scott became Gil's mother again, after years of being the distant aunt in his worldview. Together again "like cymbals in some ill-coordinated band's changing climax," wrote Gil. So, mother (who moved into Lillie's house in Jackson) and son lived together for the first time in their lives. And if it felt strange for Gil, it must have felt a little too familiar for Bobbie. Here she was, back in her now-empty childhood home in her segregated hometown, the place she had escaped from years earlier to go up north and pursue her dreams. She was back on South Cumberland Street, looking at the old familiar photos hanging on the wall, the drapery her mother used to hang in the windows, the old familiar squeaks and cracks as she walked up the stairs. She took over the front bedroom and brought in some new furniture, china, and silverware, but the house felt quiet without Lillie.

It was just the two of them, and Bobbie was getting to know Gil, learning how to love her son after all these years. She needed to trust him and to gain his trust after such a long absence. "The best way to do that, she decided, was to let me see that she was honest. No hype and no hurry," he wrote. As time passed, he saw that her love was unconditional and their bond was unshakeable. So much closer in age to him than to Lillie, she bonded with Gil over their mutual sense of humor and she shared with him her knowledge of contemporary music and literature. They developed their own vocabulary with a little Spanish, a little slang, and plenty of inside jokes.

While Gil's life was being upended, Jackson was going through its own changes, and the civil rights struggle was about to come close to home. By late 1961, a new junior high school called Tigrett opened in Jackson, and there was talk of desegregation. A petition went through Gil's elementary school asking which students would like to attend a white school. Gil signed up, though he assumed that the petition was being circulated only to comply with federal law. Though it was rejected by the Jackson school system superintendent, the black families all appealed the decision with the support of some prominent civil rights lawyers, including Avon Nyanza Williams, a cousin of Thurgood Marshall, the first black justice on the U.S. Supreme Court. Over the next two months, the debate was the talk of South Jackson and South Cumberland Street. For blacks who had witnessed a violent backlash to the civil rights struggle, there were risks to supporting integration—one of Gil's classmates, Madeleine Walker, saw her father, Frank, get fired from his job as a drapery installer at Holland's department store because he didn't back down from wanting his daughter to attend the all-white school.

On January 24, 1962, Gil's mother came into his bedroom and spoke to him in a deep voice while she twirled a pen through her hair, a clear sign to him that something serious was afoot. She told him that the NAACP had won and asked him if he wanted to go to Tigrett. If he did, he would have to start the next day. Though about forty students initially signed the petition, only two, including his buddy Glover and Madeleine Walker, decided to go through with it. Scotty could tell from the tone of her voice that his mother was upset that so many other kids had backed out. Looking up at her, he knew that this was one of those moments when courage mattered. The twelve-year-old boy decided to go.

So, on the morning of January 25, 1962, he got up early and put on a beige sweater, his best pants and shoes, and a topcoat with a fur collar. Bobbie dressed up with a double set of large pearls, a black bell coat, and black high heels. The stylish pair, along with Gillard Glover and Madeleine Walker and their parents, arrived at Tigrett with a police escort just after the school opened and walked up the steps to join 661 white students in their classes. The white students had not been informed of their new black classmates until it was announced on the intercom during homeroom. The event made the front page of the *Jackson Sun*, in an article headlined "Tigrett School Enrolls Three Negro Students." That spring, it was featured in *Crisis*, the NAACP's official magazine, which posed the three students standing behind their parents seated on a sofa. Gil, beaming from ear to ear, sporting a white bowtie, leans over his debonair mother with her cat's-eye glasses.

Though the transition into the school was relatively smooth—there were no angry mobs spitting in their faces—the new students got an unfriendly reception. "I didn't know that the reaction would be as cold as it was," says Glover. The three went through several months of isolation, with only a few white students talking to them. Gil also soon discovered how different it really was in white Jackson. While the books at Tigrett were the same as those at South Jackson, the studies were from a different perspective. When they got to learning about the Civil War in American history class, Gil remembers that it was like reviewing it "from the loser's locker room. I don't know how many classes I'd had about the Civil War up to that point, but none of them had ever been from a point of sympathy with the South. Okay, so now the South was the home team."

Gil made history by going to Tigrett, but he didn't stay long. His childhood home was about to disappear forever—literally. A new interstate highway was being built that would cut right through the heart of South Jackson, including Cumberland Street, and residents were warned to move. Bobbie had known about the highway for months and had already made plans to move them to New York, where Uncle William had already arranged a three-bedroom apartment in the Bronx for them to share with him.

One of the professors at Lane College, where Bobbie worked as a secretary in the health and physical education department, and his wife threw a going-away party for Bobbie and Gil at their house. Many of their friends in Jackson, from the college and Berean Baptist, packed their home. When someone asked Gil where they were going, the teenager quipped, "We are going to the Bronx, to the Bronx Zoo."

The night before their departure in July 1962, Gil went around the neighborhood saying good-bye to his friends and coming to terms with his loss. This community was all he knew—Jackson had shaped his emotions and the way he made sense of the world. "They were my sight, my hearing, my senses of taste and touch and smell, all together."

4.

SOUNDS OF THE CITY

The Bronx couldn't have been more different than sleepy, leafy Jackson. The apartment was located on a noisy, traffic-filled cul-de-sac near the Major Deegan Expressway, and the rumble of the subway reverberated under Gil's feet as he walked the streets. And everyone was in such a hurry, the sidewalks full of busy people on the move, even other kids rushing to school. It really was an asphalt jungle, and Gil remembers feeling how disquieting it was to move to a place where there was no grass, open spaces, or fresh air.

It was lonely in the beginning for Gil, who was used to running outside onto the porch and yelling for his friends to come play ball with him. When he first got to Hampden Place, he wandered all the way down to the dead end without seeing any other kids, and he was miserable. He spent much of his time in his room, writing short stories and essays and identifying with his new favorite team, the loveable losers, the hapless New York Mets. Gil also missed the music of Jackson: neighbors strumming guitars on their porches, the choir singing hymns in church, the R&B oozing out of his transistor radio. When he first got to New York, he learned that life in the city sometimes provided its own soundtrack. "I couldn't find any black music," he reminisced a decade later. "I thought maybe I needed a longer [antenna on my] radio. So I went out in the street and ran into one of the brothers on the avenue. And I said, "Where can I find the blues?" He said, 'Well, hey, you don't have to do anything. Just stand there.'"

Years later, he wrote a poem about the hopes and dashed dreams of southern blacks coming up north. "I would like to say, 'Brother, Come home!' and in the great north but southern Black might be slain inside by the freezing fury of winter or the slanted inquiries of his neighbor's eyes. But we have and ever shall survive as we search for morning." Eventually, the lonely teenager met some local kids, who introduced him to "the Deegan," where he played stickball and softball and hit a double in his first neighborhood game, though they made fun of his southern accent: "They would all mock my drawl, but knew I could play ball. It shows how much I need to compete." Desperate to shed his country roots, he started going by his real first name.

When Gil enrolled at Creston, the local junior high school, he knew the school's reputation: he'd heard stories of older students mugging and beating younger ones, but most of them turned out to be just myths. His aunt Sammy initially signed him up for a vocational program that was essentially a shop class for electrical and metalwork. "That was for kids who were slow and with learning disabilities," says Tony Duncanson, who along with Bilal Sunni-Ali also attended the school and later played music with Gil. "Bilal and I were in the music classes and we were having a good time and we were rowdy. . . . But Gil was stuck in that shop class. He hated that class—in some of his concert routines, he talked about how much he hated it."

That all changed when his first report card came back and Bobbie noticed the courses he was taking. Already suspicious about the fact that he never had homework, she took action. The next day, Gil was called to the office of the vice principal, who said, "Your mother is a very impressive lady" and that she had told him that remedial classes for Gil were "nonsense" and "her worst nightmare." While the vice principal spoke to Gil, slightly mocking his mother's strong opinions, Gil muttered under his breath and looked him right in the eye, trying to catch his gaze. In the end, Gil was moved to the 9-2, more advanced classes that had a focus on music. Though he still didn't consider himself a musician, his budding talent on the school piano was noticed. Later that year, he was tapped by the music teacher to play the lead role of the high executioner, Ko-Ko, in Gilbert and Sullivan's *The Mikado*.

At home, financial pressures were mounting: Uncle William soon moved out, and Bobbie was having a hard time paying the rent on the three-bedroom apartment. To help out, Gil took a job washing dishes at Jackson's Steak and Lobster House, delivered groceries to elderly neighbors, and picked up the night editions of the newspapers on his bike for the corner candy store on Fordham Road and Sedgwick Avenue.

Though he was too young to work the 8:00 P.M.–1:00 A.M. shift at Jackson's, he smeared his mother's eye shadow on his upper lip to give himself a fake mustache to convince the owner that he was old enough. He regretted that it took him away from writing his five-page detective stories, but the experience provided him plenty of creative fodder. Almost fifty years later, in his memoir, he had some fun describing how hot it was working the dishwasher in the kitchen: "Like a combination microwave oven and a dame with big tits on Spanish Fly rubbing up against you."

After being "somebody" in Jackson, he had worried about being "swallowed alive" by the city and feeling a constant struggle "against becoming *nobody*." That was what happened at his new high school, DeWitt Clinton, an eight-thousand-student behemoth that was so crowded with adolescent boys that classes were scheduled in three shifts. Though the school had an impressive legacy as the alma mater of artist and writer Romare Bearden, boxer Sugar Ray Robinson, and jazz pianist Bud Powell, it was nicknamed "Dumb Wit" due to its poor graduation rate and low test scores. And Gil soon started struggling in class, complaining about the teachers, and disappointing his mother.

He made an indelible impression on one teacher while at DeWitt, the diminutive Nettie Leef, a young native New Yorker who had an appreciation for great literature, opera, and classical music. She was committed to teaching the beauty of the arts and literature to young students. This wasn't easy at DeWitt, where most of the students didn't pay attention, ignored the books she assigned, and slogged their way through writing assignments. Gil was bored, too, with her class and annoyed at the assignments that didn't reflect his own experience. One day in class, he ripped her latest assignment, John Knowles's *A Separate Peace*, as "white noise about white people."

When Leef challenged him to bring in his own writing, Gil was ready.

He gave her some of his detective stories and essays, and she was impressed. "What struck her about his writing was that he stood out—and she thought he was immensely talented," remembers her sister, Ellen.

Leef thought that Gil deserved better than DeWitt and said she could help him get into Fieldston, a prestigious private school in the upper-class Riverdale section of the Bronx. Gil was skeptical, but he agreed to meet one of the Fieldston teachers and Leef at a Howard Johnson's on Fordham Road, where he demolished a cheeseburger and a strawberry sundae as he answered what he considered condescending questions about his ability to adjust to such a different environment. Ever the smart aleck, Gil gave sarcastic replies and thought about asking the teacher, Professor William Heller, if it was true that there weren't any black people in Riverdale.

Still, Gil realized that this was a rare opportunity, one that offered him the chance to escape the overcrowded classes at DeWitt Clinton. He agreed to take an entrance exam, but while he completed the three-hour English section, he left a third of the way through the math portion, failing that section of the test. He assumed he couldn't compete against upper-class students from wealthy families attending prestigious schools "unless a bomb was dropped on Wall Street."

Two weeks later, Heller called up Gil to inform him of his "disappointing results" on the exam, but he said he would give him another chance if he was really interested in the opportunity. He invited Gil to come meet the admissions committee. The appointed morning began disastrously: When he woke up, his mother was having a diabetic episode, the first of many she suffered for the rest of her life, and a doctor was hurrying up the stairs to give her an insulin shot. Gil almost missed his bus to the train to Riverdale, where he rushed to the campus to a well-appointed room facing a half-circle of stern committee members.

He sat and answered their questions, all the while feeling like a "bug under a microscope," being pushed and prodded by a group of people who seemed to be playing roles in a surreal play. And in one of those moments of moral clarity, he realized he needed to push back—maybe inspired by his grandmother's stubborn demand to get served in a segregation-era department store or his mother's refusal to accept unequal opportunities. As ever, his mouth almost got the better of him. One of the committee members asked, "How would you feel if you saw one of your classmates go by in a limousine while you were walking up the hill from the subway?" Gil quipped, "Same way as you. Y'all can't afford limousines. How do you feel?"

When the committee took a break, Gil rushed to a phone to call up his uncle, who gave him the grim news: Gil's mom was in a diabetic coma; he needed to go see her right away. Gil walked back in the room and calmly told the admissions committee members that he needed to be by his mother's side, and he thanked Heller for his efforts. When Gil arrived at the hospital, what he witnessed was frightening to him: his mother, her skin ashen, was lying on a gurney with tubes sticking out of her, and she was hooked up to an assisted-breathing machine. She improved and came home a few days later, but her medical condition forced Gil to take on more responsibility than just doing odd jobs to help pay the rent. His job became restocking the kitchen every week and being more careful to attend to his mother's medical needs.

She soon recovered, but was left in a much-diminished state as a full-fledged diabetic, a condition she endured for the rest of her life. She went back to work, this time taking a desk job for the New York Housing Authority at the Amsterdam Houses. It was tougher to make the payments on the three-bedroom apartment at Hampden Place, and so by September 1964, they had moved into a two-bedroom in the Robert Fulton Houses, a huge housing project on West Seventeenth Street, between Ninth and Tenth Avenues. Gil had a small bedroom, and there was an upright piano in the living room, on which he would practice his blues riffs and mimic some of the pop tunes he heard on the radio, such as Smokey Robinson and the Miracles' "Ooo Baby Baby."

The new environment was stimulating to Gil. Known as Little San Juan for its large Puerto Rican population, the neighborhood was full of families, energy, and music—music everywhere. Jose Feliciano was strumming "Mack the Knife" for quarters in front of a pizzeria on the corner of Eighteenth Street and Ninth Avenue, Richie Havens was crooning in coffee shops down in the Village, and the Latin sounds of Joe Bataan and Eddie Palmieri echoed off the pavement. It was an era of creative freedom in music, and old rules were being discarded—instead of courting the big record labels and playing at established venues, young artists were taking their music to the streets.

Just living in the neighborhood, Gil was exposed to the turmoil and energy of the 1960s. Across the hall from their new apartment lived a quadriplegic Vietnam veteran who used to talk to Gil and his friends about the war and politics for hours. He had a capuchin monkey that would fetch beers out of the fridge for him and his guests. Bodegas on the corner were selling marijuana blunts for a dollar, and shots of tequila. And local Puerto Rican gangs got into turf battles that often resulted in stabbings and shootings, when they weren't being chased or beaten by overly aggressive New York City cops.

It was far away from Jackson, and Gil was a lot different from the Scotty who played baseball and crooned calypso tunes to the girls. That was evident when he and his mother returned there to pay a visit in 1963. He was excited about going home, "anxious to walk on my streets and breathe my air" and to catch up with his friends. He felt nostalgic—Gillard Glover was the "king of the hallways" at the school they'd helped integrate, the girls were "pretty and soft," and students were singing the latest hits. Gil stopped by to visit his old friend Walter Pedro Newburn, who had an upright piano in his house. "He's playing this stuff—upbeat pop like the Beatles—and it was terrible. I thought he'd never make it with that kind of music." Near the end of his visit, Gil had a revelation: the kids in Jackson were the same, and nothing in town was likely to change much in the next twenty years. But he was now in New York, where life was tough but anything was possible and things changed from day to day. New York was now his home.

In the fall of 1965, he started attending his new school, Fieldston. Over two hundred and thirty blocks uptown, the campus felt like a royal palace, with stone buildings, nicely trimmed lawns, new classrooms and gymnasiums, and even an art studio with a skylight. Gil was one of only five black students in a class of three hundred, which definitely made him feel guarded. It was the mid-sixties, and the campus, which had a strong liberal Jewish progressive tradition, was very active with antiwar politics and heady revolutionary talk. It was an environment that welcomed open discussion and debate on the issues, but Gil often censored his growing feelings about the injustice of American capitalism and the country's endemic racism, for fear of jeopardizing his lucrative scholarship and upsetting his mother. But back in Chelsea, he was more outspoken, talking about the war and the civil rights movement with friends and neighbors, and poring through leftist magazines and political books in his bedroom.

Just as Gil had adjusted to New York, blending into starkly different neighborhoods in the Bronx and Chelsea and adapting to different circumstances at home, so he played the chameleon at Fieldston. He was immediately popular—an athlete on almost every team, involved in almost every single assembly or school play—and he had a great sense of humor. "The brooding dark qualities that later emerged as an artist and that informed his personal demons were nowhere in evidence. He was clowning around, he seemed to be part of the in crowd," says classmate Danny Goldberg.

Skinny and gangly and almost six feet tall, with hair cut very close to his scalp, Gil seemed a little older and more experienced than some of the pimple-faced boys at Fieldston. He was the starting forward on the basketball team for two years, playing a kind of street ball that the prep school boys weren't used to. The team, which had a poor record, played against most of New York's other prep schools, sparking some rumors that Gil once played against Jim Carroll, the poet whose infamous *Basketball Diaries* detailed the life of a basketball-playing teenager who shot heroin. Carroll attended Trinity, which played Fieldston several times, but there is no evidence that the two poets played against each other in high school.

Many of Gil's close friends at Fieldston, most of them white, have great memories of their time with him in school, and Gil cherished their friendship, but his experience was not always as happy. In his memoir, he writes that many students and faculty members just did not like him, and that they let him know that. Though he writes that he can't accuse them of being racist, he claims that other students weren't interested in hanging out with him because he was the new kid and they'd known each other for years. There were students and faculty at Fieldston who didn't want someone like him invading their cloistered community and who were "quietly seething" at his presence at the school, remembers Fred Baron, a former classmate.

Sometimes the naïve idealism of Fieldston's liberal students annoyed him. In an ethics class, one student started talking about how being poor made you one of the people, and Gil cut him off, snapping, "Listen, man, I've been poor and I want to be rich. I want to do what I want when I want, and you can be poor." Goldberg, who went on to become a music mogul, managing the careers of Kurt Cobain and the Allman Brothers, remembers first noticing Gil's talent early in their freshman English class over an assignment. "Everybody came in with two-page superficial essays, and then this guy reads this forty-page portrait of his life in Tennessee, and it was like literature: insanely sophisticated for a high school student, the sophistication of the dialogue and the richness of detail; it was like being on a high school basketball team with LeBron James."

But Gil was very cautious about not standing out on the monoracial campus—and that applied to his budding love life. He was flirtatious with one of the only black girls in school, but he hesitated when it came to dating white girls, says Baron. "I saw him in the cafeteria one time talking to this beautiful redhead, and you could tell they were really into each other, and I asked him, 'Why don't you ask her out?' and I could tell that he didn't feel comfortable doing that."

In addition, unmentioned in his memoir, is his first band. At Fieldston, Gil, Goldberg, Baron, and some other pals formed a rock group called the Warlords. "He was in class with us, and we were playing and sitting on the grass in the back quadrangle and singing, and he came over and started singing with us," says Ira Resnick, who sang lead. Baron played rhythm guitar, Bill Horwitz played lead guitar, David Appleby played drums, and Gil sang and played piano. Gil taught piano to Baron, who taught him how to play guitar. "We did a combination of Gil's songs—great songs, complete tunes with lyrics and melodies and rhythm—and covers of Beatles, Stones, and Kinks songs," remembers Baron.

Gil's writing, which he kept in a ring binder he often carried around, were love songs, one of which, "Sandy," was about a part-time love affair. "Writing songs came very easy to him—they were very personal, simple in a way, almost like a Motown song and kind of bluesy," says Ira Resnick. Gil's big show-stoppers were "Go Now" and "Wooly Bully," by Sam the Sham and the Pharaohs, with him doing splits onstage.

In a moment of marketing savvy that presaged his later talent for turning polemical songs into chart toppers, Gil came up with the band's name, the Warlords, taking it from one of the biggest gangs in the Bronx, since the gang had tagged its name on practically every vertical surface in the city, lending the band easy publicity. The group, which played on campus and at other local schools and got gigs at weddings and bar mitzvahs, was once confronted about the name by its namesake. Before a gig at Manhattan College, one of the gang leaders came up and demanded to know why they called themselves the Warlords: "What the fuck is this?" When Baron and Gil explained that it was easy marketing, since the gang's name was scrawled all over the city, the gang members laughed, seeming to appreciate the logic. They stayed for the gig and came to other shows, even inviting the band to play a street party for them, but that never panned out. Once, when the group was playing Jerry and the Americans' "Lock the Door (and Throw Away the Key)" at Manhattan College, a Catholic school, some gang members kept shouting out the dirty parts of the song, and the pastor supervising the concert quickly shut down the show.

The group's energy and pop sense impressed a Fieldston administrator whose wife worked at MGM and suggested that they audition for her at the couple's Central Park West home. So the band took the train down to the elegant apartment, where they played a few songs, and the administrator's wife was impressed. "You have a great sound," she said, encouraging them to sign a record deal with one of MGM's labels and hit the road to perform their songs. But she cautioned that they would have to get tutors, since they were still in high school.

The guys were excited and ran home to tell their parents—who all rejected the idea. When the boys met up for school the next day with long faces, Gil said he had an idea. "He pulled out this matchbook that had an ad inside for getting your GED in the mail," remembers Baron. "So we all did it, got our degrees in the mail and then went back to our parents." It didn't work the second time, either, and Baron's dad scolded him, saying that a Fieldston education was about more than just the degree.

With that dream gone, Gil continued playing, sang with another Fieldston band (called A Stitch in Time), and participated in many school activities. Students still remember when he sang Bob Dylan's "Like a Rolling Stone" at a school assembly, accompanied by only Horwitz on acoustic guitar, his calm, assured voice feeling its way through the lyrics. The *Fieldston*

News ran a photo of him wearing a cowboy hat at an assembly dedicated to "Cowboys and Their Songs," where he and others sang in harmony classics such as "Home on the Range." After the assembly, he and his friends pulled out skinny little marijuana joints and got stoned in the shadows of the campus quad.

Gil and Fred Baron formed a lifelong friendship, forged through the band, the football team, and proximity to each other. Fred lived in Peter Cooper Village, directly east of Gil's apartment in Chelsea. One or two nights a week, Gil stayed over at Fred's house and grew close to his father, Jerry Baron. After Fred went to bed, Gil and Jerry would stay up arguing about politics until late at night. Gil was a voracious reader, devouring everything from the Bible to Marx, and he believed in socialism. Jerry was a conservative libertarian who gave Gil copies of Ayn Rand's *The Fountainhead* and *Atlas Shrugged*. They would debate the issues of the day from the War on Poverty to Vietnam, neither changing the other's mind, but each becoming very close and respecting the other's views.

At school, Gil kept his personal politics close to his chest. Though the campus was liberal and students often talked about Vietnam and civil rights, Gil didn't really contribute. In November 1965, Goldberg and some other students organized a trip to join the March on Washington against the war in Vietnam, each student putting in five or ten dollars to pay for the expense. Gil didn't join the trip, though he had voiced anti–Vietnam War sentiment. "The politics formed in high school informed him for the rest of his life, but he had more to lose than I did, so was more careful and more private about it," remembers Goldberg.

Not that he wouldn't stand up against injustice or racism. Once, a white student used the word *nigger*, and Gil got right up in their face. "I can use that word but *you* can never use that word. That's insulting, and I won't have it." One time, on the subway, a bunch of rough-looking bikers was accosting some girls, and Gil went over and quietly told them, "Fellows, that's too far. Back up and stop it." When they mocked him, he pointed out his football teammates across the car and said, "You can either have a beautiful night, have fun tonight, and watch *Kojak*, or you'll be in jail getting fucked in the ass. So you choose." The bikers backed down. When Baron later told Gil, "You know that was stupid, right?" Gil replied, "Ah, fuck 'em!"

Bobbie *was* strict, and insisted on Gil being home at a certain time, determined to keep him away from the streets. Of course, like a typical teenager, he knew how to get around her rules. His twin cousins on his mother's side, Carenna and Carol Ransom, who lived in Brooklyn, would pick him up at the apartment in Chelsea, providing a convenient alibi while Gil went out on his own to house parties thrown in the neighborhood, where he'd drink beers and smoke joints. When he *was* at home, Bobbie often reminded him about his obligation to excel, and the extra pressure to make his family and his race proud. Gil needed some incentive, because his grades were poor; he was getting a C-plus in sociology and English, and teachers criticized his lack of discipline. His history teacher, Earl Clemens, one of the few black members of the faculty, said that Gil was more interested in making jokes and amusing his white classmates. "Gil is tremendously popular with his classmates. But no amount of popularity can, for me, compensate for his not working up to capacity more often."

Ever since he'd first started learning chords on his grandmother's upright, Gil had always been on the lookout for a great piano to play. At Fieldston, the temptation was overpowering. In a room adjoining the school auditorium sat a Steinway grand, probably the most beautiful piano he'd ever seen in his life. And it happened to be one of Fieldston's three pianos that were off-limits to students, a rule vigilantly followed by the imperious music teacher, Ari Worthman, who reminded Gil of a *Spider-Man* villain, with his hooked beak, pale skin, and horseshoe of white hair on a bald scalp.

Once, Gil was enthusiastically stomping out a Temptations song, attracting other students, who danced and sang in the room, when Worthman kicked them out. After that, for months he sneaked in to play quietly, without attracting attention, until he was busted by the teacher, who landed in the room as if he'd leapt in by "parachute," recalled Gil. When a letter announcing Gil's appearance before Fieldston's disciplinary committee arrived at the apartment, Bobbie assumed the worst, not believing that he was in trouble for playing the piano. "Did you hit someone—like the music teacher?"

When she arrived for the meeting, Bobbie gave a command performance, breathlessly narrated in detail by Gil in his memoir. "Expel him," she told the committee, adding later, "if you believe playing the piano is high on your list of offenses, expel him." And then she excused herself to go to work, leaving the committee members to think about their arbitrary rules, and Gil stunned and proud.

To help his mom pay bills and to save up for college tuition, he worked at the A&P supermarket on Eighth Avenue three nights a week, gigged as a keyboard player with some R&B bands for twenty-five dollars a night, and took a job as a seasonal worker at the New York Housing Authority, which involved being a referee for basketball games in the St. Nicholas Houses in Harlem and the Dyckman Houses on the Upper West Side. That summer, Gil met and played ball with Lew Alcindor (who later changed his name to Kareem Abdul-Jabbar), who lived in the Dyckman Houses and was two years older than Gil. Though Gil had a decent jump shot, he was routinely blocked by Alcindor during games at a court in a park uptown from the George Washington Bridge. "Same way anybody else would have done," quipped Gil.

Back in Fieldston's good graces, Gil continued to write stories and essays in his notebook as often as possible. In thrall to Langston Hughes, whose Jesse B. Semple columns he'd devoured as a boy in Jackson, he was impressed with Hughes's ability to get across a message with a dose of humor and by Hughes's mastery of so many art forms, from poetry and essays to music. "He was one of the frontrunners in capturing the ways in which black people talk and express themselves."

In his senior year, Gil wrote his thesis on Hughes and decided to interview him, finally to meet one of his heroes. The seventeen-year-old student took a tape recorder and hopped on a downtown train to meet the sixty-four-year-old writer, who was giving a speech. Hughes, whose style was considered a little quaint and dated against the midcentury literary changes, was in the sunset of his career, toiling at the *Amsterdam News* and writing a column for the *New York Post*, which was then edited by liberal scion Dorothy Schiff.

"He was very gracious and humble," remembered Gil years later in an interview with Tom Murphy. "We talked about his work and how he had come to master so many art forms. That, also, was very influential because I like to write many different things myself: poetry as well as longer pieces and music. He'd done the same. He wrote songs, he wrote that weekly column and I used to read his work in the *Chicago Defender* when I was a boy in Tennessee. It was nice to come across him still working and still just as powerful and as humorous as he was in print."

5.

UNLEASHED

When Gil met Langston Hughes, he was debating whether to attend the writer's alma mater, Lincoln University. He consistently cited the fact that Hughes sparked his desire to attend the prestigious black college founded by the Quakers in 1854. Other famous Lincoln alumni whom he admired were Thurgood Marshall; Oscar Brown Jr.; Larry Neal; Kwame Nkrumah, the first president of Ghana; and Nnamdi Azikiwe, the first president of Nigeria. But Gil was still on the fence for much of his senior year while other students were already lining up their applications to their favored colleges. Due to his indecision and some discipline problems in the classroom, he was ordered to see Fieldston's minister, the few African Americans on campus, for his nonjudgmental, calm demeanor. When they met in Nichols's church in Harlem one afternoon, Gil mentioned his interest in attending Howard, another traditional black university. Nichols told him that he was a "Lincoln man" and that "there's a long tradition of men who made a difference going there," describing the college's influence on his life and on his way of thinking about the world. By the end of the hour, Gil was convinced.

For a young, politically conscious black high school senior graduating in 1967, you could hardly pick a more ideal campus than Lincoln. West of Philadelphia and surrounded by rural towns, the school was engulfed in the tumult of the 1960s without the chaotic energy of urban campuses such as Columbia or Berkeley. Because it was halfway between New York and Washington, DC, Lincoln attracted many prominent stars of the era. Muhammad Ali, a legend among college students for his refusal to go to Vietnam, was escorted around campus. The leaders of Deacons for Defense and Justice, a black self-defense group started in Alabama, and black arts leaders such as Amiri Baraka visited and talked to students. It was a heady time on campus: black nationalist groups were demanding changes to the curriculum, black Muslims were proselytizing, and creative students were experimenting with free jazz and surrealist poetry. Gil's first year there, 1967, also marked the entrance of the second class of women at the longtime male bastion, shaking things up on campus.

The creative ferment at Lincoln, and the young black students from around the country attracted to that energy, were responsible for the Gil Scott-Heron who moved millions with the messages in his music and helped influence generations of musicians. Most of Gil's early band members, including collaborator and cowriter Brian Jackson, attended Lincoln, where they found each other, formed groups, and made music. Lincoln was somewhat insulated from the anger and rage exploding on urban campuses, allowing students to absorb the changes convulsing the country without being overwhelmed by them and to respond to it in their own ways. "Students at Lincoln wanted to get away from the maddening crowd," says Victor Brown, a singer who joined Gil on some of his first albums. "It didn't explode like Howard or Morgan State, and students could take a much more intellectual take on the changes taking place."

At Lincoln, Gil thrived creatively and socially. For once, he truly felt like he belonged: the campus was full of intellectual debate, radical politics, and black students who wanted to change the world. "He was a gawky kid from New York," remembers Carl Cornwell, who was two years older than Gil. "He had a country air about him but he was a city boy." In some ways, he was already known on campus. Charismatic and tall, with a towering Afro and blue jeans, Gil stood out. An older student, Ron Welburn, remembers thumbing through *Southern Exposure* magazine at the library in 1965 and seeing a photo of a long-legged black kid, "all arms and legs," sitting under a tree with some other students in an article about a school that had been integrated in Jackson, Tennessee. When he asked Gil about it two years later, Gil said, "Yeah, that was me."

When he was at DeWitt Clinton and in junior high school, Gil was still trying to get his bearings in the big city, and negotiate the crowded hallways. At Fieldston, he was trying to blend in and avoid trouble. At Lincoln, he was unleashed. He was voted president of his freshman class and took charge on several major school issues. "Any high-level political activity, he was in the middle of it," remembers classmate and band member David Barnes. "If there was anyone who went to Lincoln in those years who didn't know Gil, they were asleep," says Carl Cornwell.

But he also spent time in the black stacks of the library, reading up on works by authors from the Harlem Renaissance and modern poets such as Calvin C. Hunter and Felix T'caya U'Tansy. He took black literature classes with James Saunders Redding (who was also part of the Harlem Renaissance), reading authors ranging from Phillis Wheatley and Jupiter Jones to Ralph Ellison and James Baldwin. He was also active on the school's newspaper, the *Lincolnian*, where he was a news editor his freshman year.

Lincoln was creatively fertile, with many students attracted to different creative trends, from avant-garde jazz and African dance to symbolist poetry and performance art. Welburn, who was two years older than Gil, had a group called the Lincoln Literati, which held poetry readings and jazz concerts heavily influenced by the experimentation of Albert Ayler and Ornette Coleman. Sometimes those students would recite poetry over the music, alternating with some improvisatory music and then going into a poem and then back again. They would conduct impromptu rabble sessions around campus, discussing literature and new developments in poetry.

Almost every day, he and his roommate, Steve Wilson, an overweight student known for his penchant for cursing, and other friends would sit around and listen to the latest jazz: Miles Davis, Dexter Gordon, Herbie Hancock, Archie Shepp. "Gil was a real jazz aficionado," says classmate David Barnes. "We all loved jazz, but he knew more about it than anyone else."

Gil was exposed to more avant-garde jazz through Welburn, a tenor saxophonist who led a contemporary jazz group, the Lincoln Contemporary

Unit, which modeled itself after the Archie Shepp Quartet. In his room, Welburn would play for him new music by free-jazz composers such as Ornette Coleman and Cecil Taylor. But Gil wasn't interested. "He would say, 'Oh man, I don't like that.' That work was too atonal for him," says Welburn. "He was into Latin music; he was the one who first told me about Joe Bataan. And in his collection he had Bataan's *Riot* album and Willie Colón's *The Hustler* album."

Though Gil appreciated bebop and free jazz by John Coltrane and Miles Davis, his own music was much more blues-based, with simple melodies. He would tinker at the piano with a few chords and then bang out some lyrics that matched the mood. "His songs at the time were more sentimental, songs about unrequited love," says Welburn. "I remember most of the harmonies. They were similar to Joe Bataan's songs and Stevie Wonder's songs. They had a wonderful harmonic lyricism, a modulating lyricism." He remembers one song, "Who Set the Stage?" with a typically dewy-eyed ending: "There goes another girl out of my life."

Gil used to decry the casual use of drugs by other students, repeating the popular conspiracy theory that the government had introduced drugs into the black community to subdue the population and mute the chances of violent protests engulfing the country. Welburn remembers telling Gil that several students in his dormitory were smoking marijuana and that the aroma was wafting out the window. Gil snapped, "Those guys are stupid. They think they can close the door and open the window and the smell won't be around." He was outraged at the students' thoughtless ignorance and that they were falling into the trap set by the government. Gil told Welburn that true activists and revolutionaries shouldn't mess with drugs if they really wanted to be effective.

Full of energy, Gil was persistent when it came to realizing his ambitions, whether it was writing poetry, creating music, or learning about the world. In the student union, in a meeting room near the cafeteria, sat an upright piano. Several times Welburn remembers eating lunch while Gil was trying to compose songs and being interrupted by the budding musician eager for advice: "Hey, come on over here. I want you to hear this," he'd say. "But Gil," Welburn would respond, "I'm in the middle of lunch." Cornwell, a saxophonist, remembers Gil's impromptu interruptions. "He heard me playing sax in the theater and he would come in and read poetry over the music, just extemporaneous stuff off the top of his head."

Welburn tried encouraging Gil to write his music down and copyright it. "But he didn't have time for that. Mostly he just sat down and played by ear. He was too free-spirited as an artist to follow the notes and the sheet music, and he didn't have the patience for that."

There was an annual literary magazine on campus, *Axiom,* founded by former student Sam Anderson, that featured politically conscious work and prose influenced by Eugène Ionesco and the theater of the absurd. Gil wanted to start his own magazine and call it *Open Workshop.* True to his impatient nature, he produced one issue, just four mimeographed pages with poems and political commentary, before being distracted by other pursuits.

6.

THE PROTEST AND THE RAGE

On the evening of April 4, 1968, radios on the Lincoln campus crackled with the news that Martin Luther King Jr. had been shot on the balcony of a motel in Memphis. Students started to gather at the chapel. And when King's death was announced, some started to cry and others walked around in shock, commiserating with one another. Gil, who had just turned nineteen three days earlier and had been in a small theater on campus when a student rushed in and blurted out the news, wandered the campus in a daze, like so many of his fellow students.

Soon, some of America's largest black neighborhoods were exploding in anger. Riots erupted in at least 125 cities, including Boston, Chicago, Los Angeles, Newark, and Washington, DC, leaving at least forty dead and threatening to transform King's nonviolent movement into a racial confrontation.

Gil was frustrated because the campus was so distant from the protests and demonstrations blowing up across the country. So he channeled his militant energy into his writing. In a poem in the campus newspaper, the *Lincolnian*, on December 29, 1968, he anticipated more bloody riots:

Red neck enemy
of dark
who survives under

a blanket of night.
Revolts will blend
us all or
    kill us

The campus, though isolated from the action, was divided between young radicals caught up in the anger of the era and career-driven students and older veterans taking advantage of the GI Bill. And the group of radicals had its own divisions: between black nationalists and civil rights advocates, between Muslims and non-Muslims, between suburban and urban students. Though he was far more outspoken now, Gil remained skeptical of joining an organization or being affiliated with an ideology and he tried to remain above the fray. This attitude seems due both to an instinctive skepticism he inherited from his mother and to his own independence of mind. But sometimes he couldn't help letting his passions get ahead of him, though some of that bravado appeared intended to bolster his reputation among the activists on campus.

In a front-page op-ed in the *Lincolnian* titled "Black Judas," Gil thundered with indignation, adopting the role of the righteous prosecutor out to purify the campus of niggers—"Black bodies with White ideals. (i.e., money, house in Burgeiouse [*sic*] Ville, Cadillac, etc.)"—and of those who sat in the student union "masturbating under the table." He condemned the campus as a cesspool of "ping-pong, pinochle, Penn relays, sexual frustration, and mixers." In the op-ed, his solution was Maoist in its purity: to have righteous students inform on the "back-biting, bull-shitting majority" by compiling a "list of names including all niggers and people with nigger-tendencies. Know your enemy! Point him out." He even proposed prioritizing food, medical facilities, and housing for the pure radicals. "The changes will point out the Black Judases who reside on campus. They will be along for the hand-clapping but not the actual attack."

In between the political ferment on campus, Gil spent as much time as he could writing poems and stories and random thoughts, scribbling them down in a notebook over lunch or on a typewriter in his dorm room. Just after King's assassination, he started writing a novel, *The Vulture*, which he had been imagining in his head for a long time. It was fast-paced pulp fiction about a murder victim, John Lee, and it followed four of Lee's friends who may or may not have been involved in his death, drawing interweaving narratives.

By the spring semester of his freshman year, Gil was already being recognized for his writing. On May 6, 1968, he received an Omega award from the school for creative writing for his poetry and short stories. "A product of the ghetto, he writes with striking sensitivity about the shocking realities of his ghetto existence and his experiences as a Black man struggling for respect, dignity and freedom in a white man's world," noted the press release announcing the honor.

Back in the city on summer break, and during monthly trips home, he took walks around the streets near his mom's apartment with a little notebook, filling it with observations about the people he knew, their interactions and physical details, to use as material for *The Vulture*. Like a journalist, Gil would strike up conversations with his old neighbors, soaking up their verbal tics and physical mannerisms.

He also met up with his Lincoln buddies, to go to concerts and shows around the city. They would come by his mom's apartment on Seventeenth Street, where Bobbie would cook dinner for them and talk with them about issues. "You could see in his mother where Gil got his wit," says Eddie "Ade" Knowles. "She would have you laughing, very sarcastic sense of humor. The two of them would go at it, jousting, and she was sharp, so he had to be on his toes."

Back home, Mom was still in charge, giving him tasks and chores to do. Welburn remembers coming to visit and hoping to watch a game on TV with his friend, but Bobbie had other plans for Gil: go to the Laundromat, go get some groceries. "She could be a tough cookie but he loved her a great deal," Welburn says. "It was one of those kinds of things where somebody could be a big deal on campus, and at home it's like, 'Yes, Mom. No, mom.'"

In addition to jazz clubs and cafés in the Village, Gil went to the East Wind poetry collective on Lenox Avenue in Harlem. Around the corner, on 125th Street, was Pride Inc., a job-training nonprofit, where his friends Charlie Saunders and Isaiah Washington worked when they weren't playing drums. At these sessions, Gil would sit in and take turns with others reciting his poems while Charlie sat behind the conga drums, tapping out that insistent rhythm, transporting the verses to another level. Gil took this experience downtown, sneaking into coffeehouses in the Village, where his assertive voice and potent lyrics filtered through the crowd.

What struck Gil was that this performance continued an age-old black tradition going back to the African *griot*, the Mandinke word for oral historian. "When you looked at the 'Roots' thing, you may have seen the man they called the Griot," he said. "He was the storyteller and the man responsible for the history of the family. The Griot was known throughout Africa as the man responsible for the oral tradition. We've sort of picked up on that tradition."

It was a long tradition, one that had been brought to America on the slave ships. Since it was illegal for slaves to learn to write, they kept their history alive orally, through passing stories down from generation to generation. During the Harlem Renaissance, poets such as Countee Cullen and Sterling Brown held readings, acknowledging the heritage they were continuing. Fast-forward to 1967, young black writers LeRoi Jones and Larry Neal started Kuumba House in Newark, New Jersey, where poets would rap their poems to the accompaniment of drummers and musicians playing African string instruments. "Words along with rhythms: just the songs and dancing along with rhythms," Gil later told *DownBeat* magazine. "I saw a lot of people doing it."

Indeed, it was happening across the country. In St. Louis, the Black Artists' Group was experimenting with free jazz and theater, and the Watts Prophets in Los Angeles were building a following with their spoken-word poetry. And Wanda Robinson, Nikki Giovanni, and Village poet Jason Rohrs were performing and recording tough, lyrical poetry over drumbeats. These proud black artists were "using their art as a weapon to attack the oppressive system," said Gil.

"It was the season of the black wind," wrote Vernon Gibbs in his 1976 *Playboy* profile of Gil. "Proud Afro-scats bugabooed the midnight streets. Tongues lashed brimstone medleys about the coming Armageddon, when America would finally pay for her sins. Hip revolutionaries demanded the new order. Out of the fire of the Watts and Harlem battalions that took to the sidewalks of the Sixties swinging Molotov melodies, the Last Poets arose."

The Last Poets was a group of poets who particularly intrigued Gil. They included the young black nationalists David Nelson, Gylan Kain, and Abiodun Oyewole, who had been reciting poetry over conga drums around Harlem and, more recently, had read poetry at a birthday tribute to the late Malcolm X in Mount Morris Park in Harlem on May 19, 1968. The group took its name from a poem by South African Keorapetse Kgositsile, who believed that the era of poetry was ending, to be replaced by a time of violence.

Gil was excited by the Last Poets and the power of their performances, how the spare drums accentuated the revolutionary lyrics. Back on campus in September, he was determined to finish *The Vulture* and to take his music in a different direction, beyond banging out blues songs on the piano in the student lounge. And it wasn't hard to find students who wanted to join him, since Lincoln attracted other young black artists searching for experience. Eddie "Ade" Knowles, a transfer student from Bronx Community College, was playing drums and performing with African dance companies on campus. One warm night in the early fall of 1968, he was in his room when he heard a knock. It was Gil, full of energy and ideas. He introduced himself and said he was working on some poetry and music and asked, "I heard you play drums. Would you be interested in playing for us?" Ade blew him off, saying, "No, I'm not interested in being a sideman." Gil quickly replied, "That's not where I'm coming from." Ade told him that drums needed to be given a prominent place and not just used as background beats. Gil agreed and eventually convinced him to come down to the chapel to play. "I was totally dismissive, but he was persistent," remembers Ade.

Gil would not take no for an answer, excitedly telling Ade about his poetry and his ideas for music. He asked Ade to come over to the chapel and rehearse. When they got there, Gil played some of his songs. "He was very high energy, had a lot of things he wanted to do, writing the poetry and writing the novels."

Later that fall, Gil invited the Last Poets to perform at Lincoln, promising an audience of engaged students. Always eager to reach out to black students, the group quickly agreed, and Gil soon took care of all the arrangements, putting up flyers and securing a performance space. At the concert in December, the Last Poets performed their propulsive new poem "When the Revolution Comes" to a crowd of nearly one hundred students.

When the revolution comes

When the revolution comes

When the revolution comes some of us will probably catch it on TV,
    with chicken hanging from our mouths. You'll know it's revolution
    cause there won't be no commercials

When the revolution comes

Gil was fired up by the poem's radical lyrics and aggressive energy. After the show, he approached Oyewole. "I want to start a group like you guys."

"Go for it," said Oyewole. "We want to have Last Poets all over the world. It's more than a name, it's a philosophy. Get your shit together right now because we're going to have a revolution. We have to tighten up and get rid of all the negative attitudes."

Gil told Oyewole that he understood what he was trying to tell him. The tall student with the big Afro struck the older poet as a serious young man who followed through on his ideas. "He was a sincere dude. He had a certain smooth disposition about him that I noticed right away," says Oyewole. "He wanted to join this movement, and he told me he's writing poetry, and I liked his energy. We had people caught up in the movement, and they sounded like they were on fire all the time, like a bullet halfway out of the chamber. But Gil knew how to hold his trigger back if necessary."

After the group hung out for an hour, they got in Oyewole's beige four-door Impala and drove back to New York. Fellow Last Poet Kain used to tease Oyewole for driving a car, saying that he wasn't "a real revolutionary." Oyewole would snap back, "I'm driving to the revolution, motherfucker. You can take the train." Though he wouldn't hear about Gil for a few more years, Oyewole had a good feeling on the drive home. "The college scene was alive and well. The revolutionary pot was being stirred."

7.

THE BLACK AND BLUES

Gil didn't have to look far to find kindred spirits who wanted to set the world on fire with their music. Another student in his class was Victor Brown, who grew up in Boston, where he sang in the church choir and attracted notice with his strong, beautiful voice. In the seventh grade at Boston Latin, a Catholic school, he auditioned for the glee club but lost to a white student who warbled off-key. In his freshman year at Lincoln, Brown joined the glee club but attracted the ire of the imperious music director because he had never learned to read music. "He was very abusive, yelling at me, 'I don't know why you're looking at the music. You can't read it anyway.' Thus ended my attempt to be in a traditional music program." Determined to sing, Victor entered a talent show thrown by Cheney State College's Omega Psi Phi fraternity, singing a duet with a young woman, covering a Nina Simone song. Backing up the singers that night was Knowles, who was playing congas. Brown and his partner won first place. Knowles was impressed, telling the singer that he wanted to play with him at Lincoln.

On a small campus with only six hundred students, most Lincoln students knew each other, and Brown quickly developed a reputation as a singer. At the start of their sophomore year, he and Knowles jammed a few times and started a band, which they called the Black and Blues. Taking notice was David Barnes, a talented percussionist and singer who grew up in Brooklyn and was in the All-City Chorus. He was also politically active at a young age, leading marches throughout the city to protest the fact that the city had never hired an African American high school principal. Barnes first met Oyewole of the Last Poets when they were both teenagers in the Young Troopers, an artistic group that tried to keep kids off the streets. When Barnes arrived at Lincoln, he started playing music, and bonded with Victor Brown over singing. Barnes entered the homecoming talent show, singing "Human" and beating the Black and Blues, who subsequently asked him to join them.

Gil, who had already bonded with Knowles and played pinochle with Brown in the student union when he wasn't playing piano or writing poetry, joined the band in 1969. They would practice anywhere they could find a piano on campus, often sneaking into the chapel. They would hang out, sometimes get high on marijuana or hash, and come up with songs.

When Gil joined the band, he took action to get them wider exposure, contacting a number of black studies departments in the Northeast. The band would pile into a van, throw their instruments in the back, and hit the road, often skipping classes. When they arrived on a campus, they'd usually play in a large classroom or the corner of the student union, not the auditorium. "We were having less people come to see us do what we were going to do than you could get in a phone booth," remembered Gil.

But they were a hit, and soon they attracted larger crowds, mainly black students. "The music was primarily original songs, and it was right in tune with the moment," remembers vocalist Victor Brown. "If you listen to Curtis Mayfield or Sly and the Family Stone, their lyrics were visual portraits of what was going on in the real world, and Gil fit right in. He had insight and an ability to describe in real terms what he saw around him, and he was very outspoken." Gil loved James Brown, and sometimes he'd amuse the band by going out onstage and doing his best impersonation of the Godfather of Soul. The act almost got him injured during a gig at Swarthmore College, when he jumped up to do a split but the tables that made up the stage weren't locked together and he fell through to the floor. While band members looked on in shock, Gil jumped back up as if nothing had happened.

Handsome, with an easy smile, Gil attracted his share of female fans. But though he dated a few girls, he was so consumed with writing and performing that none of the relationships lasted longer than a few weeks. He knew how to charm women into bed, but he often had trouble opening up about his emotions and really connecting enough to deepen a relationship. Years later, he wrote a little ode to his college girlfriends and flings, from a "white rug embrace I'll never forget" and a "sweet village dance" with Yvette, to "love at first sight" with Toni on Route 1 one night.

In the fall of 1969, Gil was a junior, and a new crop of students arrived on campus, heads full of inspiration and hearts full of passion and anger. One of them, Brian Jackson, was a musical prodigy from Brooklyn. In high school, he grew disenchanted with the curriculum and helped lead protests to demand lessons that incorporated the African American experience. Often, he skipped school to hang out at a local cultural center in Brooklyn called the East. Brian, quiet but determined, would spend hours playing the piano at the center, where other young, disenfranchised black artists could come and feel like they were understood. Occasionally jazz musicians such as Sun Ra and Pharoah Sanders would drop in, giving impromptu performances.

Growing up in Crown Heights, Brian was captivated by the sounds of the sixties, from Eddie Floyd and James Brown to Sam and Dave. He listened to the new songs on a transistor radio under his pillow. "Soul music was the soundtrack to my adolescence," he said, "the background to the changes that were taking place all around us." He experienced a segregated school system of the type that Gil had helped integrate in Jackson. He was bussed from his black neighborhood in Crown Heights to a white school in Flatbush. "I had a couple of racial run-ins, but it didn't affect me as much as watching the news." Every day on television, he saw "people who look like me, look just like my uncle and my cousin, getting sprayed by fire hoses up against the wall, then beaten and sent to jail. Dr. King was being held responsible for all of that."

Just like Gil, Brian was a voracious reader of Langston Hughes and was inspired to attend the poet's alma mater. When Brian came to Lincoln, he would practice as often as he could—"like Schroeder," the Charlie Brown character who was always pictured head down to the keyboard, he says—finding padded practice rooms at the music school to play the piano. Gil, himself on the hunt for a spare keyboard, noticed Brian quietly performing several times and was impressed, but never interrupted him—until one day.

Brian was in the middle of practicing when he noticed Gil. "I look through the window, and I see a guy looking at me and he comes in and he has to turn sideways to get his Afro in the door," he remembers. "And he had an Adam's apple that came out halfway across the room and a big goatee." Gil sat down at the piano and played a few songs. "While the music was good, what struck me were the lyrics. They were unbelievable. I was just as taken by the lyrics as he seemed to be by my playing." Then Brian sat down at the piano and played a beautiful piece. Gil couldn't help himself: impressed with Brian's mastery of the instrument and his melodic intuition, he shouted out, "That's pretty cool! I can't play like that! Maybe you can play the shit I'm trying to play?"

When Victor told Gil he wanted to enter a talent show with "God Bless the Child" and some original compositions, Gil told him that they needed this mysterious piano prodigy. "I said to Victor, 'This guy will play anything you want! Why don't you talk to him?'" Victor went to check out Brian practicing his chords and was impressed. So he introduced himself and invited Brian to take part in the talent show.

Before Brian joined the group, Gil played most of the keyboard parts himself. But he soon stepped back to focus solely on his poetry and songwriting. That version of the Black and Blues—featuring Gil on vocals, Brian on piano and flute, Ade on drums, and Victor on vocals—became the nucleus for the Midnight Band that created and performed some of Gil's most memorable music, from "The Bottle" to "Johannesburg," throughout the following decade. But for now, they were just another band on campus, taking gigs wherever they could, each player getting paid about four dollars a night and sometimes up to fifty-five dollars a week. Back on campus, the Black and Blues may have been popular with students, but not so with the faculty, coming in third place at the campus talent show judged by Herbert Southern, the imperious head of the music department. Professor Southern respected only classical music, and he wouldn't let the Black and Blues play and rehearse in the music center, saying he didn't want to hear that "jungle music."

Desperate to practice as often as they could, the guys in the band would rehearse almost every afternoon and night, often skipping classes and meals. And they went to elaborate lengths to break into buildings to find pianos to play, including an old chapel on campus. Since the doors were usually locked, they would have to break in through a window, which took a lot of shimmying and acrobatic movements. With his lanky body, Gil was usually tasked with prying open a window and sliding through it. Then he would creep into the building and unlock the door to let his buddies in. His scaling feats on campus, along with the curvature of his spine, which sometimes made him appear to be sidling along a wall, earned him the nickname Spiderman.

One night, the band arrived at the chapel and found the doors open. Some of the janitorial staff let them come in and play the baby grand piano. But the next day, Professor Southern found out about the impromptu performance and took all the keys out of the piano to prevent them from playing it. That didn't stop the Black and Blues from breaking in another night, taking another piano, an older upright, carrying it past the narrow pews, and lifting it up onto the stage.

Spending so much time together practicing and performing, they developed a tight bond, one cemented by their mutual love of music. "It was something special," says Ade. "We were brothers; we could read each other's minds after a while." Though they may not have attended class, they learned about literature and history from one another. Victor Brown says that he got his education from his friends in the band. "I was certainly not as politically aware as Gil or as Ade. I was just a brother who could sing. But rubbing shoulders with people who are more politically conscious slowly rubbed off on me, and I began to think about different things."

Gil was constantly writing new poems and lyrics, often based on current events ranging from police brutality in the South to intimidation of voters in Newark. On the small circuit of the campuses they toured, the Black and Blues developed a reputation for strong, incisive, politically aware songs. And Gil's lyrics resonated in the world of black activists fighting

injustice and rallying for equal treatment. Kenneth Gibson, a structural engineer who was running to be the first black mayor of Newark, invited the
group to perform at one of his rallies in 1969. The Black Panthers provided
security because some local Italians had threatened to disrupt the rally,
which made for a tense performance and a quick exit for the band. "So, there
we are at this outdoor stadium," remembers Ade. "We did the event. Yeah,
'Vote for the Brother . . .' [a song Gil wrote for the event] and got out of
Dodge." Gil later returned to Newark on his own, to recite some of his poetry at a black power conference at the House of Prayer, organized by fiery
activist Amiri Baraka. His presence electrified the crowd, and Baraka later
praised Gil for being part of a movement of black people to "liberate ourselves to destroy the legacy of slavery and humiliation which has always
been our lot in white racist monopoly capitalist America."

Another time, they had a weeklong gig at the Smiling Dog in Cleveland,
a rundown storefront turned coffee shop with moldy couches and post-riot
décor. A local reporter did a feature story on the fiery young black poets
from Lincoln University, calling them a "walking talking education organization." When they performed, the local police sent extra squad cars to
patrol the area, in anticipation of riots.

Gil traced his activism back to those discussions on his grandmother's
front porch in the 1950s, and located it on a time line of socially conscious
African Americans that extended back to the eighteenth century. He often
cited historical figures such as Phillis Wheatley, the first African American
woman to publish a book, and Martin Delaney, a Civil War lieutenant and
writer who is considered the first black nationalist due to his emphasis on self-
sufficiency. Gil also cited the influence of twentieth-century figures such as
actor Paul Robeson, who sought to wield his talent to advance the cause of
workers' rights, racial justice, and socialism. Robeson "once said that the artist
has the responsibility to either help liberate the community or further oppress
it," Gil was fond of saying to explain his motivation. He was keenly aware of
his place in this long tradition of activist artists, and aspired to have a similar
impact. But he was modest enough to know how much he was indebted to
those who came before him. He described his role as just another link in a
chain—"you have to be aware of the people who made contributions, made it

possible to be at this point. Like there could be no Gil Scott-Heron if there'd been no LeRoi Jones [Amiri Baraka]; had there been no Langston Hughes, no Paul Dunbar, no David Walker, no Nat Turner . . . That's the reason they have scholarships and all is that people were getting their asses kicked and shot at and buried so that this could get done."

8.

WHO AM I?

Gil enjoyed performing and jamming with the band, and he was impressed at how the music could inspire and enlighten the people who came to their shows. But he still considered himself a writer who played music just to perform his poetry. He didn't really understand the power of music, or the musician's creative potential to transform his life and the world around him, until he heard John Coltrane. One night in the spring of 1969, Gil stopped by Ade's room and the drummer played Coltrane's *A Love Supreme* album for him. The saxophone legend had died two years earlier, and Gil had heard him only playing with other groups, never Coltrane's own compositions. He remembers the impact of hearing the album as "immediate. The first time I heard the [*Love Supreme*] chant, the spirituality, the mix of the instruments, the way the solos were set up, the way the tune was done, and the length of it at almost 20 minutes long—I got lost in it. I was literally taken aback."

The album's symmetry and cohesiveness was what Gil craved in his own music and poetry and life. At Lincoln, he felt out of balance. Though the band was thriving and winning some acclaim, his writing was not getting the attention he felt it deserved. His main reason for coming to Lincoln had been to follow in the footsteps of his hero, Langston Hughes, and to be anointed by the school as the great new black poet. Though he had received a literary award in his freshman year, the English faculty was still dismissive of his writing in later years, and their lack of encouragement of his efforts to write his novel upset and confused him, he complained to friends. Stymied in his literary ambitions, Gil channeled much of his creative energy into music and performing with the Black and Blues. "The faculty didn't take him seriously," says Ade. "He would try to get people to read the novel, and they weren't interested. Gil was really very assertive and very aggressive. He was a high ball of energy who wanted to do a lot of stuff, and some faculty was put off by that."

Soon after they bonded over music, Gil started coming over to see Ade to get feedback on his novel. He'd come by his friend's dorm room at night clutching chapters, with a jug of wine and plenty of enthusiasm: "Let's do this." So, the two of them would stay up until three or four, discussing the novel, and end up oversleeping their classes. Ade was impressed that Gil was churning out twenty-five to thirty pages a day and felt that he understood character development and plot very well. "He was dedicated; he would rewrite chapters over and over again." They grew close, and Gil told his friend, "You're the only person who takes seriously what I am trying to do with my writing."

Once he committed himself to finishing the novel, Gil felt that his studies at Lincoln were too distracting and that maybe he should take a leave of absence. "So there I was, hung up between wanting to write and reading Euripides." But he was torn: his mother, her two sisters, and her brother had all been outstanding students, and there was incredible pressure on him to go to college, excel, and do even better than they had. "When I should be studying I wanted to work on the book but when I worked on the book I knew I was wasting my time as far as the money I'd invested in going to school," he wrote. "It was difficult to explain to people. It wasn't about getting it published, it was about completing something."

What should he do: stay on campus or leave and finish the novel? He spent months trying to make up his mind—he later compared his indecision to "a jackass that was set down squarely between two bales of hay and starved to death." In the end, he felt that he could succeed only if he pursued his dreams—much like Coltrane, who inspired Gil with his mercurial independence in the face of criticism. "I knew I was going to face a lot of criticism and I might not get back to school to graduate. I had to follow my own mind. So I had to listen to people and see examples of people who had done that and been successful in spite of the criticism. I think I got that from 'A Love Supreme.'"

When Gil asked for a leave of absence, Lincoln administrators were taken aback and responded in a way that confirmed his disenchantment with the school. His adviser, the head of the English department, didn't think it was a good idea, and sent Gil to the dean, who thought he had lost his mind and told him to go see the school psychiatrist. Gil was confused but amused by the school's reaction, dutifully attending one session with the shrink, nodding and smiling, but staying committed to his plan. The biggest test of his resolve, of course, was telling his mother. On a trip back to New York City, he broke the news to her over dinner. She wasn't happy about his quitting school, but she could tell that he was determined to pursue his dream. To his surprise, she accepted his choice, but encouraged him to go back to school once he'd finished the novel. In his memoir, he notes how supportive of his writing she was and that he always took his prose and poetry and lyrics to her first before showing them to others because he knew that she would give him constructive criticism.

Gil had planned to have *The Vulture* finished by the start of the following semester, in February 1969, but he underestimated how long it would take him. By January, in between performing with the band and hanging out with new friends, he had hardly made any progress. He came up with an idea for the end of the book and figured out how to connect the four separate narratives to the opening. Now he just needed to write it. To make that final creative spurt, he moved off campus and took a job at a nearby dry cleaner, living in a room in the back with just a lamp, a bed, and a small table with an old Royal typewriter. The news spread quickly around campus: "Gil's in the back of the cleaners!" He borrowed money from friends, sneaked into the dining room, and had them bring trays of food out to him.

He later described the risk he took by staking his future on *The Vulture* as "my way of doing the high-wire act blindfolded"; if he failed, he would have nothing. No money, no school, no pride left, and "no hole that I could crawl into."

By that spring, the novel was finally finished. It takes place in Gil's old neighborhood in Chelsea and includes characters drawn from the young drug dealers, bullies, oddballs, eccentrics, and cops he knew growing up. There is Spade, a quiet, tough leader who commands respect in the ghetto; Tommy "Afro" Hall, an idealistic black militant plotting to kill local drug dealers; Junior Jones, who idolizes Spade and is disillusioned by the whole drug scene; and I.Q., a young black intellectual who quotes Greek philosophers and occasionally gets high.

The four characters reflect different parts of Gil's personality. Some of Spade's quotes could be lines in one of Gil's poems: "The acrid smell of the flaming pier was still wedged in my mind, painting my mind ugly." And Jones's putdown of the hippies who cop downers from him is imbued with Gil's sarcasm: "That stuff was for the hippy poets and folk singers who liked to go around singing the blues and talking about the total destruction of mankind and all that wild shit." Just as Gil often felt caught between the nonviolent message of civil rights activists and the violent rhetoric of black radicals, Tommy "Afro" Hall is trapped in that space, though he harbors dreams of teaching black students about their culture.

But the character that most reflects the real Gil is I.Q., who is first encountered lounging in Central Park "dressed in a dashiki, blue jeans, moccasins, and wire-rimmed glasses" and reading Euripides' *Alcestis*. His intelligence and scholarly knowledge reflects the Gil who spent hours reading literature in the library, soaking up philosophy and poetry.

Determined to find a publisher, Gil focused on Ramparts Press, which had a reputation for edgy material and had recently released *Soul on Ice*, a collection of essays by Eldridge Cleaver, an imprisoned leader of the Black Panthers. After talking his way past the secretary at the front desk, he dropped off his novel with editor Robert Scheer and promised to come back in two weeks. When he returned, he sought to make a good impression, wearing a blue dress shirt under a leather jacket and carrying a briefcase. Right away, he saw on the editor's desk that his manuscript had been accepted, he later wrote.

Through a haze of cigarette smoke, the rumpled editor offered him an advance of two thousand dollars—but only on the condition that he rewrite all the ghetto dialogue in proper English and switch the order in which two characters' stories appear. After sitting in shock for a few minutes, and before questioning the editor's suggestions, Gil started thinking about how the money could pay for his room and board and tuition. Scheer then said that readers would be more interested in the danger of the ghetto experience than the mystery. His tone insulted Gil, who sat in silence for a few more minutes.

He was torn—it was tempting to go back to Lincoln with two thousand dollars in his pocket and the opportunity to "shove copies of a book with my name on it down the throats of the big-mouthed jokers" who had mocked him for dropping out of school. Not to mention how proud it would make his mother and uncle. "All I had to do was sign that paper and walk out."

Gil got up, picked up his manuscript, and walked out of the room. With only a five-dollar bill in his pocket, he left the building and wandered downtown, full of panic and in a "thickening wall of April gloom." In front of the Twenty-third Street YMCA, he ran into his Fieldston buddy Fred Baron and Fred's father, Jerry. They invited him back home for dinner, where he told them all about the disastrous experience. Jerry began reading the manuscript, and when Fred left the room, Jerry "pulled out a fifty dollar bill and handed it to me," Gil wrote. Smiling, Jerry said he was going to keep the manuscript: "I'm going to hand this over to my friends and have them get in touch with you."

Gil used the money to take the bus back to Lincoln, where he waited and worried. Ten days later, he got a phone call at the dry cleaner, where he was still living, from Lynn Nesbit, a literary agent, who offered him a five-thousand-dollar advance for the book. "He was overjoyed and very grateful," remembers Nesbit. "I saw that he was an immensely talented writer and that he could be an important cultural figure. He was new to the whole process and was eager to hear suggestions for what changes he should make, that this was sort of a miraculous opportunity."

The publisher, World Publishing, also bought the rights to *Small Talk at 125th and Lenox*, a collection of Gil's poems. Gil was elated, and told friends that it was the highlight of his life. Since his childhood in Jackson, scribbling detective stories in his notebook, he had dreamed of getting his stories published and making a living as a writer like Langston Hughes.

9.

BROTHERS IN ARMS

When Gil returned to campus in September 1969, the school was on the verge of revolt. As a rural school, too far away from urban unrest, Lincoln didn't experience the explosive rage blowing up on other black campuses such as Howard University or Morgan State. But there was plenty of anger directed at the conservative school administration, which looked down on political demonstrations and some of the free-form creativity taking place on campus. The school had started admitting female students only the year before, and some of the older students and faculty were still resentful at the changes taking place on campus. But Gil and his friends kept pushing for even more change.

Among them was Carl Cornwell, a student who occasionally jammed with the Black and Blues and who had his own band, a jazz quintet that played a lot of contemporary music by Herbie Hancock and McCoy Tyner. Called the Harrison Cornwell Limited after Cornwell and trumpeter Joe Harrison, the group had originally included Brian Jackson, until Gil snatched him away to play with the Black and Blues. Cornwell, whose father taught at Lincoln, grew up in town and was imbued with the school's pride and heritage. But once he became a student, he saw firsthand that the college was lacking essential services and wasn't responsive enough to the needs of students.

At midnight one Friday in November 1969, at the end of a rehearsal,

Cornwell's group was packing up their instruments when drummer Ron Colbert started having an asthma attack and his inhaler wasn't helping him catch a breath. The group walked to the school infirmary but it was closed. So they took Ron back to his room. By the time the ambulance arrived, it was too late. "He died in my arms," remembers Cornwell. "I'll never forget it." The tragedy could have been avoided if the infirmary had been staffed and open around the clock. Colbert's death brought to a head some issues that had been simmering for years: Gil's neighbor in his freshman dorm had died of an aneurism that had gone untreated after being detected, and several students had had their medical problems misdiagnosed by the campus doctor. When Gil returned on Sunday night from a weekend in New York City, he quickly found out about Ron's death and decided to take action, demanding adequate medical facilities. The student body united around the demands, especially after the administration started to claim that Colbert may have been getting high, though there was no evidence that the young man used drugs.

Gil made up a list of seven demands, including a 24/7 infirmary, the purchase of a fully equipped ambulance, and the firing of the on-campus physician, Dr. Davies. The next morning, the student body boycotted classes, and hundreds of them met in the school chapel, where Gil spoke, explaining the need for the changes. The protest grew angry, culminating with some students hanging the doctor in effigy from a tree in his front yard and setting it on fire. The doctor came out of his house and swore that he wasn't responsible for the deaths. As he proclaimed his innocence, he had tears in his eyes. When Gil arrived at the protest, he stood between the students and the doctor, looking at the doctor's children staring out the window in fear. "A cold flash scampered across the back of my neck," wrote Gil later to describe his sudden fear that events could spiral out of control into violence, a fear which was allayed only when the students went back to their dorms. The realization that radical action sometimes leads to unintended consequences and violent overreactions haunted Gil, and that image of a distraught Dr. Davis lingered in his mind for months to come. The experience reinforced Gil's instinct to avoid violence and militant action in the struggle for social change.

Though the school agreed to most of the demands, fully stocking the infirmary and buying a brand-new ambulance, the students continued their boycott into a seventh day. At one point, Gil claimed that a young administrator at the school threatened to kick him out if he didn't stop the boycott. Gil was sitting in the basement of the student union, trying to take it all in, when he was informed that a young doctor who had applied for the job opening would take the position only with Gil's approval. He liked her, she took the job, and Gil decided to end the boycott.

Not that things calmed down on campus. The next battle involved student demands for a black president to replace Dr. Marvin Wachman, the longtime white president of the school. "He wasn't the right color and he wasn't doing the right things for Lincoln," said Cornwell. "There was a real emphasis on black power, and the student body really wanted a black man running the school." Students marched and circulated petitions to pressure the trustees to find a new president. They did get their black president: Herman Branson, the scion of a prominent black family in Philadelphia, came in as president in 1970, but the conservative-minded Branson didn't approve of the school's rampant activism.

At the turn of the decade, two tragic national events took place that served to define the 1960s. During a peace rally on May 4, 1970, at Kent State University in Ohio, the National Guard shot and killed four students. The moment was captured forever in a photograph of a student crying for help over a dead student's body. And on May 15, 1970, two black students at Jackson State University were shot and killed by members of the Mississippi State Highway Patrol, who fired through the students' dormitory windows. Outraged at the muted reaction by U.S. attorney general John Mitchell, Gil wanted to shut down all campus activities to protest the shooting. He saw how the violence at Jackson State impacted him and his friends at Lincoln—if it had happened there, it could happen on their campus. And if they didn't protest the killings, their silence would only embolden reactionary forces that sought to quell student unrest by any means necessary.

The whole campus was riled up that day, and some students shouted, "Let's march on Oxford!" That was the sleepy town just down the highway, where blacks had recently been refused accommodation at a hotel. Gil was outraged about the killings, but he feared that a march on Oxford could provoke a violent reaction and considered calling up officials in Oxford to reassure them that the approaching marchers were peaceful and were "not a realization of the fear that many of them had always held in their most secret places, like a town with a penitentiary on its outskirts." He never made the call, but he was worried about the potential for violence.

"Hundreds of students were all lined up, ready to march down Route One," remembers David Barnes. "We were getting ready to march into Oxford, an all-white town, which was really dumb. Somehow word spread, and we saw trucks drive by with shotguns and rifles in the back. We had no weapons for the revolution. And some of us wised up. Cooler heads prevailed. Gil told everyone to calm down. We weren't ready for that type of revolution." Rather, students headed back to their rooms and later held a vigil in the chapel.

Not that the calm would last. In some of the rural towns surrounding Lincoln, there were small units of the Ku Klux Klan. Just a few years earlier, the Klan burned a thirty-foot cross one night near the college campus. Concern grew that the local Klan might take revenge on students for the riots in Philadelphia. So, Gil and some buddies decided to form an impromptu defense squad and went "out prowling in the fields with rifles," remembers Cornwell. At one point, Gil sat with a rifle and a bandolier about 100 yards from the spot of cross burnings in 1962 and 1966, determined to confront Klansmen if they attempted it again. When it started to rain, he linked up with Brian and two fellow students, stashed a few rifles in the trunk of the Rambler and headed out on the highway, one of them clutching a machete. They were headed to a gas station to get some coal oil to make Molotov cocktails. Just four miles north of campus, going sixty miles an hour, one of the tires blew out and the convertible screeched across the four lanes, smashed through a chain-link fence, and hit the corner wall of an insurance company office.

Gil flew out of the car and hit the pavement, leaving a gash on the side of his head, but he was conscious—"the driver's side door handle was still in his outstretched left hand, though the car was now some twenty feet away"—and the other three also survived the accident. They quickly grabbed the rifles and shells out of the trunk and hid them across the highway. When a state trooper stopped to help them, he didn't suspect anything and gave them a ride back to campus. Battered and bruised, Gil and his friends recovered from their injuries, drank a few beers, and plotted their next move.

Later that year, campus unrest boiled over and students took over the administration building to demand a variety of changes, everything from overhauling the curriculum to male students who wanted the right to stay in women's dorms overnight with their girlfriends. Some administrators were alarmed by the intensity of activism on campus and cooperated with law enforcement agencies, who were investigating radical students at colleges around the country. And Lincoln was rocked by scandal the next year, when it was reported that a Citizens' Commission to Investigate the FBI had broken into the FBI's offices in a nearby town and found records indicating that Lincoln's vice president for student affairs was an informer for the Bureau. It was not surprising that the Bureau had targeted Lincoln, which was a hotbed of student activism and was home to political refugees from around the world, including South Africa and Zimbabwe. Most of them were older, and some had been involved in revolutionary activities in their homelands—one student even had pictures of himself posing with Mao Zedong and Che Guevara.

The Bureau, which kept tabs on student activists and militant organizations through the controversial COINTELPRO program, targeted some members of the Black and Blues. When Ade returned to his home in the Bronx to recuperate from an illness, his mother was called by the FBI. The Bureau informed her that Ade's name was on a list of surveillance targets. As far as his friends knew, Gil was not targeted and never mentioned being targeted by the Bureau. After his death, the FBI claimed that it did not have a file on him in its records.

Gil later wrote a poem that captured his rage over his college's role in helping the FBI conduct surveillance on its own students:

> *But something else was happening and students weren't supposed*
> *   to know.*
> *Lincoln's state relationship included COIN-TEL-PRO.*

As now that you've got background and a certain point of view,
I'm awarding you a scholarship to go with me to Lincoln U.

The anger and resentment Gil felt about Lincoln and the tumult reverberating on other campuses inspired his second novel, *The Nigger Factory*. The provocative title refers to colleges that take young black men and turn them into obedient members of a bourgeois society. Though some of his fellow students and friends at Lincoln became characters in the novel, most of the action was based on the student unrest at Columbia University, Kent State, and his mother's alma mater, Lane College in Jackson, Tennessee. By visiting campuses and meeting students through exchange programs, Gil was well informed of the demonstrations and protests that were exploding on campuses across the country. "Where students were trying to find themselves in one direction were getting pulled in another by folks who can't remember being young," Gil told the *Denver Westword*.

Gil did marathon writing sessions, staying up for days, taking a break every once in a while to play cards in the student union. Again, he would stop by his friend Ade's room for late-night sessions to talk about the book. He spent a few weeks questioning Ade about one of his characters: "He's a student leader. What would he say?" Ade gave him answers and realized only later, after reading new chapters, that the character was based on him. "Gil was a great listener, he had a good ear, and that was obvious in the way he wrote things. He could capture the way things sounded; that was true with his poetry and the songs he wrote."

By the summer of 1970, Gil's circle of friends and collaborators at Lincoln was going through some changes. David Barnes and Victor Brown had graduated and headed off in different directions, which basically disbanded the Black and Blues. That left Gil and Brian, with some help from Knowles, to write music just for themselves. As would be the pattern for a decade to come, Gil focused on the lyrics and some simple melodic riffs, and Brian composed most of the music. But Gil was distracted that summer by the long-awaited publication of *The Vulture*.

When it was released on June 25, 1970, the novel attracted some notice for its raw street-smart vibe, though it was never destined to dominate the bestseller lists. Some critics described *The Vulture* as a cross between the work of reformed pimp Iceberg Slim and crime writer Donald Goines for its tough ghetto slang and pulp fiction style. The review in the publishing trade magazine *Kirkus* praised Gil for using flashbacks to ratchet up the tension, with scenes of distraught parents at a kitchen table, though it wasn't impressed by his character development. Still, the reviewer wrote that "the patois rings true, giving a movement and strength the characterizations lack, existing as they do for just that time, place and action."

Almost as satisfying as the critical approval was the monetary reward. Gil used the five-thousand-dollar advance to pay his tuition, buy textbooks, and treat himself to a car: a used white 1965 Nash Rambler convertible with a hundred thousand miles on it. Back at school, he drove the band to gigs in it and took road trips to explore the rest of the country beyond New York and Pennsylvania.

Publication of *The Vulture* validated Gil's focus on writing, but he still enjoyed performing and playing music. By the start of the decade, he realized that he could have the best of both worlds without compromising his ideals. Poetry fit into the African American tradition of the spoken word, and many of his poems became lyrics for songs that he composed with Brian. "A lot of times, people can say in poems things they can't say to you personally, but they need to get that information across," he told James Maycock. "I don't think poetry will ever lose its place in the community. I think it's more important than ever." He realized that writing poetry and song lyrics was its own challenge, compared to the breadth of long-form prose or novels. "To do 8 lines and tell a story, it puts you to work."

Gil's experience in Jackson and the blues he heard coming out of local clubs and on the radio shaped his writing style: the pathos and gut-wrenching emotional honesty of the blues. And the rhythm of the blues shaped the way he wrote poems—"lotta hittin' on the one down there," he said, meaning that he would emphasize certain words on certain beats, anticipating by a decade the revolution of hip-hop, with its emphasis on rhythmic speech over music. Gil also borrowed some of the styles used by Langston Hughes and other poets of the Harlem Renaissance to get the intended effect in his poems and lyrics, which was to convey his own observations to the man on the street, who wasn't necessarily equipped with a master's degree in English literature. He was heavily influenced by the way Langston Hughes used humor and wordplay to highlight contradictions such as the reality of life in America versus the way people thought things were. Some of Gil's compositions also seemed to borrow some of Hughes's style, adopting a preacherly cadence to mock old elitist traditions. In "Comment #1"—"And the new word to have is revolution / People don't even want to hear the preacher spill or spiel / Because God's whole card has been thoroughly piqued / And America is now blood and tears instead of milk and honey"—Gil takes aim at the black church, echoing Hughes's attack on academia in "Letters to the Academy," in which Hughes challenged "all you gentlemen with beards" to "come forward and speak upon / The subject of the revolution."

By 1970, Gil had written a few dozen poems that worked as song lyrics, most of them political and social commentary such as "Brother," "Who Will Pay Reparations on My Soul?" and one song that will define him forever. That spring, he and Brian and some friends were sitting around watching TV one night in one of the dorms when a news report came on about a demonstration. The newscasters started talking about how many people were taking part. "We said, 'People ought to get out there and do something; the revolution won't be televised," Gil later recounted. "A cat said, 'You ought to write that down.'" Over the next few weeks, Gil started writing down lyrics in his notebook, and he and Brian started paying more attention to what was actually being shown on television. They noticed the commercials, and the friends commented to each other on the insidiously persuasive power of ads for everything from toilet cleaner to breakfast cereal. The contrast between the commercials and the demonstrations in the streets could not have been more glaring: one was on TV, and the other was live. When he was finished writing, he titled the poem "The Revolution Will Not Be Televised."

10.

"WHITEY'S BEEN KICKING MY ASS FOR TOO LONG"

Like most artists, Gil and Brian were eager to get their music heard. They initially assumed that they would just write the songs and the music for other artists. But who would sing their radical lyrics? By the late 1960s, top R&B stars such as James Brown, Curtis Mayfield, and even the Temptations were responding to the tumult in American society by releasing more politically conscious songs, such as "You're a Winner" and "Ball of Confusion." But the songs weren't that hard-core; they functioned mostly as laments about the black ghetto, with noncontroversial exhortations in the chorus to take action. Which singers were prepared to deliver a harsh message like Gil's recent poem "The Get out of the Ghetto Blues," in which he jokes about escaping the ghetto in a "pine box" after "shooting that stuff in your arm"?

"Who the hell are we going to get to do this?" Brian joked with Gil, naming some of the R&B artists dominating the charts at the time. "The Stylistics? The Chi-lites? Teddy Pendergrass?"

Gil was wary of the major record labels such as Columbia and RCA, assuming that they would not be receptive to his lyrics. He was intrigued by Flying Dutchman, a small New York label started by longtime producer Bob Thiele, who had worked with artists as diverse on the jazz spectrum as Louis Armstrong and Archie Shepp. Thiele had started the label in 1969 after departing from ABC/Impulse! And Gil knew that Thiele had worked with poets, recording work by Angela Davis, H. Rap Brown, Pete Hamill, Stanley Crouch, and Beat writers such as Jack Kerouac.

Starting out as a hard-living dilettante born to wealth, Thiele established a reputation in the music world as someone who could instantly recognize genius, signing saxophone giants Lester Young and Coleman Hawkins, as well as taking a chance on a young guitarist from New Mexico named Buddy Holly after first hearing the teenager play "That'll Be the Day" in 1957. Though the label executives labeled Holly's tune "hillbilly garbage," Thiele persisted and released the future rock-and-roll classic on Brunswick Records, a label devoted to "race music," the term for rhythm and blues. "When he was around genius, he made sure that they were given free rein to do whatever they wanted to do and he would just fight the fight at the record label to get the music out there," remembers Bob Golden, Thiele's longtime assistant.

But Thiele's claim to fame was his role in building and cultivating the legend of Gil's musical hero John Coltrane, at Impulse Records. Coltrane was Thiele's resident genius and his personal priority. He promoted the saxophonist's albums, such as *Africa/Brass* and *A Love Supreme*, with their challenging rhythms alongside mainstream artists such as Ray Charles and Duke Ellington. The duo developed a strong rapport, with Thiele promoting his star and Coltrane taking Thiele to nightclubs to hear up-and-coming musicians such as Albert Ayler and Archie Shepp who were breaking boundaries in jazz. "Even to this day, I thank Coltrane for being," said Thiele many years later. "Because he carried me on into jazz music. I think I would have just faded away—I was a swing cat, you know."

On July 17, 1967, Coltrane died of liver cancer at Huntington Hospital in Long Island. Less than two years later, Thiele left the label and launched Flying Dutchman, eager to sign up emerging artists in jazz, rock, and the spoken-word scene. Always on the hunt for genius, Thiele would go to nightclubs every night. He was very aware of what was happening and who was hot. It's possible that he saw Gil perform some of his spoken-word poetry at a club in Harlem before they actually met, says Golden.

When Gil went to Thiele's office near Columbus Circle and got a glimpse of the legendary impresario in his office, surrounded by towering stacks of papers and records and the occasional salami sandwich, he paused for a second to catch his breath. After calming his nerves, "I told him I was a song-writer and had a few songs I felt some of his singers might be able to use."

Thiele was impressed by the "militant black poet," explaining in his memoir that Gil had carefully orchestrated the meeting. "A book of poetry he had written arrived at my office minutes before he somehow burst in," wrote Thiele. "It was all I needed to hear from an authentic spokesman of the militant community, and I instantly said, 'That sounds great, great idea.'"

Four days later, Thiele called up Gil and told him he didn't have enough money to record an album of music but was interested in doing some "spo-ken word stuff." Referring to the book of poetry Gil had sent him, "If you do that and make any money, maybe we can get some money together and do an album of music." Thiele was very excited about Gil's potential. "Gil was oozing with talent," says Golden. "A composer and a writer, though he was a greater wordsmith. I've known a lot of people in the arts, and he was the first Renaissance man I ever met. He showed up and had an immediate impact, basically representing the entire history of black music and telling stories about the black experience."

Since Thiele just wanted to do an album of poetry, he wanted to record Gil on his own, with his voice accompanied by some simple percussive beats. At first Thiele didn't want Gil to use the percussionists from his band, Ade and Charlie Saunders and David Barnes, but Gil insisted on using the trio, and Thiele ultimately agreed. It was an expression of Gil's loyalty to his friends that he would repeat many times over in the decades to come.

The summer before the recording session, Gil refined the lyrics of his poems and rehearsed with the drummers, gathering them at his mother's apartment in Chelsea to practice. Gil was nervous, and he later admitted that he was unsure whether he could carry an album on his own—until then, he'd only been one part of a bigger group, and he usually wasn't even the lead singer. But Thiele's quiet confidence in Gil bolstered the young poet's belief in himself. "Bob was a very nice guy, and he saw creativity in Gil— that's why he invited Gil to be on his label in the first place," says Barnes. "He let him do his thing, and that strengthened Gil's resolve."

Part of Gil's motivation to record an album was his realization that it was a much more effective means of getting his message and ideas across than a novel. He believed strongly in the civil rights movement, redressing inequality and tackling injustice. Though the revolution may not be televised and may not be read, it could certainly be propelled through the sound of music. "I got into recording," Gil wrote, "as part of the consideration that there are a lot of our school children and a lot of our adults, too, who do not read comprehensively enough or often enough to really enjoy dealing with novels," Gil later told a reporter. Gil's motivation anticipated rapper Chuck D's statement twenty years later that hip-hop was the CNN of black neighborhoods. Gil felt that he was informing his community about issues and events they were not being told about on the network news programs. "I'm trying to say that anytime that people are susceptible to ideas that relate to change, then they are in contact with the revolutionary spirit," Gil later told the *Black Panther*, the group's eponymous newspaper. "You see, we place a lot of values on where people over here place their values. We're not just exposed to the things that Black folks are saying, 90 per cent of the time we are exposed to what White people are saying, and we still don't believe them."

The album, *Small Talk at 125th Street and Lenox* was recorded in the late summer of 1970 in front of an intimate crowd of twenty friends and family sitting on folding chairs, whose applause and laughter can be heard in the background. It sounds like it was recorded at a small nightclub—an effect sought by Thiele and Gil—and that immediately became the accepted truth about the legendary session. Reviews of the album all noted that it was recorded at a nightclub at the intersection of 125th and Lenox in Harlem. The truth is far more mundane—it was actually recorded in a midtown studio owned by Atlantic Records. Gil wanted it to be as much a live recording as possible, so he invited some buddies from Lincoln and other pals to sit in on the session while Thiele sat on the side and watched the band do its thing. Gil's voice was full of youthful fervor tempered with a sense of bemusement, as he balanced political salvos with witty rhymes. As with any live session, there were mistakes. When Gil rapped "Whitey on the Moon," there is supposed to be a pause before the punch line "Air mail special to whitey on the moon," but the drummers kept playing, and the punch line was lost as some audience members chuckled. "It was special," remembers Barnes, who played maracas during the session. "There were friends of ours there and they were clapping and whatnot. It was a totally acoustic experience with no pretensions. What went down was it."

The album cover hailed Gil as "A New Black Poet," with a dramatic photograph by Chuck Stewart: young Gil, confident and clear-eyed, sporting a little goatee, leans by the opening to a dark alley in Harlem. It is just a close-up of the full photograph, which showed the view down to the end of the alley, where an older man is seen squatting on a toilet. "We found a spot near these apartments above one hundred and twenty-fifth street," remembers Stewart. "I took a picture that I thought would do the job." The sleeve notes proclaimed, "I am a Black man dedicated to expression; expression of the joy and pride of Blackness." In the liner notes, jazz critic Nat Hentoff called him a "protean phenomenon," noting the "continually organic interplay between music and writing in the life of Gil Scott-Heron" as a hallmark of young artists' ability to mix genres. "It's all one to them—expression in any and all forms." Among his influences, Gil cited Richie Havens, Coltrane ("the time-defiant nature and thrust of his work"), Otis Redding, Jose Feliciano, Jimmy Reed, Billie Holiday, Malcolm X, and Huey Newton. Gil told Nat Hentoff that he wrote a poem, "Revolutionary Prayer," with Huey in mind:

> If I must die
> Let me die looking for freedom
> Instead of ways to keep from dying

Gil had written the poem "The Revolution Will Not Be Televised," the best-known track on the album, long before stepping into the studio, but when he first put the words to paper, he already saw it as a piece of music, a classic twelve-bar blues song. On three of the tracks, Gil played piano, but otherwise his poems over conga beats were indebted to the Last Poets. Gil's tracks were more charismatic, livelier, while the Last Poets' lyrics were stern and hard-core; Gil laced his critiques in "Revolution" and "Whitey on the Moon" with plenty of humor. As James Maycock writes, he "skillfully switched from sparkling satire to deadly solemnity in the blink of an eye." Not everyone saw the difference—in its review, *Billboard* called it "a solid soundalike" of the Last Poets. Other critics grouped Gil in with a new wave of socially conscious black musicians but felt that he stood out, since "his imagination is much more sophisticated, literary and formally compact," noted the *New York Times*'s Craig McGregor. In his review, he reprinted some of the lyrics to the album's track "Liberals," noting that most of Gil's lyrics were unprintable in the *Times* due to their use of profanity.

What was striking was Gil's blend of radicalism with humor: a pie in the face followed by a left hook to the jaw. "Whitey on the Moon" was the other song that stood out to critics, a ninety-two-second gem of a prose poem contrasting Neil Armstrong's walk on the moon with life in the ghetto, where "a rat done bit my sister Nell." Amid the patriotic and reverent coverage of the moon landing, "Whitey on the Moon" was devastating in its harsh counterpoint. Every line is punctuated by "And whitey's on the moon," and for the last line, Gil pauses dramatically for about three seconds before uttering the line. "It had that kind of ironic twist to make people understand how bad things were in the ghetto," says Amiri Baraka. "It was very funny but sobering to think about what that really meant."

Gil said that he wrote the poem that summer, inspired by Eldridge Cleaver's description of the moon landing as a "flying circus" intended to distract America from its problems at home. Gil added, "Just something to hold down the pressure and revolt in America." The memorable punch line and title of the song was actually suggested by Gil's mother, Bobbie, who also said that he should mimic Langston Hughes by repeating in the middle the opening line of the poem, "A rat done bit my sister Nell."

In some ways, the album was anachronistic—after all, the classic spoken-word poetry in coffee shops in Greenwich Village was already passé. And Gil's militant and angry poems were a world away from the self-absorbed dreamy lines that Kerouac and the Beats used to perform at clubs in the Village. Gil's poetry was infused with the honesty and humor of the blues, the militant rhetoric spouted by black radicals and the strong and confident conversational banter overheard on the streets of Harlem. Uniquely suited to its era, the lyrics were filled with dropped names of most of the major black figures, from H. Rap Brown and Martin Luther King Jr. and Malcolm X to Charles Mingus, Pharoah Sanders, and Mongo Santamaria.

Much like Langston Hughes, Gil was able to see the comedy in the tragic and profane, and he knew enough not to take himself too seriously.

He saw plenty of fellow activists and students whose stern manner somehow diminished the effectiveness of their message. "If you've lost your sense of humor, I think you've lost your sense of humanity," he told *Wax Poetics*. "It connects me to some of the people I most admire, people who either mixed comedy with art or art with comedy, people such as Dick Gregory or Richard Pryor. You can't just start screaming at everybody. Everybody knows there are things wrong with this planet. But in order to make it through all the things that are going to happen to you in your life, you need to maintain humor. It's the most important aspect of yourself."

The track that is most responsible for his reputation as a political singer, "The Revolution Will Not Be Televised," is distinguished by its comic asides and sarcastic tone. Gil himself characterized it as satire rather than a political diatribe. "People would try and argue that it was this militant message, but just how militant can you really be when you're saying, 'The revolution will not make you look five pounds thinner'?," he told the *Telegraph*. "My songs were always about the tone of voice rather than the words. A good comic will deliver a line deadpan—they let the audience laugh."

Gil's verse was transformed and energized in the move from the page to the stage, through his use of dramatic pauses and the way he enunciated certain words. And on the album, he included some atmospheric touches that added to the power of the lyrics. On the first track, "Introduction," Gil has a close eye for detail, quietly taking in the hustle of conversations at that busy intersection of 125th and Lenox in Harlem: "I don't know if the riots is wrong / But Whitey been kicking my ass for too long."

Much of the political activity that animated Lincoln and the coffeehouses in New York City informed Gil's poetry. He wrote about the "Rainbow conspiracy" on the introduction to "Comment #1" and "Enough," later explaining that that was a term used derisively by the establishment in an attempt to stoke fear in white communities about the threat posed by different groups such as the Latino Young Lords, the Black Panthers, and the white-led Students for a Democratic Society. Gil was just as critical of blacks who advanced their political careers by assuaging white power brokers and then posing as radicals when they visited black neighborhoods. In "Revolution," he mercilessly skewered then-NAACP head Roy Wilkins, who was considered a sellout by militant black activists, describing him as "strolling through Watts in a red, black, and green liberation jumpsuit that he has been saving for just the proper occasion."

On "Small Talk," he ruthlessly mocks the vanity and posturing of black militants—"We deal in too many externals, brother. Always afros, hand-shakes and dashikis"—and condemns the violent rhetoric directed against whites. With the same biting wit he displays on "Revolution," he skewers militants who are tough on other blacks, rushing them with their "super-black bag," and exposes their hypocrisy:

> *I think it was a little too easy for you to forget that you were a negro*
> *before Malcolm*
> *You drove your white girl through the village every Friday night*
> *While the grassroots stared in envy and drank wine,*
> *Do you remember?*

In "Who Will Pay Reparations on My Soul?" Gil took a step forward in his self-expressive capacities, linking his own personal trauma as an abandoned child to other forms of oppression in America, including the treatment of Native Americans:

> *What about the red man*
> *Who met you at the coast?*
> *You never dig sharing,*
> *Always had to have the most.*

The album was an amazing early example of a creative work going viral, decades before the advent of Twitter and Facebook. Though the album got very little airplay due to its content and style, except on a few black stations in urban areas, it caught on in progressive and black neighborhoods. Through word of mouth, *Small Talk* was the talk of campus coffee shops and night-clubs in West Philadelphia, Harlem, Watts, Chicago's South Side, and At-lanta. Poet Nikki Giovanni, who was twenty-seven at the time, remembers seeing Gil perform poems from the album at Liberty House in Harlem, a store that sold crafts made by black cooperatives in Mississippi, and feeling good that another talented poet was on the scene.

Just two weeks before the release of *Small Talk*, Gil came back to Lincoln to visit and talk to students. He had been Spiderman, the tall and overly energetic student who liked to play piano and read his poems and play pinochle but seemed a little too eager for his untested talents. Now he returned as the conquering hero, already playing the role of griot with lengthy late-night sermons that served several purposes: to speak truth to power and to help promote his upcoming album's poems that spoke truth to power.

In one late-night session featured in the *Lincolnian*, in a story headlined "Spiderman Raps," Gil was described like a revolutionary prophet—and his fiery words only bolstered that reputation. He lashed out at the school's insularity and distance from black neighbors in surrounding towns and cities. He used almost biblical language, for dramatic effect, to describe "black citizens" living in "the village": "I mean, there are people down in the village who are near-starving." He condemned the traditional fraternities on campus, saying that they should become less Greek and more black. "The guys could wear dashikis, the girls could wear the long garbs and they could adopt African names." That same year, Last Poet member Abiodun Oyewole did just that with his Yoruba Society, traveling to traditional black colleges and urging students to make those changes.

With the tone of a preacher, Gil urged respect for black women and condemned materialism. And he was clearly adopting some positions espoused by black nationalist groups such as the Black Panthers, telling students to stop dancing and buying records and to read more books about their culture. He had come a long way from his days in high school—or maybe he felt liberated enough to unleash his true feelings. The teenager who used to love imitating the Godfather of Soul onstage now declaimed that "we are being eaten up by black capitalists like James Brown. We spend our money on foolishness that fades away in weeks; solid black things live on and on—these are the things we need to invest in—not 45s or learning the 'latest dance craze.' We got to watch out for the bullshit liberals. If they really were sincere they'd be out on Times Square with a machine gun now."

To condemn record buyers two weeks before your debut album is released is either brilliant or naïve. But Gil didn't feel like he had much to lose, not expecting much of a reaction to the album. He remembers being surprised at its success. "We didn't think we'd get airplay. We didn't think about how much reach we would have. We wanted to play something different."

Slowly, album sales grew, and some larger record store chains started picking it up, though many radio stations still wouldn't play it because of its profanity. The album never made the charts, but sales in urban centers and college towns were strong enough to help pay for the recording of another album, as Thiele had promised. As the word of mouth spread, Gil was soon doing his first media appearances, with WRVR's legendary "jazz priest" Father Norman J. O'Connor and on Ossie Davis and Ruby Dee's radio show in New York City. "When it first came out, I heard it and people were talking about it in the streets and quoting it. It became part of the language," said Amiri Baraka. "Gil was more popular than the Last Poets because he was taking a pop form and using it to the extent that it could be used as a message."

The message and his music had a special appeal for the Black Panthers and other black radicals, some of whom saw Gil as the ideal popular artist to spread the revolution. Though James Brown rapped about black pride and Curtis Mayfield exhorted black Americans to take action, Gil's lyrics were more radical. And he was tapping into a tradition of spoken-word performance, from ministers rapping sermons in church to singers who would talk between songs. In a way, it was secular preaching. "I'm like a gospel and R&B fan, so when I heard Gil for the first time, I said to myself, 'Man, this brother has taken this whole thing and moved it a whole other level,'" remembers A. Peter Bailey, a founding member of the Organization of Afro-American Unity and editor at *Ebony* magazine. "For those of us who came out of the movement, out of the Malcolm X wing, we jumped on it right away. He was using music the way it is supposed to be used. If you want to reach black folks, you've got to have some music, and Gil's music was that."

Though he disavowed violence, Gil shared the sentiment of black militants that the civil rights appeals were dated, says historian Leon F. Litwack. While Martin Luther King Jr.'s followers chanted "We Shall Overcome," the new militants yelled, "We Will Overrun," and recited Gil's lyrics in

"Evolution": "We are tired of praying and marching and thinking and learning / Brothers want to start cutting and shooting and stealing and burning."

By the fall of 1970, the album was a favorite among hip black college students across the country, who were hungrily absorbing the fiery lyrics of the Last Poets and radical poets Nikki Giovanni and Sonia Sanchez. Gil was invited to perform in August at San Francisco's first Black Expo, a cultural event featuring musicians and artists that included playwright Ntozake Shange and Sly and the Family Stone. "It was an artistic renaissance, and those artists were helping fuel the anger and the rage and the passion of the political movements," says Ahimsa Porter Sumchai, a pre-med student at San Francisco State University and the outdoor stage manager at the expo. At the time, the Last Poets were better known than Gil, and Sumchai barely knew who he was when long, lanky, angular Gil loped up to the stage. "He was very good-looking," she remembers, "with a big Afro and very pronounced features. His physical appearance was very commanding, and as he approached the stage he hit on me. Then he got up there and performed and just blew my mind."

After the show, Gil and Sumchai hooked up and dated, seeing each other several times a year after he returned to New York. She was captivated by his charm, and he was intrigued by her beauty, intellectual energy, and defiant attitude. Gil could be arrogant when it came to dispensing political opinions, and Sumchai would challenge him, knocking down his arguments and forcing him to frame his views more carefully. But she had no illusions and just enjoyed being his "San Francisco girl." "When he came to town, I'd get him a cab to pick him up at the airport, and he would stay with me. To be perfectly candid, there was a girl in every city, to help him in every place. I didn't see myself becoming Mrs. Gil Scott-Heron."

The intense schedule of recording and performing around the country transformed Gil's life in innumerable ways. Not only did it expose his poetry and music to a vast audience beyond the confines of Lincoln's canteen student union, but it took away Gil's quiet anonymity. No longer was he able to be impromptu—take a week to hang out with his buddies, cancel plans to watch the Mets play the Phillies, or to smoke a blunt and roam New York City's nightclubs. All those wonderful spontaneous moments became much more difficult—they had to be planned in advance and coordinated according to the new priorities of his recording career. It was all a lot for a twenty-one-year-old freethinker and college student to handle.

Though he had effectively dropped out of Lincoln (again) when he first toured for the *Small Talk* album, he made the decision final in his senior year. When he told his mother about his decision, Bobbie wasn't surprised, but she was disappointed. "She was just concerned that he would not be able to make a livelihood and worried about what his future would look like," remembers cousin Carenna Ransom. Yet Bobbie understood and identified with his artistic aspirations; she knew what he had to do. "Scotty wanted to sing and he wanted to march to a different drum—and you couldn't change his mind," says Ransom. She remembers that Gil pulled her and her twin sister, Carol, aside soon after the album was released and urged them not to call him Scotty anymore. Always sharp with her tongue, she shot him a look and deadpanned, "Okay, Gilbert."

Some of Gil's friends at Lincoln also objected to his leaving Lincoln, urging him in late-night sessions at the canteen not to drop out. "We were protective of each other and thought that it would make better sense to 'get his education first' and then get into the risky field of entertainment," says classmate Gloria Dulan-Wilson, who says that they were deeply suspicious of the recording industry and how it treated black artists. "Particularly because they felt he 'couldn't sing all that well' and did not want to see him get hurt and disillusioned in the white world."

II.

REVOLUTION OF THE MIND

"The Revolution Will Not Be Televised," the poem that anchored *Small Talk*, was Gil's first hit. Though its provocative content and minimalist structure kept it out of most record stores and off Top 40 radio, it started to get airplay on college radio stations around the country. "That poem was everywhere," remembers Nikki Giovanni.

Like many great works of art, the poem that served to define Gil's life and legacy has been misused and misinterpreted since it first hit the airwaves. "The Revolution Will Not Be Televised" has become such a cliché that it has lost much of its original force. Often removed from its lyrical intent, the title has served so many countless headline writers and ad copywriters in search of an easy pun that most people don't even know the original reference. "Everyone knows that title. People use it all the time," says Aldon Lynn Nielsen, a poet and Penn State professor. "But it's clear that they haven't heard anything more than the title—ninety-nine percent of the time, they never quote a single line."

Gil felt that most critics missed the point of the song—it was less about condemning commercialism and more about criticizing cultural racism, how black people viewed the TV shows they watched, which didn't include their views, let alone their faces. "We're always digging on Ozzie & Harriet and Donna Reed as the ideal American family trip," Gil wrote, "and that in no way epitomizes *our* thing," he told Ray Townley of *Down Beat*. "The logical conclusion is that our thing must be off if it's not like that, that it must not be correct. My attempt was to put those daily images in perspective, in a *real* perspective, which is pretty much where black people end up having to come from."

Gil later explained that too many listeners took the poem's title literally, believing that it meant that the protests that led to the overthrow of the government would not end up making the network news. For him, the point of the title was different: that the first change has to take place in your mind, and that makes it difficult to capture or record. He told PBS: "You have to change your mind before you change the way you're living and the way you move. The thing that's going to change people is something that no one will ever be able to capture on film, it will just be something that you see and all of a sudden you realize that I'm on the wrong page, or I'm on the right page but I'm on the wrong note. And I've got to get in sync with everyone else to understand what is going on in this country."

Though the seven-inch single of the track did not sell that many copies, "The Revolution Will Not Be Televised" did invite inevitable questions about whether it was hypocritical to release an anticommercial jeremiad on a record that was played on the radio in between advertisements for shaving cream and chewing gum. Gil's answer perfectly captured the intention of provocative works of art, from Picasso's *Guernica* to George Orwell's *1984*, and placed the power of the message in the hands of the audience. "The question is what you deem the message to be, what you decided I said after you heard it," he later told journalist Ray Townley. He was only putting the message out there; what happened next was up to the listener.

The poem and its provocative title had an immediate impact on the culture and on those critics and observers who kept their ear to the ground. Less than a year after its release, *New York Times* music critic Craig McGregor used lyrics from the song to preface his May 9, 1971, essay declaring the end of Woodstock Nation. He then interspersed the lyrics throughout the essay, which functioned as a virtual obituary of sixties rock. Describing the tragedy of Altamont, the infamous 1969 Rolling Stones concert at which a Hells Angels security guard stabbed a black man to death, McGregor fumed that "we must beware surrogate Revolutions . . . because what America, and the world, need right now is the real thing," and ended his rant by reprinting the last six lines of Gil's "Revolution." Later that year, radio station WBAI featured snippets of the song throughout the Network Project, its eight-part series on the impact of television.

The enduring force of the poem and of its title already ranks Gil among the greats, says writer David Rigsbee. He recalls once talking to poet Mark Strand in Rome, who told him, "There's only one reason for poetry to exist and that's to write an immortal line." Gil did that, believes Grigsby. "That title has entered the language. That's an amazing achievement—to write a line that everyone in the universe knows."

Some of his old friends in Jackson, Tennessee, were shocked when they first heard the song, not linking it with the sweetly smiling Scotty they knew as a child. One of Portia Hegmon's former boyfriends gave her a copy of the *Small Talk* album and she couldn't believe it was Gil's. "I thought it was so un-Scotty. It was like it was the opposite of the person that I knew," says Hegmon. "He was quiet but kept things to himself. Now, he was so in your face. But I liked it and I realized what he was saying in it."

For the Last Poet who inspired the poem, the revolution took a detour. Abiodun Oyewole's experience proved to be a cautionary tale for Gil, demonstrating the real-world risks faced by a young black man who chooses to promote radical political views. Just months before Gil released the song, the Last Poet was arrested for robbing Ku Klux Klan members at gunpoint in North Carolina.

So the Last Poet was sitting in jail on a three-year bid when he first heard "The Revolution Will Not Be Televised." He thought it was an inspiring poem, and he was a little envious of the song's success, since it was so closely based on "When the Revolution Comes."

"Gil was blowing up, and I was sitting in jail," Oyewole says. "If I were out there, I would have taken that position, because I was the only one who could sing and do poetry. And the only one who could do that as well was Gil, and he was getting the flowers that I wasn't getting." But ultimately Oyewole felt a connection to Gil, and his songs became a regular part of Oyewole's music rotation in and out of jail, particularly the haunting lyrics on the title track of Gil's next album.

12.

"I SAW THE THUNDER AND HEARD THE LIGHTNING"

By the time the *Small Talk* album was released, Gil's percussionists were splitting off in different directions. Eddie "Ade" Knowles graduated and taught music classes in the Bronx. Charlie Saunders went back to Bronx Community College and became a sheet metal worker, later working on the construction of the new World Trade Center in downtown Manhattan. David Barnes went to graduate school and then taught in Brooklyn. And Gil moved back to Lincoln, where he lived off-campus with Brian Jackson, in an old double-wide trailer full of beer cans and cigarette butts, and worked on his next novel.

Since *Small Talk* performed well, Thiele lived up to the promise he had made to let Gil record, for his next release on Flying Dutchman, a music album with Brian. He called Gil and asked him, "Whom do you want to perform with?" Gil jumped at the chance and reached for the stars. "Let's get Ron Carter on bass and Hubert Laws." Carter had risen to fame as part of Miles Davis's quintet in the 1960s, and Laws was a bandleader whose versatility had earned him respect from jazz and classical music aficionados alike. Brian wanted Elvin Jones, but when they got to the studio, Thiele asked Gil, "Let's try Purdie." Legendary R&B drummer Bernard "Pretty" Purdie, who'd jammed with James Brown and Miles Davis, was working downstairs at Atlantic Records, and was playing with King Curtis, who was backing up Aretha Franklin. So Purdie joined the session.

On April 19, 1971, this group of all-star musicians strode into the studio in New York and wondered who the hell these two college dropouts were. "They had no idea who we were or what we were doing," Gil told the *Daily Swarm*. "When they came in and saw us, they wondered what the hell was going on with Bob because it was two high-school guys, well two high-school-looking guys." When Carter showed up, he said, "Look, well fuckers, you know, look, let's see what we got here." Looking down at the set list and noticing the title "Lady Day and John Coltrane," he said, "They got a song here about two of my favorite people; let's see how this song works out." Then he pulled out the chart for the song and played it with the band. Afterward, Carter seemed satisfied: "Alright, this is going to be alright." Then they played "Or Down You Fall," a personal song about insecurity. After playing the opening a few times, the musicians felt that it sounded off. They turned around and asked Carter, "This ain't right, is it?" Ever the jazz improviser, Carter quipped, "If he does it again that way, it's right." Though Carter was dismissive at first of the duo's youth, and skeptical of Gil's vocal chops, he soon became a believer. "He wasn't a great singer, but with that voice, if he had whispered, it would have been dynamic," Carter told the *The New Yorker*. "It was a voice like you would have for Shakespeare."

Legendary arranger Johnny Pate was brought in. Pate, who had worked with Curtis Mayfield and B. B. King, was struck by Gil's vocal delivery. "He wasn't singing but rapping, long before rappers even knew what it was all about," says Pate. "It was a pretty unique and hip thing for me." Purdie brought in a young bassist, Jerry Jemmott. While Purdie hit the sticks, Jemmott would play a bass line counter to that beat and develop some chord progressions on several tracks. "Purdie was perfect, absolutely perfect for what we were doing and a great guy," remembers Gil.

The album was named *Pieces of a Man*, after one of the album's tracks. Though credited to Gil, it was really Brian and Gil's masterwork, and Brian cowrote seven of the album's eleven songs. The album kicks off with the now-seminal version of "Revolution," which transforms the song that was first recorded on *Small Talk* by adding Brian's lilting flute, a muscular bass line, and Purdie's crackling drums. Though it starts with a politically explosive bang, the rest of the album consists of romantic ballads and reflective soul-jazz compositions. It was a musical leap forward, with Gil's rich baritone propelled by strong rhythms and great melodies. All of that was due to Brian, said Gil: "You know, on the first one, I was playing piano. And on the second one, Brian was! There's your leap right there!" The album also marked a mature step forward for Gil's lyrical voice, which had moved from the angry young rebel of *Small Talk* to a sharp observer of society's tribulations.

The title track, for instance, was based on a story that he heard from band member Ade, whose father went crazy when he lost his job. "He was a bricklayer and he couldn't get in the union because it was all-white," says Ade. "He wound up working as a bellman at the Times Square Hotel . . . the fact that he couldn't manifest what his real talents were [it felt like] a piece of him was stripped away." Some of the lines are hauntingly prophetic of Gil's later arrests for drug possession:

> *And now I hear the sound of sirens*
> *Come knifing through the gloom*
> *But they don't know what they're doing*
> *They could hardly understand*
> *That they're only arresting*
> *Pieces of a man*

"Home Is Where the Hatred Is" marks Gil's move into stark new terrain. One of his most-cited songs, though it never topped the charts, the devastating portrayal of a junkie resonated with audiences. Its lyrics seemed to prophesy Gil's later drug problems (though he was not a heroin addict). He later explained that he based the haunting song on a young man he knew from New York City, where he refereed basketball games during the summer. He said that the kid was an All-City high school basketball star and a bike delivery boy who started hanging out with some heroin addicts in Gil's Chelsea neighborhood.

"Over the course of that summer, he went from who he had been and who he could have been to who he never should have been but inevitably became," he explained. Gil based the lyrics on the expectations placed on this young man by his family. Though his brother had a good job at a bank and his sister was getting married, the highest hopes were for the boy, and he started avoiding going home because "that's where the hatred is."

Though Gil never revealed the boy's name, the song seems to be based on Michael "Cet" Tabor, an All-City star basketball player who was a legend on the courts in Harlem. He got clean, joined the Black Panthers, and was later charged by federal prosecutors with taking part in a conspiracy to blow up buildings in the city and kill policemen. Four months into his trial in 1971, he fled to Africa, where he remained for the rest of his life, hosting a radio show in Zambia before dying of stroke-related complications in 2010.

Gil says he wrote the song in the first person, rather than the third, to avoid making it sound accusatory. "If you do things in the first person, then even people with those kinds of problems can look at them because you're not talking about them. You're talking about yourself. They can look at themselves by looking at you."

When soul singer Esther Phillips, a recovering heroin addict herself, first heard the song, she told Gil point-blank that he "knew too much about junkies not to be one." She even bet some of her sidemen that Gil really was a junkie. But when Gil met up with Philips one day, he had just come from playing basketball and was wearing shorts and a sleeveless shirt, which exposed his healthy arms and legs. "Damn, I lost the bet," she said. In 1972, Phillips recorded her own version of the song, a moody and haunting one that brought her acclaim and a Grammy nomination. Gil was proud of her performance and incredibly flattered that she had chosen his poem to cover. "It brings it to life and that's a helluva thing for a writer to be able to hear in one of his songs."

Gil liked to say that his poems weren't just personal but that they represented the people he knew and saw around him in his community. "Some of them were angry, some of them were upset, some of them were parents, some of them were in love with their children, some of them were trying to get jobs, some of them were working with their jobs, some of them had problems with their women." By adding rhythm and blues to his message-laden music on *Pieces of a Man*, Gil went even further in crafting a distinct sound that merged serious lyrics with funk music. "It was a way to structure the message without hitting you over the head with it," says historian James B. Stewart, and it went beyond what conscious soul singers were doing at the time. "With Marvin Gaye and Curtis Mayfield, you had the uplifting lyrics but you can't picture a lot in your mind. They were dealing with generalities and not specific realities. Gil takes you through the storyline and beyond."

As noted by many music critics, Gil's voice anchored the music, despite the fact that he didn't have a great singing voice. His baritone, in the middle register, was narrow, and he had difficulty hitting high notes or finding the right key to sing in. Jazz critic Ray Townley compared his narrow vocal range to that of Dylan, who also was able to match captivating lyrics with strong melodies, noting, "There are moments when Scott-Heron's off-key phrasing and simple melodic sweep truly enhance the word content."

The album attracted plenty of notice and sold twenty to thirty thousand copies, an impressive number for a work that led off with one of the most incisive critiques of American consumer culture ever recorded. "Revolution" was released as a B-side to "Home Is Where the Hatred Is," but the single never made the charts. But as with *Small Talk*, strong word of mouth racked up sales, and the album reached No. 25 on the *Billboard* soul album chart two years after its release. Those sales were helped by strong airplay on the FM stations (such as WDAS in Philadelphia), which were starting to shove aside the longtime AM standbys on the radio dial.

WDAS's Dan Henderson was one of the first deejays to introduce a new style of playing records, weaving together an eclectic mix of records from hard rock to gospel and establishing a cult following with his audience. Gil was one of his favorite artists, and he played "Revolution" and "Lady Day and John Coltrane" almost every day. Henderson invited Gil to come on the show, and he accepted; he came to the studio clutching a giant joint filled with liquid hashish that he called "The One." It knocked him out for two hours, rendering him unable to move. "I was petrified and ossified," Gil later wrote, claiming that he had been handed the drug by someone else. Despite (or perhaps because of) the high, Gil bonded with the well-connected deejay and hired him as his manager. Henderson soon got the group good gigs, including one playing with blues legend John Lee Hooker and R&B singer Donny Hathaway at Temple University later that year.

13.

THE URBAN STRANGE

Even after the critical and commercial success with *Pieces of a Man*, Gil still considered himself first and foremost a writer. The disappointment he felt about being dismissed by the English faculty at Lincoln hadn't blunted his dream of writing for a living and achieving some modest fame. Steve Wilson, his former roommate at Lincoln, told Gil about a friend who had been admitted to the writing fellowship program at Johns Hopkins. Gil was impressed, and they drove down to check it out, clutching their youthful dreams and a bottle of Jack Daniels Black that Gil had stolen from a local liquor store.

In his retelling of the story, Gil expresses his doubts about his true talent, whether he was really qualified to write for a living like his hero Langston Hughes. He explains that part of his motivation for the trip was to check out whether Wilson's buddy, the writing ace dubbed "B. More," was actually qualified or whether "the brother had gotten into Hopkins the way I had gotten into Fieldston," essentially an affirmative action admission, a "local-Black-makes-good type."

When they arrived at Johns Hopkins, Wilson and his friend got drunk while Gil ate his lunch. In a heated debate over who was a better writer, B. More insulted Gil as an "Afro-wearin' chump and a "fuckin' prep." At one point, Wilson stood up for Gil, pouring a shot of whiskey and telling his friend that Gil was more talented than them because he didn't drink, though hitting the bottle would make him more of a "real writer."

Gil later claimed that he went to the department's admissions office, determined to drop off his application, but was told that all twenty-seven openings had already been filled, even though the deadline was still a month away. In his sweetest voice, he asked the secretary if he could just say hello to poet Elliott Coleman, who ran the program. Coleman, a poetry giant who mentored prominent writers such as Russell Baker and John Barth, was a "great man" in Gil's opinion. Part of his admiration for the Waspy scholar stemmed from Gil's desire to buck the black intelligentsia, to defy the pressure being placed on him by racial separatists to ignore or repudiate nonblack artists.

When he stopped into Coleman's office, Gil was prepared. He handed the "great man" his two books and the *Small Talk* album and told him that "if any of the twenty-seven you've awarded has done as much work as I have, maybe I don't deserve one like I think I do." The theatrics worked, and Coleman opened up a slot for him in the program, to Gil's everlasting pride. Over the next decade, Gil loved to brag to students, colleagues, and friends about how he was able to get a master's in creative writing without having a bachelor's degree.

From the moment he stepped into class in the fall of 1971, Gil had a commanding presence. As one of only two African Americans in the program, he stood out with his dashikis and towering Afro. He was even more exceptional due to the fact that he had already published a novel and a book of poetry. "He was an intimidating guy, and he played that up," remembers fellow student and poet David Rigsbee. "He liked that edge of menace, though it was obviously a protection for him, too." Gil brought a black briefcase to class that contained his novel and poetry collection, almost out of a need to show off to the other students that he had already been published.

Typical of many writing seminars, the class got caught up in pretentious discussions about semantics and structure. Gil quickly realized that he didn't have the time or patience for such pretentiousness (and some of the faculty seemed suspicious of him, assuming that he was just a dilettante who'd gotten lucky). A few weeks into class, he presented a poem that received "the usual workshop critique, and he didn't come back," says Rigsbee. "I remember being appalled that people were nitpicking. Well, he's already got a fucking book, so shut up!" Rodger Kamenetz, another fellow student, remarked. "It was so clear that he was not going to sit around and say, 'I like the word "yellow" more than the word "almond." We would sit in class talking about line breaks, and it would end up in a journal read by maybe thirty people. Gil didn't have time for that."

Gil's resistance stemmed from his experience at DeWitt Clinton High School and Lincoln, dealing with pretentious English teachers who insisted that difficult books made great books. At a 1980 concert, Gil riffed on a ninth-grade teacher who made the class read a poem that included the line "What now shall I see on the wall a shadow of an image." While Gil tried to make sense of the line's meaning, another classmate said, "This must be deep." Gil thought that the line only seemed deep because it was in a book that had been handed out by the teacher. "Ordinarily, you read that and it don't mean anything to you, you say, 'Hey, this must be nonsense' . . . what happens is when a lot of folks get ready to write poetry, that's what they decide they are going to be—deep. They decide they're going to be poetic . . . people feel that the way to be poetic is to make sure there are certain little parts can't nobody understand. Why would you need a poet to make things *more* complex? Two winos can make things more complex."

Rather than reach for abstraction and abstruse lines to impress graduate school writing seminar teachers, Gil sought to use ideas and words that everybody could understand. "Of course, this poetry was always put down as street poetry. Because that's where the people were, the people were on the street and that's who you want to communicate with." After exiting the seminar, Gil spent most of his time writing outside of class and rehearsing with the band. He also toiled at his thesis, "Circle of Stone," a thirty-five-page semi-autobiographical story about a day in the life of a restless young photographer living in Harlem who makes plans to return to his hometown in Tennessee to find his bearings.

The novella, which was never published, is preceded by a poem titled "Abstract," which sums up some of Gil's contradictory feelings about his heritage and the tense mood in America at that moment. The powerful poem was a few steps beyond early poems such as "Get Out of the Ghetto Blues," slipping even deeper into the dark side of the American dream:

> *Him growed up*
> *with warindianreservationbirthcontrolrottingearthnigger.*

The story centers on Nathaniel B. Glass, a photographer for a black advertising agency, who burns with rage at the compromises he's made in his career. In brutally honest prose, Gil describes Nate's desire to repair his "damaged sense of values" and his sense of incompleteness at his effort to build an independent life in the city.

After a night of unsatisfying sex with his girlfriend, Josephine, Nate returns to his fourth-floor one-bedroom apartment at the corner of 145th and Amsterdam Avenue and lights up a joint.

> *Horns blared up at him from the street, babies cried in other apartments, someone upstairs was called a jive muthafucka and he could swear he heard a rat clawing at the baseboard beneath the sink.*

While the marijuana smoke relaxes him, Nate ponders what his "mother, father, sister, granny" would think of his drug habit, foreshadowing Gil's own ambivalence toward drug use in later years. Echoing a question the latter-day Gil might ask, his character muses: "Was that one of the moral things to ask . . . ? If you're surviving in New York, who deserves to get high more than you?" Nate looks out the window and sneers with disgust at the rush-hour crowds streaming out of the subway, "skin moist and flabby like fish skins drenched oily by Metropolitan sweat." Finally, he decides that he needs to escape the "elbow scraping holocaust and claustrophobia" of the city and head back down South.

The details of Nate's life and family mirror Gil's experience—he was raised in Tennessee by relatives, later enrolled at DeWitt Clinton High School in the Bronx, and was abandoned by his father, who "had made it clear that he wanted nothing to do with mother or son when he left. . . ."

In a way, the novel may represent an unfulfilled desire of Gil's, even in his young twenties, to reverse his migration to the loud, chaotic city full of cynical people and complex realities and to move back to Jackson, the only home he truly loved, where he could "laze around all day on the back porch drinking cider or something stronger." That was familiar to him, where people greeted him with open smiles and easy manners in contrast to the tough life in New York: "The urban strange was attacking him. The strangeness of urban life and the coldness and suspicion."

After throwing some clothes and some pot into a bag, Nate pauses to question his constant need to run away from himself: "Run away from college! . . . Run, nigger, run!"

It all directly speaks to Gil's own life—running around to parties in New York, stealing wine from a liquor store on his way with Lincoln roommate Stevie Wilson to visit John Hopkins in his freshman year, dropping out of Lincoln twice. "Run, nigger, run!"

But, unlike Gil, Nate actually goes home again, throwing his bag and a box lunch into the back of his secondhand VW on a rainy evening and heading out over the George Washington Bridge for the fifteen-hundred-mile drive to Tennessee. From there, the novel jumps clumsily into a profile of Nate's boss before ending abruptly.

Though Gil often cited his two novels, the unpublished "Circle of Stone" remains a mysterious footnote to his career. But the experience was valuable in at least one respect. He needed to make his mom proud, so as soon as he got his master's degree at Johns Hopkins, he sent it to Bobbie. It worked. She found a special place for it on the wall of her small living room in the apartment on Seventeenth Street.

14.

SPIDER AND THE STICKMAN

Gil was growing more confident as a musician, buoyed by the critical acclaim he was receiving for those first two albums and the feedback from the audience at shows in 1971 and 1972. Though he respected Thiele, he was chafing under the control of the legendary producer and he wanted to take charge of his own music. He was eager to buck Flying Dutchman after his next album, which would complete his three-record deal with the label. So he rushed through *Free Will*, which featured poems that didn't make it onto *Small Talk*.

In addition to some of the Lincoln crew, a few members of the all-star team from *Pieces of a Man*, including Bernard Purdie and Hubert Laws, returned for the New York session on March 2 and 3, 1972. The album was split, with the first side focusing on lyrical soul-jazz pieces such as "Did You Hear What They Said?," and the other side delivering more tough political tracks, such as "No Knock" and "The King Alfred Plan," over spare percussion and Brian's flute. The two parts represented both halves of Gil's personality, the personal and the political, the reflective and the aggressive.

The album also reflected Gil's growing political education. As he became more aware of the hidden forces that shaped society, he became more committed to vocalizing his opinions. "The whole idea behind those sort of things at the time was to put some information in front of people that they couldn't get any other way." In tracks such as "No Knock," Gil spotlights

the police use of no-knock warrants to storm homes in black neighborhoods, an issue that he once discussed with Nixon's attorney general John
Mitchell in a meeting with other student leaders. In "Ain't No New Thing,"
a fast-paced poem accompanied by flute and percussion, Gil lacerates white
culture for exploiting and oppressing black artists, naming musicians such
as Billie Holiday, Charlie Parker, and Jimi Hendrix. And in "The King
Alfred Plan," he articulates a long-simmering conspiracy theory about the
government's plans for a black uprising. That plan, a fictional scheme to put
blacks into concentration camps in the wake of racial strife, was first described in a 1967 novel by John A. Williams. The theory spread quickly
through black neighborhoods after Williams made photocopies of the section describing the King Alfred Plan and left them on subway seats in New
York City.

"The Get out of the Ghetto Blues," anchored by Brian's bluesy piano
playing and David Spinozza's tough guitar, became one of Gil's best-known
performances. His voice was in rare form, raw and emotional but laced
with his sardonic attitude: "I know you think you're cool / If you're getting
two welfare checks." Gil was out there: conspiracy-minded and paranoid,
angry and righteous, and often telling uncomfortable truths. After all, the
injustices he discussed, from police abusing people's constitutional rights, the
FBI's COINTELPRO program to infiltrate and destroy black nationalist
groups such as the Black Panthers, and white artists' theft of black rhythm-
and-blues music, were really happening. Years later, he regretted the decision to split the album thematically, saying that he should have dropped the
poems and made the album all music. But in the moment, he was rushing
to complete the album and exit his deal with Flying Dutchman.

The album cemented the partnership that would create Gil's most last-
ing music. The duo Spider and Stickman (Gil's name for Brian Jackson) felt
that they completed each other musically. "Gil with his deep relationship
with the English language, and me with my fierce loyalty to the principles
of good music," says Brian. There was a symbiosis to the way they worked.
In general, Gil would come up with a few chords, a spare melody, and Brian
would then take over and complete the track, adding complexity and depth
to the piece. Other times, Brian pointed Gil to a certain theme or topic for the
lyrics that would accompany his melodies. Though Gil is always associated

with the content of the lyrics, Brian often conveyed his ideas through music. He would play a tune, and Gil would ask him what was on his mind at the time he played that particular chord or progression. Sometimes Gil's provocative attitude in his lyrics was too much for some of his friends, including Brian, who at times felt that Gil was "a little too blunt, he kinda beat people over the head with it." It may not have been Brian's style, but he certainly agreed with the sentiments expressed in the songs.

Brian was meticulous about his performing, sitting behind his four-keyboard setup (a Rhodes, Clavinova, Elka string, and a Minimoog) and endlessly tuning them to his satisfaction. Gil, who wasn't a trained singer, was challenged vocally by some of Brian's compositions, but they also stimulated him and inspired some of his best work. "Gil is primarily a poet, secondarily a vocalist, thirdly a composer, and fourthly a musician," says longtime producer Malcolm Cecil. "That's why he and Brian worked so well."

They also connected on a personal level. Like Gil, Brian had been raised as an only child by strong women. "It shaped our views of ourselves. We considered ourselves loners, on the outside of society," said Jackson. And the two of them often preferred being alone to being around other people. "What he saw in himself, he saw in me," says Jackson. "The stubbornness, the honesty. A lot of people around him would kiss his ass, but not me. Creatively and emotionally, we were brothers." The two helped support each other through the tumultuous 1970s and the intense transformation in their lives. They "sheltered each other" from the tricks and temptations of the often-cutthroat music business, says Jackson.

Brian also identified with Gil's abandonment by his parents because his own father, Clarence Robert Jackson Jr., had walked out on him and his mother when he was a little boy, moving across the river to Harlem. Just like Gil, Brian was raised by women: his mother and grandmother. Just as Gil drew inspiration from Albert Porter, an educated and politically aware man who gave him his first typewriter, Brian had his uncle Reggie, who had lived in Denmark and exposed him to different forms of music and to the world of ideas.

On March 24, 1972, just weeks after Gil and Brian finished recording *Free Will*, Dial Press published *The Nigger Factory*. Around the same time,

Gil went back to Lincoln to perform a triumphal concert. Students on campus treated him with awe, and some of the professors who had dismissed him showed up out of curiosity. Critics were less kind: "An offensive novel by a young black writer who should know better," slammed *Kirkus Reviews*. "Full of machismo, didacticism, conventional liberalisms, not helped by any of the absolutely mundane pseudo-reportorial ('7 P.M. Phone Call') style and Uncle Remus dialect ('I wuz callin' befo' cuz we were gonna like confer wit'choo befo' we handed the shit to the Man).'"

As was the case with *Nigger Factory*, Gil's novels have received occasional praise but they have never received critical respect, often being dismissed as early experiments by a songwriter. In recent years, some scholars have paid renewed attention to the works as serious examples of "vernacular realism." At the time, Gil was disappointed by the scathing critiques, but he knew deep down that those critics had a point. His anger and energy were full of youthful self-righteousness, but they were not grounded in real-world experience. On campus, radical theories and ideologies taught in class and repeated in late-night dorm room discussions set hearts on fire, but they existed in a vacuum. Students eager for a taste of revolution might march in the quad and protest against the school administration just to feel alive, but that type of rebellion felt shallow and self-centered. For Gil and Brian, it was time to go where the real action was.

15.

FREE JAZZ AND WILD STUFF

They soon got their chance when some black artists in DC invited them to move into a rundown Victorian mansion once owned by President Grant and later occupied by members of Duke Ellington's family. The legendary jazz bandleader's nephew Henry Letcher had teamed up with a cousin, photographer Leon Collins, to take over a dilapidated former vocational school for blacks at One Logan Circle and turn it into an artistic community. When they moved into the four-story pile, where Letcher's father had once educated GIs returning from World War II, they found it overrun with homeless people. The cousins cleaned up some rooms and built a platform out of some tables on the first floor and made it a small performance space, where musicians would come and jam, play free jazz or anything that came to mind. Other rooms were turned into studios for photographers and artists. Letcher and Collins dubbed the space Free Art. "Some musicians were frightened to come by," says Collins. "They'd say, 'You guys do some wild stuff here.'"

At a time when many freethinking college students such as Gil and Brian were disillusioned with the world of academia and dropping out of college, One Logan Circle functioned as an alternative campus. Collins and Letcher started a band, and they would rehearse and perform on the roof, occasionally causing traffic accidents by rush-hour motorists trying to locate the source of the music. One of the housemates, Vic, owned a black Cadillac

hearse, and they would all pile in and drive around the neighborhood looking for adventure. The cousins had some vacant rooms and a mutual appreciation for Gil's music. "I was in tune with Gil's message and the
politics," says Collins. "Growing up as a native Washingtonian, everything
is a conspiracy theory. We would go and see him perform in the city. To us,
he was a spoken-word hero more than a musician."

Letcher went up to Lincoln, where he saw Gil and Brian perform. After
the show, he asked them, "You want to come to DC? We have this musicians' house." A few weeks later, they packed up their things and drove
down to DC, moving into a second-floor room. Gil and Brian would rehearse in the music room, which featured two drum kits. "They were very
diligent about what they were doing, they would rehearse from nine to five,"
says Letcher. At the end of the day, someone would stir up a big pitcher of
piña coladas and everyone in the house would do barbeques on the roof. Gil
loved to rhetorically spar in conversation with close friends, almost like "playing the dozens," the traditional African American rhyming contest. "Gil used
to talk crazy and make up his own words—the circle became the 'squircle'—
and the conversation would ping-pong back and forth," remembers Gary
Price, a photographer and filmmaker who lived in the house. "A lot of his
lyrics came out of that."

In a city that attracted protesters, organizers, and activists of every
variety, debating issues across the political spectrum and with a huge population of black people, the messages in his lyrics were received with enthusiasm. "This was Chocolate City. People in DC were pretty sophisticated and
they liked his political wit, and I think he liked speaking truth to power
in the heart of the government," says housemate Leon Collins. The city may
have been quieter than New York, but parts of DC were like a war zone in
those days, with National Guard troops armed with M-16s watching from
the rooftops and riot police tossing tear gas canisters to break up the looting
in poor neighborhoods. "People were very poor and hungry and angry,"
remembers Letcher. "We saw looters get shot and killed right around the
corner from the house. And Gil was deeply affected by that. He was a sensitive cat."

The political tumult that Gil had been soaking up in books and newspaper headlines on campus at Lincoln was now right in his face. And that

intense exposure to injustice and poverty at the heart of America propelled him into radical activism, prompting him to hang out with the Black Panthers and raise funds for political prisoners, in the years to come. For now, he constantly debated the issues of the day, from ending the war in Vietnam to redistributing wealth, and the effectiveness of protests with his housemates at One Logan Circle. Letcher shared Gil's beliefs, but he was more cynical about the possibility of actually effecting change in government and society. "I used to caution him, 'Look, there is not going to be a revolution. It's dangerous to even say that.' And he would get a little mad at me. He was fully engaged with what he was saying."

The group in the house could get a little paranoid, which may be a natural instinct in a town filled with government officials, soldiers, and radical activists. They were well aware of the FBI's COINTELPRO program to infiltrate and conduct surveillance of artists and activists. And they suspected that some of the unmarked vehicles parked across the street were watching them and that their phone was tapped—they never paid the bill and yet their service was never cut off. One morning, more than a dozen policemen raided the house and searched every room on a tip that it was a drug factory. Later that day, a lieutenant from the local precinct came over and apologized.

In 1972, Gil and Brian reunited with their Lincoln buddies Ade Knowles and Victor Brown. The bond they all shared with one another helped the band thrive artistically. There was a comfort level going back to their days in the Black and Blues sneaking into the chapel to rehearse, and they still spent hours together shooting the shit and brainstorming ideas for songs. "It was a hive mind, a collective consciousness," remembers Gil's girlfriend Sumchai. "I remember some conversations where it was like a basketball team passing the ball, with ideas bouncing around the room, along with plenty of inside jokes."

16.

BLUESOLOGY

Soon after getting his master's degree in 1972, Gil was heading to New York one morning aboard a crowded Amtrak train. He was on his way to meet Grace Shaw, his editor, when he found himself standing next to Leslie Lacy, the author of *The Rise and Fall of a Proper Negro: An Autobiography*. Born in Louisiana, Lacy lived the life of a self-aware black revolutionary to the fullest during the 1960s, joining West Coast militant groups and going back to his roots by moving to Africa. They got to talking, and Lacy suggested that Gil look into teaching at Federal City College, a relatively new school in DC that was attracting many of the black intelligentsia as students and faculty members, including socialist theorist C. L. R. James and historian Ira Berlin.

The idea appealed to Gil, who had been increasingly thinking about taking a college teaching job, a gig that would allow him freedom and time to write and perform. Though he had been disappointed with his experience as a student at Lincoln and Johns Hopkins, his intellectual curiosity drew him to the academic life. The dismissive attitude and pretentiousness of the faculty he'd encountered had frustrated him, but it also made him wonder if he could do a better job. Gil often told friends that he dreamed about becoming an English professor. The gig also gave him a reason to stay in DC, a city he had truly come to love. With its active fan base, dynamic

African American community, and politically charged atmosphere as the nation's capital, it energized him.

Upon Lacy's recommendation, Gil was offered a job teaching a creative writing class at FCC in the fall of 1972. The two men taught alongside each other in the "shoe box" building at E Street and Second Avenue, and spent long afternoons discussing politics and racial dynamics at Lacy's apartment on Sixteenth Street.

Aldon Nielsen, a conscientious objector to the Vietnam draft who was interested in creative writing, showed up for Gil's first class and found only two people in the room. The teacher's seat and desk were empty and there was a young woman waiting for the class to begin and a tall man sitting in a chair scribbling notes on some sheets of paper. Nielsen went over and sat next to the woman, and they made small talk for a few minutes. Finally, they started to wonder if the teacher was going to show up. Nielsen turned to the young man and asked, "Hey, do you know when this class is supposed to start?"

The man stood up and walked to the front of the room. It was Gil. He introduced himself and gave a brief description of what he wanted to teach in the course, for which about twenty-five students had registered though only a few showed up at that first class. "Let's go over a few things and the other folks will just have to catch up," Gil said.

Over the semester, the class tended to follow a loose structure, with Gil assigning books and stories and having open discussions with the students. "What struck me about Gil was his real love of genre stuff but also a real intellectual vigor," says Nielsen. "We spent about an hour on a Robert Blake movie, *Electric Glide in Blue*, discussing how the movie was put together." Gil was casual in his manner as well. He always carried a beat-up leather briefcase spilling open with a shuffle of papers and one of his novels. When Nielsen saw Gil perform twenty years later and they went backstage, there was the same briefcase, and he told his wife, "There it is."

"He never said, 'This is my approach to writing.' It was more like a workshop," says Aldon Nielsen, who was a student in Gil's course. "He showed how in *The Vulture*, you can give away certain information without revealing too much. How to get from A to B, diagramming and the shifting viewpoint." To describe how he developed the plot in *The Vulture*, Gil drew a chart on the blackboard with little boxes that represented each character's point of view. He then showed how he had decided to have the action move through them, charting the plot from each different point of view.

At the time, Gil was still writing song lyrics and poems, but he didn't tend to share those with his students. Once, he explained to the class his theory that most history books were Eurocentric in their description of events, such as the "discovery" of Africa. That lesson became part of the "Bluesology" monologue that he included years later on his album *The First Minute of a New Day*:

> And yes there was love and medicine and religion and intertribal
>   communication by drum,
> but no papers and pencils and other utensils and hell these folks never
>   even heard of a gun.
> So this is why the colonies came, to stabilize the land.
> The dark continent had copper and gold and the discoverers had
>   themselves a plan.
> They would discover all the places with promise,
> you didn't need no titles and deeds.

While he may have remained secretive about his own lyrics, he was open about his methods to his students, some of whom had become fans after picking up his albums. He showed them how to start with a verbal kernel that had an interesting sound to it and to keep developing it further and further, adding nuance and depth. One of his assignments was a common one in creative writing classes: asking students to write about a remembered experience in vivid detail. It elicited a powerful description from a woman who had been in labor for ten hours giving birth to one of her four children.

Though he would spend hours sitting with certain students, carefully going through their manuscripts, Gil liked to impart tough love and would sometimes try to shame his students by talking about how much he'd enjoyed composition classes at Johns Hopkins because those students were so hungry and talented. One of his students was David Nicholson, who went on to become the books editor at the *Washington Post*. He remembers Gil bragging about how he had gotten into the MFA program at Johns Hopkins without having a bachelor's degree. "He seemed very proud of that accomplishment." Gil was also dismissive of writers and artists who used hard drugs. While talking to Nicholson about their mutual appreciation for Jimi Hendrix, he declared, "Boy, all that talent, and he just gave it away for a bag of cocaine." Nicholson doesn't remember much about Gil, recalling that Gil was often late to class or absent, adding that, "I learned more in a five-minute conversation with [author] Larry McMurtry outside his bookstore in Georgetown than I did in a semester with Scott-Heron."

17.

THE PRINCE OF CHOCOLATE CITY

At the time in the early 1970s, the black music scene in DC was dynamic, with local funk and soul bands such as Parliament and Trouble Funk developing a reputation in the city and then hitting it big nationally. Other area bands didn't have to top the charts to make a living, with plenty of clubs such as Ed Murphy's Supper Club and other venues from Blues Alley to the Cellar Door, with a support network of talent managers and promotional photographers. Murphy's club became a home away from home for Gil and the band, and students and faculty from FCC often stopped by to hang out or check out Gil's performances.

Gil and the band regularly performed in the tristate area around Washington. Soon, he linked up with Norris "Bruce" Little, a local legend in the music scene and promoter who booked talent and had relationships with all the major record labels. Little's production company booked shows for Roy Ayers, Stanley Turrentine, and trumpeter Hugh Masekela, and his family was involved in almost every aspect of his business—his sister often cooked meals for local bands.

Little's Charisma Productions was in the Shaw neighborhood, on Seventh Street, with an office dominated by a giant color mural of all the musicians they worked with. For a couple of years, from 1971 to 1972, Gil's morning routine was to stop by the office. Donning a beige fedora, he would walk in carrying a Granny Smith apple, a bean pie, and that day's *Washington Post*.

"He would sit at the desk, eat his apple, read the paper, and talk about politics," remembers Little's niece Sheila Smith-Williams. "Whatever was going on in the news, he wanted to discuss it."

It was truly a unique time for young African Americans in the nation's capital, who were coming of age in the wake of the freedoms won by the civil rights movement and were yearning to make their mark in politics, the arts, and journalism. "It was a feeling that you could do anything," remembers Ivan Brandon, who was then a reporter at the *Washington Post*. "People saw a brighter future, and we were all enjoying it. Young black folks had a spirit and a feeling that they were headed in the right direction. Gil was part of that; he was our poet."

Soon after recording *Free Will*, Gil started calling the band members about gigs around the country. Earth, Wind and Fire, which was still a jazz-funk band at this point—they hadn't yet turned into the R&B colossus of the mid-1970s—was asking the band to support them on tour. Most of the band members were not prepared for the traveling, the commitment, or for performing onstage in front of thousands of people. But they went. "All of a sudden, we're playing all over the country," says Ade. "It wasn't really organized, because we didn't have a manager." Soon the band was playing baseball stadiums and giant theaters, opening for other chart-topping groups such as KC and the Sunshine Band and Mandrill. They'd come a long way from playing gigs before a few dozen people in the student union at Lincoln.

On August 10, 1973, Gil and the band performed at a late-night tribute concert for jazz trumpeter Cal Massey at the Apollo Theater. They exploded onstage, playing cuts from *Free Will* and some of Gil's poems from *Small Talk* to a lively audience. Between songs, the crowd started to scream. Gil turned and saw Muhammad Ali stride out of the stage entrance, smiling and scowling at the same time. The heavyweight champion was at the peak of his popularity, especially to black fans who admired his civil rights advocacy and his refusal to go to Vietnam. Ali walked up and hugged Gil, and the pair discussed music and racism and current events before a rapt audience. For years afterward, Gil reminisced about that night, saying that that was the moment he knew that his life would never be the same.

Back home and off the road, Gil looked forward to recording again. The contract with Flying Dutchman fulfilled, he left for Strata-East, a progressive jazz label known for recording contemporary black jazz musicians including Pharoah Sanders and Charles Tolliver. He always maintained that the impetus for the departure was Thiele's refusal to add Brian's name to the album cover. Brian says he didn't know that Gil was pushing to add his name, explaining that he was actually satisfied with the credit he was given. Whatever the reason, the split was not an agreeable one, with Thiele insisting that the duo was obligated to deliver another album. They agreed to release a greatest hits collection called *The Revolution Will Not Be Televised*.

Released in the summer of 1974, the album garnered excellent reviews and spent five weeks on the *Billboard* jazz chart, peaking at No. 21 on October 12, 1974, even though all the songs had been previously released. Critics swooned, with the Los Angeles *Daily News* giving it an "A" rating. *Ebony*'s Phyl Garland said the album was "mind-blowing" and praised Gil, writing that "He does not merely posture and pacify, but presses on one to consider the uncomfortable truths of contemporary blackness." The album was released as the developing art form of hip-hop "took its first breaths of South Bronx air," writes music scholar William Jelani Cobb.

Gil and Brian's next album, *Winter in America*, on Strata-East, was credited to both Gil Scott-Heron and Brian Jackson. It was originally planned as a concept album called *Supernatural Corner*, in reference to the haunted vibe of the house at One Logan Circle. The record was intended to tell the story of an African American soldier coming home from Vietnam to an America that was indifferent to his experience and hostile to his race and who eventually loses his mind. The narratives in the song were taken from the soldier's therapy sessions in a psychiatric ward, Jackson later explained. One of the original songs, "White Horse Nightmare," is about the veteran's heroin addiction. But the label considered the album too morose, and Gil and Brian took out some of the songs, leaving "Rivers of My Fathers," "Back Home," "The Bottle," and a few new pieces.

They had recorded the album in the beginning of September 1973, at Dan Henderson's D&B Sound Studio, in Silver Spring, Maryland. The space was so small that there wasn't enough room for both of them in the studio, so Gil would sing in the studio while Brian played flute in a hallway next to a water cooler. The tight quarters only added to Gil's discomfort, and he complained about how long the sessions were taking. True to the ethos of the impromptu jams and poetry readings he'd soaked in as a teen-ager at jazz clubs in New York, he felt alive when he was performing and disliked the recording process. Whereas some musicians love to tweak their songs and do multiple takes in the studio, Gil tried to get it done as quickly as possible. Engineer Robert Hosea Williams, who had recorded Roberta Flack and funk guitarist Chuck Brown, recalls, "Gil was one of the hardest I've ever recorded. He had to do everything at once." Not only would he resist multitrack recording, in which each section of the song is isolated and separately recorded, but "he never shut up," says Williams. "When he would sing a verse and then start talking, it was crazy to record. We'd have to erase those things later." Sometimes they would leave the mistakes in there. When drummer Bob Adams skipped a beat at the 1:40 mark of "The Bot-tle," the band wanted to rerecord the track, but Gil said, "No, that's okay."

The album, the first one that Gil and Brian produced on their own, is quieter, more subdued and reflective than previous albums. The duo per-formed most of the cuts by themselves, and they used only a small group of session musicians, drummer Bob Adams and bassist Danny Bowens, on the last day of recording. Again, it was anchored by Brian's musicianship, with a sound that combined the organ with African and free-jazz influ-ences. Some of the songs, "A Very Precious Time" and "Peace Go with You, Brother," feature just the two of them, with no other backing musicians. "They were put together that way to give people the further idea of what Brian's songs were really about," Gil told James Maycock. "I think they were really beautiful and we wanted to make sure his [Brian's] name was out front so that people could understand how much influence he had, not only on that one, but on 'Pieces of a Man.'" The album also marked the duo's embrace of the Fender Rhodes keyboard, which was used by more and more popular musicians, from Herbie Hancock to the Doors. On their first few albums, the band wasn't able to afford the state-of-the-art instrument and used a Farfisa, a Wurlitzer, and whatever other synthesizer was available.

The album's title had a special meaning to the band, who had lived through the tumultuous and tragic events of the 1960s. Gil pinpointed the killing of JFK as "the day that started the Winter in America. The deaths of Robert Kennedy, Malcolm X and Martin Luther King were all part of that." He explained: "America was in a dark period because all people who had been trying to do something positive had been lost . . . all those people had been killed. We were trying to say that's how you get to winter. You put out the lights. People who were trying to bring sunshine to us had been extinguished." Jackson felt that the song was their version of a warning, like Orwell's *1984*, to look at a grim future that was rapidly approaching and to impel people to take action. "People were still trying to effect change en masse and we were just hoping that if we put it out there, people would say, 'Oh yeah, the window is closing rapidly.'"

Though *Winter in America* was a powerful image that resonated with them, Gil and Brian declined to include a title track, in contrast to Thiele's preference of doing so on albums for Flying Dutchman. The partners felt that "Winter in America" should not stand as its own song, separate from the other tracks, but should, as the album's title, convey the theme and the mood of the album.

Some of the songs reflected the duo's sense of alienation from the music industry and the pressure to sell records. On "Back Home," Gil wrote, "I never thought I'd be lost and searching for a warm friendly smile / I never thought I'd be running through the city streets like a newborn child." In the lyrics to "A Very Precious Time," that feeling translated into nostalgia for a past that didn't really exist, said Jackson. "Was there the faintest breeze? / And did she have a ponytail? / And could she make you feel ten feet tall, / Walking down the grassy trail?" Jackson explains that he and Gil had both felt isolated during their adolescence, and they longed for an experience that made them feel loved and supported. "None of these things had happened. It was things we wished had happened."

In "Back Home," Gil also revisits the nostalgia for the South explored in his Johns Hopkins thesis, "Circle of Stone." The lyrics seem imbued with his family history, the Herons moving from Jamaica to the tough streets of Detroit, and the Scott men and women leaving Tennessee for Chicago and New York. Though autobiographical in feeling, the lyrics seem to recall the story of his mother's younger brother, William, with whom Gil stayed after arriving from Jackson in 1962. Nicknamed B.B., Gil's uncle served with the U.S. Air Force in Germany and then took a top job with the Social Security Administration, arriving in New York in the 1950s. Smart and ambitious, he seemed to epitomize the success of that northern migration experienced

by millions of southern blacks. But ten years later, he had lost his job and
was forced to move into an apartment on the second floor of a building on
a grungy block in the South Bronx. And B.B. missed his old home back in
Tennessee.

> *There's been a whole lot said about your city livin'*
> *They told that the streets were paved with gold*
> *And some of us believed them, left our homes and came lookin'*
> *But that was just another story they told.*

The album's penultimate track is often cited as one of Gil's wittiest and
most incisive political satires. Throughout the previous year, he had devoured the *Washington Post*'s coverage by Bob Woodward and Carl Bern-
stein of the developing Watergate scandal. He had been reciting the "H_2O
Gate Blues" as a monologue in his shows for over nine months since debut-
ing it at the Berkeley Jazz Festival in April 1973. He was going to leave it
off the album because he thought that the poem would not resonate outside
the nation's capital—"nobody outside of Washington seemed to know what
the hell I was talking about"—but drummer Adams convinced him to include it, telling Gil that even if most listeners didn't understand the particular political details, the poem was still "funny as hell." In addition to
explaining Gil's understanding of the significance of Watergate, the poem
also demonstrated how much political insight he was gaining from living
in DC.

Recording the poem in one take, Gil read off index cards and impro-
vised some of the lines, such as his description of the "three thousand
shades" of the blues, while the band played a slow blues jam. On "H_2O
Gate Blues," he ventured beyond "that cesspool Watergate" to chronicle
American misdeeds and atrocities around the world, from the overthrow of
Allende in Chile to the bombing of Laos. Though the references are dated
(most people under fifty would have a hard time recognizing any of the
names in this delicious rhyme: "Haldeman, Ehrlichman, Mitchell, and
Dean / It follows a pattern if you dig what I mean") the power of the critique still stings. Gil took weeks to build a monologue, skillfully turning
the words on their head. "He might start talking about Reagan, and each

night, he would add more to it, started with one small circle, and that small circle kept getting wider and wider," remembers Ade.

On "Rivers of My Fathers," Gil poignantly traces the lyrical and musical journey of African Americans, starting with a blues-style introduction featuring Jackson's big chords and Bob Adams's rim shots. In the song, he expresses his desire to find a "way out" of the harsh city, someplace where he can "lay down by a stream . . . miles from everything." Instead, he's stuck in the urban jungle where the "concrete is my smile."

Though it may have been a depressing environment, the gritty streets of Washington gave Gil plenty of inspiration for his lyrics. One of his most famous and infectious songs on the album is "The Bottle." It captures Gil's ability to tell a powerful story and send a message while getting your attention with propulsive rhythms. Behind their house on Logan Circle in DC was Paradise Liquor, where a group of alcoholics would gather each morning at 6:30 or 7:00 to trade in the empty bottles they'd collected the night before. Gil and Brian would sit on the building's lawn to get some fresh air and watch the alcoholics, prostitutes, and homeless stragglers roam Logan Circle. "Gil would follow their conversations, listening and taking mental notes all the time," says Letcher.

He started talking to some of them and learned their personal stories, quickly realizing that none of them intended to be where they ended up. As he told it, one of them was a doctor who had lost his license and then his family for performing an illegal abortion on a teenage girl—someone had begged him to do the operation and then ratted him out. One was a military air traffic controller who had misdirected a flight, sending a plane into the side of a mountain and killing four people; he left work that day and never went back. And one was a social worker who saw one of her clients overdose; she fell into despair and couldn't take it anymore.

"No one set out to be an alcoholic," Gil told writer Patrick Sisson. "All of them had something happen in their lives that turned them around. This was right at the time when doctors were starting to determine that alcoholism and drug addiction was an illness, not just a social feeling or something weak about your character. It struck me that something needed to be done to help these people, not just jump on down on them like that."

By the time of the recording session, Brian had become quite agile with the flute and suggested adding it to the song. His flute playing on "The Bottle" gives the track its catchy hook, and along with the propulsive rhythm, is one of the key factors in the song's appeal. But it almost never became a hit. Gil was opposed to releasing singles, preferring to have the audience experience the album in its totality. When engineer Williams first heard the song, it reminded him of hit songs by Johnny "Guitar" Watson. "It's got a hook with a whole story," he recalls. "I went to Gil and Brian and said, 'You have to make this a single.' They didn't think so."

Williams told them, "Even if you don't think so, this will become a hit song on its own." He was right. The song got a lot of airplay on the Howard University radio station, WHUV, and producers at the influential station convinced Gil and Brian to release the song as a separate single on 45 and as a twelve-inch single. The song did indeed become an underground hit before hitting the mainstream, reaching No. 15 on the R&B singles chart. Unfortunately, because Strata-East was a small label with few resources, it was unprepared for the demand and wasn't able to press enough copies of the single.

One of the song's early fans was Clive Campbell, a Jamaican-born dee-jay who moved to the Bronx in November 1967 and joined a graffiti crew called the Ex-Vandals, taking the name DJ Kool Herc. He and his sister started hosting parties in 1972 in the rec room of their building at 1520 Sedgwick Avenue, playing records with funky breaks, such as the Jimmy Castor Bunch's "It's Just Begun" and James Brown's "Give It Up or Turn It Loose." He kept the dance floor packed by playing songs with heavily per-cussive drum breaks, playing one break and cueing up another record's break on another turntable, extending the break into what he called a "merry-go-round." Soon his parties were legendary in the neighborhood, and he started deejaying at local clubs and schools. The two tracks that Herc often played were "The Bottle" and "Johannesburg," two of Gil's more per-cussive songs. But it was the words in Gil's music that had a special appeal for Herc, who would blend "The Revolution Will Not Be Televised" with other beat-heavy tracks, emphasizing certain lyrics. "When Gil cursed, he cursed in certain ways that I could respect it," Herc says. "It had power and strength and rhythm to it."

Eventually, Herc's style spawned imitators, such as Grandmaster Flash and Afrika Bambaataa, who extended the break and started cutting and scratching the records, to all kinds of effect. Those deejays attracted friends who would grab the microphone and emcee the party, flattering girls in the audience, taunting rivals, or exhorting the crowd in ever-more-creative ways. When hip-hop parties featuring break dancing started to spread throughout the city, Sylvia Robinson was watching carefully from her office in New Jersey. A former R&B singer, Robinson had found success recording soul and disco groups such as the Moments, and had a good ear for new trends in music. When "The Bottle" started to shake up dance floors, Robinson got one of the groups on her label, Brother to Brother, to do a percussion-fueled disco cover of the tune, with more emphasis on the rhythm, within weeks of the original's release.

As demand for the "The Bottle" grew in the summer of 1974, and Strata-East was unable to supply the vinyl, mob-connected record-pressing firms flooded the market with bootleg copies. Sugar Hill Records' copycat version, "In the Bottle," was competing for sales, robbing Gil and the band of money and attention, and also topping the charts. The label was known for its hardball business tactics, and though Strata-East complained to Robinson about the brazen cover and considered legal action, it quickly backed down. Musically, Gil wasn't happy with Brother to Brother's version, which had just slapped a hard disco rhythm onto the basic riffs and rhythm of the original song. Even when one of his musical heroes in college, Joe Bataan, recorded a disco version of the song, Gil wasn't impressed, preferring his original song's bluesy feel.

"The Bottle" became Gil's most successful recording, in regular rotation on urban radio. Frankie Crocker, the most popular R&B deejay in New York, used the song's intro, "Uno, dos, uno, dos, tres, cuatro," as his own signature drop to introduce a new record. Due to its slow build-up, the song became an infectious hit on dance floors and is still considered a classic by club deejays, ranked No. 92 on *NME* magazine's list of the top 150 singles of all time. "It works so well if you're playing in a club," says British deejay John Kay. "There are so many elements that make sense—it builds and builds like house music, before there was such a thing as drum machines. It's fantastic."

The success of the song propelled the album's sales. Strata-East, as a cooperative label, didn't have a promotional budget, and the album was sold in only three cities, New York, Philadelphia, and Washington, but it ultimately sold an impressive three hundred thousand copies and hit No. 6 on the *Billboard* jazz albums chart. The album holds a special place in the heart of many of Gil's fans. "Ultimately, *Winter in America* is an album of extraordinary beauty, a balm for the black nation, struggling with the disintegration of the civil rights movement and the post-Watergate recession," writes James Maycock.

Gil and Brian had asked their friend Eugene Coles to create the cover art for their original conception of the album, and the resulting collage-type painting, titled *Supernatural Corner*, was used. The massive four-foot-by-eight-foot work is anchored by an image of a coconut fragmenting into pieces, based on an analogy Gil once made to Cole about a coconut being hard on the outside and juicy on the inside. In the wake of the album's release and subsequent critical acclaim, friends convinced Gil and Brian to record a song titled "Winter in America" for their next album.

As their music careers started to take off, Gil and Brian realized they couldn't keep living amid the chaos of One Logan Circle, with impromptu concerts on the roof and occasional visits from homeless vagrants. They were getting more focused and organized, recording and performing on a tight schedule, and they needed a more stable environment. At first, they moved elsewhere in Washington, to a two-bedroom apartment on E. Capital Street just down from the Library of Congress. Later, they moved to a large home in the leafy suburb of Arlington, Virginia, in a cul-de-sac a few doors down from a four-star general in the U.S. Army, who gave them disapproving looks when he would see them in their backyard. Gil and Brian may have looked intimidating with their towering Afros and dashikis but they often surprised people with their generosity and communal spirit. When a teenage boy went missing in their neighborhood of Arlington, they joined the general and others to search a nearby hill, winning the respect of their new neighbors.

18.

THE RHYTHM OF REBIRTH

While the band became a fixture in the DC nightclub scene and on larger stages, Gil kept the down-to-earth ethos of the Black and Blues alive—he couldn't say no to any student group that invited him and the band to perform. Paul Chandler, an activist and friend of jazz drummer Max Roach, brought Gil up to the University of Massachusetts in 1973. (Chandler and his friends were part of the Third Word Alliance, an interracial group that occupied the UMass campus to protest what they claimed was discrimination against them for their political beliefs.) "He took jazz and R and B and soul and the blues, all of it, and created this powerful music," Chandler says. "You can hear it in the bottom. In music, they talk about the bottom, 'Listen to the bottom.' He knew it. And he could put it into poetic form in a way that spoke to many of us activists. When we were going through a lot of stuff, it was cats like Gil who kept you going."

Those gigs often ended up costing the band, since they played either for free or for minimal fees that barely compensated their transportation expenses. When the black student union at St. John Fisher College in Rochester, New York, invited them to perform in 1973, the students couldn't afford to pay hotel accommodations for Gil and the band, so they spent the night in a student's dorm room. It didn't matter to them where they slept—they just wanted to get the music in front of an audience.

In the spring of 1974, Smith-Williams found a house for the band so they could also rehearse without so many distractions. It had a rich history in music: Roberta Flack's split-level home in Alexandria with a swimming pool, which had previously belonged to South African trumpeter Hugh Masekela, was on sale for $80,000. They plunked down $50,000, from their royalties on "Winter in America," in cash to win over the broker. Brian took the upstairs bedroom; Gil grabbed the downstairs room, arranging African art on the walls and stacks of records on the floor; and the band used the basement as a performance space. After years of crashing in dorm rooms, a trailer, and the artistic commune at One Logan Circle, they felt like they'd finally arrived. This was a real home.

Over late-night conversations with the band fueled by cognac and plenty of marijuana at the house in Alexandria, Gil and Brian would discuss African culture, such as the boot dance and myths such as that of the *guaguancó* (the history of the snake). The fourteen-minute-plus extended version of "The Bottle" became a highlight of his performances. Gil would introduce the track by announcing, "About this time every night, the snake gets loose in here. The snake is referred to as *guaguancó*, the rhythm of rebirth and regeneration. The snake was named this because it had the power to shed its skin every year and appear to be reborn or renewed." For the last half of the song, the band's percussionists, Ade Knowles and later Barnett Williams and Tony Duncanson, would break out into an Afro-Cuban improvisatory jam, pounding the congas, cymbals, and drums in a trancelike rhythm.

Some of these song arrangements weren't rehearsed beforehand, so they were often improvising them onstage during a performance, which forced the musicians to be at their best. "We'd be on the road and we're doing a sound check and Gil would say, 'Yo, man. I want you to hear this. Hey, let's get the sax in there and the drums,'" remembers Ade. "And he wants to do it the next night! Every night playing with Gil was like an experience." Gil knew he didn't have a great voice, and still assumed that he was a writer who had just happened to land a recording contract. But when he started to get validation from music critics, he grew more confident in his singing ability, taking more chances with traditional songs that required actual singing and not just spoken-word vocalization.

Fond of spontaneity, Gil would mix up the set list at the last minute. "They would ask us, 'What are you going to play tonight?'" says Knowles.

"And we'd say, 'That's why we came—to find out.'" Ever mischievous, Gil sometimes refused to lay out a set list, telling the rest of the band only what the first song would be. When band members pressed him on it, he'd say, "Okay, what do y'all want to play tonight?" The band would put together an itinerary, post it on the stage, and sit in front of the instruments they were supposed to play. Gil would come out and say, laughing, "You think we're going to do that?" and he'd mix up the program. He'd even joke with the audience after announcing a song, "Watch the movement to my immediate right," while the band members ran around the stage getting into the proper position to play the song Gil had just selected.

The spontaneity could be exhilarating. On one tour with the Headhunters, jazz pianist Herbie Hancock's jazz-funk band, Gil's band mixed up its playlist from night to night while Herbie Hancock's group played the songs off their self-titled *Headhunters* album at every single show. After three nights, Hancock's drummer, Bill Summers, told Gil and the band, "You guys, every night you come and do something different. I've been playing this damn album every night and I'm tired of it."

The set list may have been loose, but Gil had high expectations for a tight performance, and he didn't abide any exceptions. "When we're not onstage, everybody can do, like, whatever they want to do," he once said. "But when we're onstage, and when we're working, we have to work together to get it right. There's just no two ways, 'cause we've done everything else."

The success of their live shows wasn't just in their spontaneity of the set lists; Gil was simply charismatic onstage. Though he could be an intensely private person and often kept to himself, he was transformed onstage, reveling in the music and the mood of the crowd. "Whenever the band kicked in, he threw his head back and no one looked happier to be there," noted writer Drew Hubner, a longtime fan. "He looked like a six-foot-seven homeless guy leading the band. He also looked like a three-year-old kid."

You wouldn't know that a half hour earlier he'd shown up in his beat-up gray Mercedes sedan—which broke down in the middle of a tour so often that it became a running joke for the band—in street clothes and needing to borrow a shirt from friends just minutes before going onstage. Basically, he was the same Gil his friends knew from college—until cocaine started slowly to invade his life.

Drugs are endemic in the music world. And they were especially so during the 1970s, an era of freethinking artists and looser drug enforcement. Many musicians in jazz and rock felt creatively liberated when high, shedding their inhibitions and feeling free to explore the depths of their imaginations. It also helped distract them from the pressure to sell records. "It's about the idea of escape, to get away. To be able to download, so to speak, what's on high," says Jerry Jemmott, a bassist who played with the band and later overcame an addiction to freebasing cocaine. "Drugs open you up. You want to get with the spirits."

As far back as 1972, members of Gil's group would break out the coke and do some lines after rehearsal or in between gigs. It started to divide the group, some of whose members didn't indulge. "We all did drugs, we smoked marijuana, we all inhaled, but when stuff got a little more sophisticated, then I drifted off," says David Barnes.

"Gil would say, 'I don't understand. Take a toot. You act like it's the boogeyman,'" remembers Ade. Many of the activists in their circle felt that drug use wasn't compatible with their revolutionary goals. For them, it was a decadent and destructive distraction, and conspiracy theories abounded that the government was pushing drugs into the ghettos to narcotize the restive poor and disenfranchised. Gil shared those views with fellow activists, who had no idea that he was using cocaine. "People would go into shock mode when they made their way into the dressing room and saw Gil snorting cocaine," says Ade.

When they were onstage, the energy of performing and the high of the drugs were exhilarating. But offstage, Gil and Brian and the rest of the band saw firsthand the excesses of the music industry, from egocentric headliners to out-of-control groupies. They vowed they wouldn't give in to the allure and power of the music industry. And their impulse was to control their own music—knowing all too well the history of blues artists and other black musicians who had given up the rights to their creations for a few dollars. In early 1974 they left Charisma because it couldn't handle the demands of a national tour. Eager for independence, Gil and Brian started their own firm. It was a smart move, cutting out the middleman and putting money from concert promoters and ticket sales directly into their own pockets. Calling their booking agency Spice Incorporated, they traveled in what was called the "chitlins circuit," playing in front of small crowds and crowded nightclubs in black neighborhoods and on college campuses throughout the South; the band really sought to keep the ownership of the music within the black community. That challenge became much more difficult once they were swallowed up by Arista a year later.

Things started to change with the release of their first real hit, "The Bottle," in the summer of 1974. The song's popularity exposed them to audiences in urban areas around the country, from Los Angeles and Chicago to Miami and Atlanta, and soon the band was forced to hit the road even more. Gil had his share of groupies waiting for him in those cities, but he still had a special place in his heart for Ahimsa Sumchai, his girl in San Francisco. By 1974 she had gotten tired of their long-distance relationship and of Gil's arrogance—"He could be a little belittling and tense with you"—and she was involved in another serious relationship when Gil and the band arrived to perform at San Francisco State that summer. Sumchai and her future husband threw a party for the band at their loft in a Victorian-era building on Fulton Street. Gil was stung by the rejection and didn't say much that night, shedding his confident exterior and acting awkwardly.

Not that he didn't have other romances to keep him busy, and he seemed to have an eye for beautiful journalists. "Gil never dealt with dumb women; every one was smart and accomplished," says friend Tony Green. "In the early days, Gil wouldn't even talk to a woman who didn't have a B.A., someone who could get what he was saying."

In the fall of 1974, Gil met Lurma Rackley, a striking twenty-four-year-old reporter at the Washington *City Star*, with intelligent eyes and a background in the civil rights movement. Her mother, Gloria Blackwell, was a fearless activist in the fight to desegregate schools and the hospital system in South Carolina. She inspired Lurma, who joined her on the picket lines and was arrested so often that the teenager was eventually sentenced to reform school. One evening at a nightclub, she saw Gil walk in with an entourage and introduced herself. Gil felt an instant connection and they started dating, and soon fell in love. After working all day, Rackley would leave the *Star*, pick up Gil at his office at FCC, get dinner, and then head back to his place or her apartment in Silver Spring, Maryland. They both shared the same political beliefs and a commitment to civil rights activism. "He was trying to make people understand that we hadn't finished, that while we made some gains, we couldn't lose ground," she says. "He was always wanting to make people understand what was going on and to keep a sense of outrage about injustice and economic inequality."

Though they were in love, Rackley was not naïve about Gil's loyalty to her while on the road. "I knew that a lot of women on tour liked him and I knew that this was a 'Love the one you're with' era, so I didn't have any false expectations that I was the only one in the whole wide world," she says. "But I was sensitive that I didn't want to be the type of person who was whiny."

In December 1974, *Essence* magazine writer Pat Kelly came backstage at one of Gil's concerts in New York to interview him, and he invited Kelly to visit his writing class at Federal City College. She soon came down to DC and attended the course, sitting in the back of the room and taking notes. Afterward, he invited her to lunch, picking up some bean pies at a Muslim grocery store and driving over to his house in Alexandria. They started dating, and Gil would sometimes invite Kelly, who was a student at Howard University, to sit in on rehearsals in his studio. At the time, he also briefly dated a news producer at Baltimore's WJZ-TV, through whom he met the station's news anchor Oprah Winfrey.

His growing fame and visibility also made Gil a sex symbol for some of his more impassioned fans. On tour, female groupies would show up at shows, knock on his hotel room door in the middle of the night, and wait for him outside his tour bus. He started dating one, Julia Jones, who wouldn't leave him alone; sometimes he'd be forced to lock her out of his hotel room to get a moment's rest. Others could be more resistant to his charms, wrote Gil, such as the "pain in the ass Dallas debutante who you finally manage to isolate in that hotel room at 3:00 A.M. who suddenly remembers all the bullshit she's supposed to take you through if you want to have sex."

Between the relationships and his busy tour schedule, Gil had little time for his students at FCC, and he started missing classes for weeks at a time. When he did show up, he was often unprepared and had to improvise a syllabus as he walked to class. "I was just doing a shitty job, as far as I was concerned, as a professor," he later wrote. "I was marking the papers on planes. I wasn't available for the students to come in and talk and that kind of stuff." As his music career soared, his academic ambitions (writing his poetry and working with students, and only moonlighting as a performer onstage) shifted. The massive crowds singing along to his lyrics and buying his albums made him realize he could have a much greater impact as a performer. He was hooked.

With a strong grassroots following, Gil and the band had dedicated fans in cities around the country, many of whom eagerly anticipated their next show. When the band came to play at Pittsburgh's Stanley Theater in August 1974, the rowdy 3,700-strong crowd got out of control, trampling concertgoers and pushing and shoving people. So many fans were smoking dope that the next day's *Pittsburgh Courier* joked that the "Steel City chapter of United Marijuana Dealers" was going on vacation "as a result of unprecedented sales during the week leading up to the concert." Gil and the band were the stars of the "Midnite Special" show, outperforming the headliners, jazz flutist Bobbi Humphrey and Donald Byrd and the Blackbyrds. After a rousing start, Gil's rendition of "H_2O Gate Blues" "held a rowdy, stage door busting audience in rapt attentiveness. When it's good, it's good!" wrote the *Courier*. Part of this was due to Gil's ability to command a stage and control hecklers. At a performance in Springfield, Massachusetts, a woman kept requesting "The Bottle," while the band ignored her. After her third request, Gil shouted in frustration, "Do I come to McDonald's when you're working?"

The success of "The Bottle" attracted the attention of record labels, including soul music hit factories such as Motown and Stax, who wanted to sign Gil and the band. But Henderson says he turned them down because "I didn't want to put him in that kind of pigeonhole" by making him a soul music entertainer, and he was worried about limiting the range of Gil's audience.

19.

"BLACK BOB DYLAN"

In 1975, Clive Davis was already a legend in the music business. The son of a tie salesman from Brooklyn, the sharp-dressed executive was a lawyer for ten years before being plucked to run Columbia Records in 1967. Like Bob Thiele, he had an unerring eye for talent and signing a string of future stars, such as Bruce Springsteen, Billy Joel, Chicago, Pink Floyd, and Santana, doubling the label's market share in three years. Davis and Thiele were opposites in almost every other way: while Thiele was secretive, shy, casual in dress, and prone to a hands-off approach with his artists, Davis was gregarious, extroverted, always wore a suit and tie, and liked to get involved in the production process.

Davis kept his ear to the streets and often went out to nightclubs in New York and Los Angeles to check out the latest music. He was familiar with Gil's *Pieces of a Man* album and had been impressed by "The Revolution Will Not Be Televised" when he first heard it in 1970. "To me, it was obvious that he was someone with a new voice, a fresh take on things, coupled with the shimmering rage of the Nixon years and how he and Brian fused funk and jazz and spoken word." Still, Gil's band was too underground for him and his pop sensibilities.

It was the summer of 1974 when Davis heard "The Bottle" playing all over radio stations in New York and realized that Gil's appeal could be much broader. He was just starting his own label, Arista; was looking for new talent to sign; and he wanted to check out Gil in concert. Davis, along with Stevie Wonder, went to go see Gil and the Midnight Band perform at New York's Beacon Theater that December. "I remember it vividly and I remember being floored," says Davis. "He was such a charismatic, compelling, striking young artist, very much of his moment in time. I was very taken with him." He compares it to the first time he saw Patti Smith and Whitney Houston perform. "This was someone whose impact would be profound."

Davis went backstage and met Gil, and they met again in Davis's office, where they traded stories and established a warm bond. "He knew about my background, when I was head of Columbia,'" says Davis. "Gil knew of my role in broadening the audience for Miles and Herbie Hancock." Gil was impressed with Davis's confidence and ambition—"there was definitely a power there, a magnetic shimmer. He was an Aries, and maybe it was nothing more than an extra luster to the aura of the fire at his core," wrote Gil.

The partnership was unique: not only was an established music industry giant taking a chance on a politically controversial spoken-word black poet with militant leanings, but the two crafted an unusually generous contract. Gil's manager, Dan Henderson, negotiated for inclusion of the publishing rights to his songs. "Clive embraced it," says Henderson. "Part of the attraction I'm sure for Clive is that I didn't want any money up front," Gil wrote. Arista had tried picking up the *Winter in America* album and the single "The Bottle," which Clive liked so much for its commercial appeal, but Strata-East asserted its rights to the distribution deal it had signed with the band.

Davis had big plans for Gil, envisioning him as the voice of his generation, with the potential to top the charts. Soon after signing him, he took Gil to see Elton John at Madison Square Garden. "I think he was trying to show me what he saw me doing without making that speech." Davis was obsessed with getting another hit like "The Bottle," which had been written by Gil, and he wasn't that interested in Brian's contribution to the group. Wary of Clive's point of view, and of the lawyers at Arista, Gil and Brian set up a publishing company, Brouhaha Music, to which all their royalties were paid, and they shared a joint bank account at Virginia National Bank.

They called that first album *The First Minute of a New Day*, to mark the new chapter in Gil's career and Davis's new company. Though they discussed the album cover and promotional efforts, Davis left Gil and Brian alone during the recording. They quickly assembled some of the old gang that had created the original magic on the first albums. Victor Brown had been back in Boston, teaching classes and enjoying his apartment in the South End, when he got a call from Gil to come to DC. "I'm putting a band together—how soon can you get here?" Victor was down there the next weekend, reuniting with Lincoln buddies Ade Knowles and Danny Bowens and meeting a few new faces, including fiery saxophonist Bilal Sunni-Ali, a member of the Black Panthers.

In June and July 1974, they returned to D&B Sound Studio in Silver Spring to record, this time backed by the full resources of Arista. On *Winter in America*, they'd been able to afford only a few days of recording time in the studio with Strata-East's limited budget. But Clive's expectations knocked up the pressure to succeed a few notches and made time in the studio nerve-wracking. "Every time that I was in the studio with Gil, it was a little more tense, because I needed to get my part right," says Victor, who harmonized with Gil and sang stirring verses on "Liberation Song," "Must Be Something," and "Western Sunrise." "We all were nervous. As soon as the tape started to roll, you could feel the tension."

The album represented an important step forward for the group, with Gil and Brian maintaining their control over the production even at a major label. It was a strong statement: that they had the intellectual capital to become a real force in the industry. Up to that point, many recording artists hadn't had that kind of control and were usually partnered with producers brought in by the label. But Gil and Brian had insisted on helming the album, much as they had done with *Winter in America*, and on maintaining control over other aspects of the recording process. Though Davis wanted to feature Gil's profile on the album cover, Gil didn't like having his picture taken and pushed to use an image of a gorilla, playing off the fact that it was a homonym for "Guerilla," one of the album's tracks. The ape sits in a wicker chair, mimicking an infamous photo of Black Panther Huey Newton. Years later, Gil explained his choice by saying that gorillas are peaceful creatures until they're provoked into violence. "They're only hostile when attacked. But when attacked, they're extremely hostile," he said with a laugh. "That's where we're coming from."

The politics of the album reflected Gil's growing awareness of global issues and his interest in Afrocentrism. The most uplifting song is "The Liberation Song (Red, Black and Green)," which refers to the colors of the pan-African flag, a symbol of liberation, which was emphasized in Gil's stirring lyrics:

> I've seen the red sun in the autumn
> And I've seen the leaves turn to golden brown
> I've seen the red sun in the autumn
> And I've seen the leaves returning to golden brown
> I've seen the red blood of my people
> Heard them calling for freedom everywhere

The album evoked the inspirational mood of the civil rights movement on "Must Be Something" and "Western Sunrise," but it also reflected the harsh reality that the dream of Martin Luther King Jr. had turned dreary ten years on. Just as in *Winter in America*, the tone was mournful, with Gil decrying the growing apathy and self-absorption of young Americans, including young black Americans: "What ever happened to the protest and the rage?"

Using the previous album's title as a new song for this album, Gil had scribbled the lyrics to "Winter in America" in a notebook over a few days in the spring of 1974—and it became and remains one of his most memorable works, poignantly evoking a low point in American history and the faded dreams of the 1960s. He paints a dismal history, from the mistreatment of Native Americans and the near-extinction of the buffalo, to overdevelopment, "the forests buried beneath the highways," and environmental catastrophe. Somberly, he concludes: "It's winter, winter in America / And ain't nobody fighting because nobody knows / What to save."

Gil and Brian had been left alone during the recording, but they learned a crucial lesson about the music business when Davis objected to the album cover. Their original idea prominently featured "The Midnight Band," with Gil and Brian's names in much smaller type, down in the lower right-hand corner. "That bothered me," says Davis. "After seeing them in person, I thought that the spotlight should be on Gil." He compares his choice to how he pushed then-unknown rock group Big Brother and the Holding Company to highlight Janis Joplin on the album cover and in their promotional efforts, which led to massive record sales.

"I never meant any disrespect to the contributions of Brian and the other players, but to me, the star was Gil," says Davis. He felt that Gil could have an enormous impact on society through his powerful lyrics and public statements, and branded him the "black Bob Dylan," encouraging his promotional executives to use that term in their publicity material. Gil didn't appreciate the comparison. He really felt that the work he was doing with Brian stood on its own, and though he was a Dylan fan, he resented being labeled as the folk singer's black counterpart. "Clive said that so people could relate to what we did," he later explained. "But he never said that to me. As far as I knew, Dylan played harmonica and I played piano, Dylan couldn't sing and I could, that made a difference right there." And the influence may have flowed the other way as well. Soon after *Small Talk* was released in early 1970, Dylan's next album, *New Morning*, featured two "monologues set to music in precisely the style used by this wave of powerful, socially committed black artists" such as Gil, the *New York Times* noted in a March 1971 feature.

When journalists started to make the comparison in interviews, Gil tended to reply with anger or amusement, depending on which mood he was in. When *Playboy*'s Vernon Gibbs brought it up in an interview in 1976, Gil told him it was an insult, giving him a "deadly glare" and snorting "contemptuously" before spitting: "I'm doing something else altogether and I would guess that anyone with an adequate amount of perception would be able to dig that." His anger seemed more calculated than genuine, fueled less by resentment of Dylan than out of frustration with the media's lazy comparison. "No, I'm not into him, man. I heard 'Blowing in the Wind,' but I don't know what he did for white folks. I'm not trying to do nothing like 'Blowin' in the Wind' or 'Just Like a Woman.'" Gil neglected to mention to Gibbs his own soulful rendition of "Blowin' in the Wind" to an auditorium of students at Fieldston. When Gibbs pressed, insisting on Dylan's significance by stating that Dylan had taken up the mantle from Woody

Guthrie and helped start the protest movement, Gil shot back, "Man, we got protest songs that go all the way back to the 1700s." And he explained for the umpteenth time that he didn't consider himself a protest singer and that he was tired of fans showing up at performances expecting "to see some wild-haired wild-eyed motherfucker because that's the impression they get of me from my songs."

Released in January 1975, the heavily promoted *The First Minute of a New Day* earned near-universal praise. In its review, *Rolling Stone* gushed over Gil, writing that "the eloquent literacy of his melodic songs speak with extraordinary insight, anger and tenderness of the human condition." The *Washington Star-News* called it "Black music of the future," and the Los Angeles *Herald Examiner* described the album as "an angry sound and a celebratory sound, tinged with Latin street rhythm and pulsing with the urgent beat of his African heritage." The review concluded that "Gil Scott-Heron is a voice we cannot afford to ignore." The San Francisco *Sun-Reporter* added a cautionary note: "Whether or not Gil Scott-Heron has the resiliency and musical depth to last in the high-pressure, extremely fickle world of commercial music remains to be seen. But with this LP, he has already made his mark." Not all the critics were so kind. Dave Marsh praised Bilal Sunni-Ali's "superb" saxophone arrangements in *Newsday* but wasn't impressed by Gil's political lyrics, saying that the "rhetoric, presumably meant to be chilling to honkies such as I, seem old-hat and off-hand."

With Arista's marketing and promotion muscle, album sales soared into the 100,000–200,000 range over the next few months. Clive Davis was thrilled, calling the reaction "unusually strong, defying any conventional categorization, as we continue to see enthusiastic response at progressive music, rhythm and blues, and FM levels." But lacking a hit single, the album didn't do quite as well as *Winter in America*, which had sales of 300,000 copies, propelled by the success of "The Bottle." Still, the album made it to No. 5 on the jazz charts and No. 10 on the R&B charts, numbers that Davis can still recite from memory.

Davis brought some of his friends in the music business to Gil's concerts, bringing Stevie Wonder with him to see Gil perform at clubs and venues around the country. In a photograph taken after Gil's debut performance as an Arista artist at New York's Bottom Line in February 1975, the music impresario confidently looks at the camera with a cocky grin as he stands between Gil, young and intense, and Stevie Wonder, smiling ecstatically in his black sunglasses. "Stevie admired Gil so much," says Davis. During the same show, the dashiki-clad Gil sang through his hits, including "Ain't No Such Thing as Superman," and ended with "Pardon Our Analysis," which condemns President Ford's pardon of Richard Nixon, a biting and sarcastic sequel to "H$_2$O Gate Blues." After the show, Wonder told *Newsweek*'s Maureen Orth, "Gil says things a lot of people are afraid to say." The writer was impressed, praising Gil's ability to enlighten *and* entertain during an era when "mindlessness and recycled rockers dominate the hit charts."

But the band was also self-aware enough to know that there was a flip side to that adulation from the sophisticates in Manhattan and the black intelligentsia in DC. "We were radical chic," says Brian Jackson, explaining that some of that praise was more about appearance than genuine admiration. "We were also being commodified. A lot of people came to our shows because they wanted to be seen coming to our shows. We were too hip for words." Gil played up that image. "Black people, all Black people are always in a revolutionary state of mind," he told *Players* magazine in November 1975. "I'm saying that I am the Black man, capable of damn near anything I set my mind on." That militant attitude endeared him to genuine radicals. The official Black Panther newspaper hailed the group in a lengthy profile and interview in 1975: "Through the creative genius and revolutionary foresight of the leader of this hard-driving group, Gil Scott-Heron, they have come forth with music that is both pleasing to the ear and healthy for the oppressed mind."

Stevie Wonder was a fan of Gil's even before Davis brought him to shows, having first heard *Small Talk* and *Pieces of a Man* a few years earlier. After they met, the R&B superstar became a sort of guardian angel for the younger musician. Wonder knew that with his politically challenging lyrics, Gil would never top the charts or get the respect he deserved. So, over the objections of the executives at Motown, Stevie often requested that Gil and the Midnight Band open for him at his arena-filling concerts so Gil could be exposed to larger audiences. "Steve took care of Gil when he could," says lighting designer Neil Fleitell. "If he could do a gig and get Gil on the bill, he would. And Gil was loyal to a fault."

A few band members who rejoined Gil on *The First Minute of a New Day* were hardly prepared for how things had changed now that the band was on a major label. Instead of playing in front of hundreds of students in an auditorium at the University of Connecticut in Stonington, they were opening for Earth, Wind and Fire at the Roxy, before an audience of thousands, and performing at Carnegie Hall. The band had gone from gigging every other month to being away on the road for almost six months a year. Brown remembers his first big show, playing at the Cole Field House basketball arena in Columbia Point, Maryland. "There was a huge screen where I could see myself as I was performing—I couldn't look at that and be able to perform. I had to close my eyes!" The group was in the big time, playing at the Greek Theatre in LA and at the Roxy. Victor remembers playing with Taj Mahal at the Hollywood Bowl; for the giant finale, the two bands joined forces for a twenty-five-minute percussion jam. "I can't imagine what that does for an audience. Even our roadie came up onstage with a cowbell."

With Arista's resources and Clive's pop ear, Gil and Brian's music became more rhythmic and percussive. But they were still the same band that used to practice in the chapel at Lincoln; five of the nine members of the group were Lincoln students. "Gil was still the same rebel that he was in college," says Victor. "The pressure had not quite got to him yet." And his monologues were just as discursive and incendiary as ever, even to mainstream audiences that only knew his radio-friendly hits. Often his charisma won over legions of new fans, who would roar with enthusiasm when he hit his rhetorical highlights and punch lines. Once lashing out at President Ford's recent pardon of Richard Nixon, who got to keep his pension, Gil thundered, "Do not pass go, go directly to jail, do not collect 200,000 dollars." When Gil performed at Carnegie Hall in February 1975, he was like "an old-line country preacher receiving the correct fervent response to his call," noted the *New York Times*.

Davis's business smarts and connections in the music world—the label signed Barry Manilow, Dionne Warwick, and Melissa Manchester—propelled Arista within a year to one of the top record labels in the world. To celebrate, Davis, ever the showman, threw a giant party at Madison Square Garden, with Gil and the band playing a show in the afternoon with other jazz artists such as Anthony Braxton. When singer Eric Carmen's bus overturned on the New Jersey Turnpike, Davis asked Gil and his band to play to fill in that slot as well. The band was exhausted but marched back onstage to run through their repertoire, including "The Bottle." The venue, enormous for a band used to playing jazz clubs and smaller auditoriums, had a special significance for Gil. The last time he'd set foot on that legendary floor, he was playing basketball for Fieldston against conference rival Collegiate. During the gig, the applause and crowd chatter were so loud that he sometimes had trouble hearing the other instruments. But that didn't bother Gil. He paced the stage, clutching the microphone and flashing a huge grin. Not all the critics were impressed with Clive Davis's black Dylan—Gil's singing and demeanor were "limited and self-satisfied," wrote the *New York Times*'s John Rockwell, who otherwise praised the band's percussion-fueled energy. None of that could dampen Gil's mood. He told friends in the following days that the show was the highlight of his career, the moment when he knew he'd really arrived.

20.

WHAT'S THE WORD?

With his outspoken support for progressive causes and his overtly political lyrics, Gil was often asked to play benefit concerts. He rarely declined, often covering his own travel expenses and playing for free. He played to raise support for people and groups as diverse as Congresswoman Shirley Chisholm; Newark's first black mayor, Kenneth Gibson; the Zimbabwe African Nationalist Union; and inmates at the Memphis State Penitentiary. In between performing some of his hits onstage, he would talk about the particular cause being showcased, sometimes improvising his monologues to match the cause.

One cause particularly struck Gil and his friends, as it had galvanized the entire black community and women's rights advocates during the mid-1970s. Joan Little, a troubled teenager, had been sent to jail in North Carolina in 1974 after a string of burglaries and shoplifting arrests. On August 27, 1974, a white guard was discovered dead and partially nude in Little's cell, with ice pick wounds to his heart and head. And Little was gone. She later turned herself in, claiming that she had stabbed the guard, Clarence Allgood, in self-defense when he sexually assaulted her. Gil kept up with the case through Howard University's radio station, WHUR. One night in February 1975, he and Chris Williams, who had owned the popular Coral Reef Club in DC, and legendary radio deejay Petey Green threw a fund-raiser for Little's legal defense. Despite a huge snowstorm that blanketed the city, crowds packed Ed Murphy's Supper Club, a small venue, for a concert by Gil and the Midnight Band that raised $2,500, including two $100 donations by some of the neighborhood's street hustlers. Little was acquitted the next year.

Davis made sure that millions of people were exposed to "that wild-eyed motherfucker" Gil by twisting a few arms. He pushed to get Gil and the band on network TV. When NBC producers were reluctant to take a chance on the young protest singer, Davis convinced them to feature Gil on *The Midnight Special*, the network's musical variety show, hosted by Barry Manilow and Loggins and Messina. On March 14, 1975, Gil and Brian once again played to an audience of millions, performing "The Bottle" and "Must Be Something."

At the end of *The First Minute of a New Day* tour in the summer of 1975, Brian told Gil that there was a DC-based drummer, Barnett Williams, who might be for the group. After checking with Knowles, Gil agreed to take on the new player for a few shows. Barnett, whom Gil dubbed the Doctor of Drumology, introduced him to some other drummers, Tony Duncanson and Reggie Brisbane.

For Gil and Brian's next album, *From South Africa to South Carolina*, they took the revolution global, connecting the struggle at home with those happening across the globe. At the three-week recording session at D&B Sound in Silver Spring, Maryland, in June and July of 1975, Williams and Duncason sat in on the sessions, presaging a new direction for the band. A few weeks later, Brian dropped the news and pink-slipped longtime drummers Ade Knowles and Charlie Saunders, replacing them with the new percussionists, including Reggie Brisbane. "We wanted to take it to a whole different level," says Duncanson. "Our style was a lot more Afro-Cuban. We had worked with masters from Guinea and Senegal and took some of those rhythms like you hear with Mongo [Santamaría] and put that in Gil's music." To increase the African focus on the new album, Williams brought in a South African rhythm called the *gambu*, which added a new element to the band's sound. Typical of Gil and Brian's improvisatory impulses, the musicians didn't have charts but came up with the music while recording.

On the album, Gil was able to most effectively achieve his goal of marrying a message to a catchy groove. As black nationalism started to fade in the early 1970s (due to splintering ideas, intense government surveillance, and the arrests of the Black Panthers), pan-Africanism came into vogue. That philosophy was for black people to take pride in their African roots and seek inspiration from the newly independent countries on the continent. In some ways, it pushed the black community not just to turn inward but to look out at the world, beyond American shores to the hundreds of millions of their brethren in Africa. One of the pivotal moments in the movement was when Black Panther leader Stokely Carmichael moved to Guinea, changed his name to Kwame Ture (to honor the African leaders who became his patrons), and denounced the Panthers for forming alliances with white radicals. Carmichael traveled the world and published essays to advance his new ideas. Soon after moving to DC, Gil started to read his books and later traced his interest in pan-Africanism "absolutely" back to Carmichael. Gil became more aware of the struggles faced by blacks in South Africa, where the white minority maintained a system that treated the majority blacks like second-class citizens. Gil told friends that it reminded him of the worst days of Jim Crow in the South and that he flinched when he read stories about black activists beaten and killed in that country.

For the first six months of 1975, Gil had been thinking about a song that brought attention to the antiapartheid struggle in South Africa. He was looking for a catchy chorus and didn't have to look far. Since the 1930s, anyone living in black neighborhoods was familiar with the radio ads for Thunderbird, the cheap wine sold by Gallo Brothers in the ghetto. "What's the word? Thunderbird." The jingle was so catchy that children would chant it in the streets:

What's the word? Thunderbird
How's it sold? Good and cold
What's the jive? Bird's alive
What's the price? Thirty twice

Gil took that jingle and expertly subverted it, turning the chorus into "What's the word? Johannesburg." That lyrical switch provided a memorable

and easy chorus to anchor the song and turn a depressing tune about oppression in South Africa into a radio-friendly hit. It also served to under-
mine the allure of a commercial jingle for a rotgut wine that was destroying
black neighborhoods, as Gil had so poignantly denounced in "The Bottle."
The chorus also mimicked a greeting used by members of the Black Arts
movement: "What's the time? Nation time."

"It was genius," says former FCC student Alden Nielson. "People would
walk around humming that jingle. It was everywhere." The Thunderbird
jingle had previously been appropriated by Red Prysock, tenor saxophonist,
in his 1957 single titled after the chorus. But Gil took it to a whole new
level, with a funky percussive rhythm driving the chorus. "Gil was always
finding something that could be reread as commentary," says Nielsen. "With
'Johannesburg,' what he's doing is taking it as a community greeting and
making it broader to the international community."

Soon after they finished recording the new album in the fall of 1975, Gil
got a call from Richard Pryor, who invited him to be a musical guest on an
upcoming episode of *Saturday Night Live*, which Pryor was going to host in
a few weeks. Pryor invited him after hearing a story about Gil that impressed
the comic: A few months earlier, Gil had been invited by singer Roberta
Flack to perform on *The Tonight Show* when she guest-hosted for Johnny
Carson. A few days later, the plans changed, and Gil was informed that
Carson was going to keep hosting. When he found out that Flack wasn't
going to be there, Gil says he told the show's producers not to book him,
rejecting one of the most coveted gigs in entertainment. It's not clear how
much of this story is true, since Gil liked to embellish stories that polished
his reputation. Flack insists that she never met Gil, though she knew his
music, and insisted that she never invited Gil to be on *The Tonight Show*.

Ten days later, Gil got a phone call from someone who asked him, "Are
you the man who didn't go on the Johnny Carson show because Johnny was
gonna be there?" Gil responded that he hadn't really looked at it like that.
The caller dropped the phone and screamed with laughter, adding, "Look,
this is Richard Pryor, when I heard you weren't going to go on because
Johnny was going to be there, I thought it was the funniest thing I ever
heard." Pryor told Gil that he wanted him to perform on *SNL*, adding that
Gil had free rein to play any songs he wanted.

Much like Clive Davis and Stevie Wonder had done, Pryor fought for Gil and championed his music. But he soon encountered some resistance from NBC producers, who weren't thrilled to have Gil as a musical guest, hoping that Pryor could bring in a more popular group. Pryor insisted on Gil, at one point threatening to quit if he didn't get his way, and the producers soon accepted his choice. Gil and the band were excited about the national exposure, though the now-iconic show was still unknown to many viewers.

When the band arrived at 30 Rockefeller Center and came out of the elevator on the eighth floor, they came upon John Belushi dressed as an out-of-control samurai chef. The band had never seen the character before and had no idea what to think. Belushi started waving his sword, speaking his fake Japanese, while giving them directions and never coming out of character. At one point, Gilda Radner followed Duncanson into the men's room, taunting him with a carrot. Chevy Chase surprised the band with his piano-playing skills. "I looked up on the stage and it was him playing a Chick Corea piece," remembers Brian Jackson. But host Richard Pryor was very quiet and shy offstage, standing in the shadows and quietly taking in the frenetic activity around him.

The episode featured several racially charged skits for the show's first black host, skits that would be hard to imagine on network television in later decades. In one, Chevy Chase conducts a job interview with Pryor that involves a word-association test with increasingly racist responses. When Chase says, "Tar baby," Pryor responds with "Honky," and they continue to elevate the insults to ever-more-offensive levels. At the skit's climax, Chase says, "Nigger," and Pryor responds with "Dead honky." The audience was stunned before breaking into applause.

Introducing Gil and the band, Pryor held up a promotional copy of their upcoming *From South Africa to South Carolina* album and told the audience, "This is the man I wanted on the show and his organization. His latest album is Gil Scott-Heron and here he is!" Wearing a dashiki over a blue turtleneck and skinny dark jeans, Gil confidently announced, "A song for the brothers and sisters in South Africa," before the band launched into a dynamic performance of "Johannesburg." Later in the show, Gil sat at the piano and played "A Lovely Day," a song he insisted on playing over the objections of the producers, who wanted to hear hit songs such as "The Bottle." It was their biggest audience to date: approximately twenty million Americans from every corner of the country. In the wake of their appearance, sales for *The First Minute of a New Day* climbed and fans eagerly anticipated the band's next chapter.

21.

MY FATHER'S HOUSE

Throughout his life, Gil was haunted by his father's abandonment of him as a baby. That loss may not have been on his mind all the time, but it always hovered there. He rarely mentioned these feelings, even to close friends and lovers, burying his resentment in work or silent rage. "He didn't talk about his father," says Lurma Rackley. "It was way too painful for him to talk about," says Brian Jackson. "There was a lot of bitterness and anger." Deep within Gil, those feelings burned. And everything he heard about Gillie made it worse. His mother told him that his father had remarried and had another family, and the old man had never sent a letter to young Gil, not even a birthday or Christmas card.

This was despite Bobbie's efforts to keep Gillie updated on his famous son. She had tracked down his address and sent him copies of Gil's first books, the poetry collection *Small Talk at 125th and Lenox* and the novel *The Vulture*, as soon as they were published. Later she sent him Gil's first album on Flying Dutchman, magazine and newspaper reviews, and even a copy of the 1971 U.S. Senate report on equal opportunity in education, which cited "Whitey on the Moon."

But Gillie did not seem to be impressed. While in Glasgow playing professional soccer, he had met and married a white Scottish woman, Margaret Trize. According to Jamaica's complicated racial dynamic, which prized white skin, light-skinned Gillie considered himself white. (Once, Margaret wrote to Bobbie, "Hope Scottie's hair doesn't grow too tall. Gil abhors the Afro look," noted biographer Goffe.)

At that time, Gil knew his father only through that three-page story and a few family photographs. He was rarely discussed in Gil's grandmother's home, and that served to largely squelch any curiosity the boy may have had about his dad. "Any question I asked about him was answered immediately, honestly, and without negative connotations, but only that. There was nothing further. . . . He just wasn't important."

Gil may have told himself this, but a son never really forgets his father's abandonment. As he grew up and realized his talents, it itched away at him that a father wouldn't have an interest in his son's accomplishments. In quiet moments, feelings of rage, impotence, confusion, and loneliness would burn through him. For all his charisma, Gil was essentially a loner, someone who knew how to entertain people, what strings to pull to make them laugh, but deep down he preferred quiet moments in his own company. "Nobody could really get close to Gil," says friend Tony Green. "It was hard for him to deal with real relationships because that person might disappear or die or abandon him. The key people in his life—his mother, father, Lillie—disappeared."

For his part, Gillie had set up a new life in Detroit with his new family and didn't tell his other children about his first child. His oldest daughter, Gayle, found out only as a teenager, when she overheard her parents talking about Gil. They told her about Gillie's previous marriage but claimed that Bobbie had left Gillie, taking Gil with her. They also told Gayle that they had no address or phone number for Gil and his mother. But Gayle was curious to learn more, and she soon followed her half-brother's career, digging up his records and reading about him in music magazines. She was in high school when she first heard "The Bottle." Curious, she wrangled some friends to go to one of Gil's shows.

It was the winter of 1975, and Gil was playing in downtown Detroit, at the Fort Shelby Hotel. Gayle wanted to introduce herself, but she was nervous. "I didn't know he would accept me, because people react differently to that kind of news," she says. She got up the courage, though, and went backstage after the concert. When she told Gil that she was Gil Heron's daughter, he fell back against a table. "He couldn't believe it," she says. "And when

I told him that I had brothers—that really tripped him out." Gil was excited, gave Gayle a hug, and brought her up onstage to meet the rest of the band: "This is my sister. This is my sister."

"I was impressed that he accepted me the way he did," Gayle says. "From that point on, we were brother and sister. We had just missed a lot of years." That evening she proposed that Gil come see his father. Gil was resistant—"It wasn't something he wanted to do," remembers Brian. "Gayle kind of roped him into it, and he couldn't say no." So, the next night, Gayle picked up Gil and Brian and drove them through the light snow to the family's house on Washburn Street so Gil could meet his father for the first time since he was a baby. Gil ran through the whole course of emotions—from anger and fear to ambivalence and pride. For the first time in twenty-eight years, he was going to meet his dad.

The exact circumstances of their reunion are lost to memory and injured pride. In one version, Gillie was still at work when they got to the house, and they had to wait for the old man to come home. "It was devastating to Gil—we walk in the door and his father's not there yet—he's still at the factory—and didn't come home for hours," remembers Brian Jackson, who accompanied Gil that night. But Gayle, ever protective of her father, insists that Gillie was upstairs when they got home and that he came down to meet his son and have dinner with him. In either case, Gayle did the introduction—"Daddy, Gil. Gil, Daddy"—and father and son shook hands. "It was like he met him but he didn't know him," Gayle later recounted. "Here was a man who raised another family, but didn't raise him. He met him because of who he was, and that was that." It was equally uncomfortable for both father and son, says younger half-brother Denis, explaining that Gillie felt so removed from his younger and sometimes irresponsible soccer-playing self that he wasn't prepared for the arrival of Gil, a potent reminder of that time in his life.

As they got reacquainted, Gil told his father about growing up down south in Jackson, and Gillie talked about his soccer career. He also told Gil about his Jamaican heritage, and how their ancestor Alexander Heron had owned six hundred slaves. And he told his son that he, too, was a poet, showing him some of his simple verses, emphasizing that he didn't write about radical politics but focused on his own experiences. (Gillie had had his poems published by a small publishing house in Detroit, largely because he shared the same name as his famous son, a fact that was well displayed on his book's front cover.)

On the way out, Gil handed Margaret a few tickets to the next show, and that was it. Gil and Brian walked out into the snow and drove back to their hotel. "I was expecting that it would be a big moment; it certainly was for Gil," recalls Brian. "But it didn't seem to be much of one for Gil Sr. It was anticlimactic; it was not really what anyone expected. His father was less than overwhelmed. I would like to think that it was too much to handle for him emotionally. As for Gil, that encounter probably troubled him for the rest of his life." Back in 1971, four years before their reunion, Gil may have anticipated his own disappointment. In "The Needle's Eye" on the *Pieces of a Man* album, he wrote:

> *So I went to see my father*
> *Many questions on my mind*
> *But he didn't want to answer me*
> *God, the whole world must be blind*

Gil rarely discussed the encounter with "the old man," as he referred to Gillie, although he hinted that it had been a mistake to go see him. It took Gil two years to express his feelings about the actual reunion, in the only way he really knew, through song lyrics:

> *It was on a Sunday that I met my old man.*
> *I was twenty-six years old.*
> *Naw, but it was much too late to speculate*
> *Hello Sunday, Hello Road*

The estrangement over all those decades had hardened Gil. "He had a problem with authority based on the fact that he did not grow up with a father," says former manager Dan Henderson. "That contributed to his flaws in his adult life. He really did struggle with authority. And Gil was a nonforgiving individual. If you let him down, he never let you forget it." Lighting designer Neil Fleitell believes that the disappointing reunion with his estranged father in Detroit probably made his despair worse. "He became a shell to protect himself."

The only benefit to the ill-fated reunion was that Gil got to meet one of his half-brothers and his half-sister. It may have been too late for the only child to lose his perpetual fear of abandonment, but Gayle and Denis became family to him. Gayle's down-to-earth attitude and occasional sarcasm instantly bonded the two, and Denis started hanging out with Gil and was captivated by his older brother and the energy of the band's performances. Denis, twenty-four, had worked the morning shift at the Ford plant with his father and attended classes at the University of Michigan. But he wanted to see the world beyond Detroit, so when Gil called him with an invitation to join him on tour, he jumped at the chance, starting off as a roadie. "That was college for me," says Denis.

As their relationship developed, Denis talked to Gil about their father, revealing his own mixed feelings about Gillie. The stories he told gave Gil insight into the childhood he'd missed, drawing a picture for him of what it would have been like to grow up with his father. They confirmed Gil's suspicions about Gillie's tough personality and also made him grateful that he had been raised by Lillie. "It wasn't a bed of roses," Denis told Gil, telling him that Gillie had been a taskmaster, that he'd expected his sons to play as many sports as he had. When ten-year-old Denis came in second in the sixty-yard dash at the Youth Games held by the City of Detroit, his father scolded him: "What happened? Did you have a bad start?" Another time, Denis was kicked out of Little League after Gillie, blind with competitive rage, punched out an umpire. Denis told Gil that the lessons he learned from his father were more about what behavior to avoid than what to emulate. "He always had an extremely fiery temper that could ignite in a moment—having seen it firsthand, I was shy of raising his rankle and I learned to control my temper."

22.

THE GRIOT

It was a busy time for Denis to join the band, which in January 1976 was heavily promoting and performing the songs off the just-released *From South Africa to South Carolina*. Immediately, "Johannesburg" became the breakout song. Though it had obvious potential to burn up the dance floor, it wasn't a planned assault on the charts. Gil actually cut it back during recording in June 1975, editing it down to three minutes and twenty seconds (shorter than most twelve-inch dance singles). As with "The Bottle," the song almost never became a hit due to Gil's obsessive focus on the album format and his opposition to releasing individual songs as singles. Engineer Robert Hosea Williams saw the song's potential, but for it to be a single it had to be longer for the dance clubs. But Gil wasn't interested in releasing it as a twelve-inch single. This time, the executives at Arista stepped in to push for the radio-friendly song to be released on its own. After discussions with close friends, Gil agreed to let the song be released as a single—that way, it would bring more attention to the antiapartheid cause.

The single blew up, getting played on the radio and hitting No. 29 on the *Billboard* R&B charts, a rare instance of a message song becoming a popular hit. It was "a paradigmatic instance of the ways that Gil Scott-Heron's obsession with popular culture joined with his populist and progressive politics . . . that had the benefit of being great music at the same time," notes Aldon Nielsen. The song had a broad impact, especially in cities and on college campuses, where the antiapartheid movement was still in its infancy. Arguably the first pop song to address apartheid, the track resonated with activists and black Americans, many of whom weren't aware of the situation in South Africa. "If it's happening to any of us, it's happening to all of us," said Gil, describing his passion about the issue.

Rapper Chuck D, who was a fifteen-year-old sophomore in high school when he first heard the song upon its release in 1976, ties "Johannesburg" back to the griot's impulse to inform, going all the way back to villages in tribal Africa, "or to pass code on the plantations of the South in America." The urgency of the apartheid issue and the lack of awareness among African Americans about it had propelled Gil's desire to write the song in the first place. "When we released 'Johannesburg,' people didn't want to talk about South Africa; so we were taking a chance," he later explained. "I felt somebody's got to bring it up, but I didn't necessarily intend it to be me. I would have rather it was a congressman or those intended to talk about these things, but they wouldn't." There were a few lawmakers who raised the issue, but they were often ignored in the halls of Congress. (In 1972, Rep. Ronald Dellums [D-Calif.] introduced a bill calling for trade restrictions against South Africa and divestment by American corporations, but it lingered for fourteen years before it was finally passed in 1986.)

The album's tight focus on political issues, ranging from apartheid in "Johannesburg" to nuclear waste disposal in "South Carolina," distinguished it in a music environment that had turned inward and superficial. Earlier in the decade, chart-topping pop artists such as Cat Stevens and Jefferson Airplane were releasing political paeans and protest songs. But by 1976, amid post-Watergate malaise, many bands had retreated into an escapist phase in the rhythms of disco and funk or self-absorbed apathy. On "South Carolina," the song about the dumping of nuclear waste in poor rural areas of the state, Gil summed up his frustration at the prevailing mood: "What ever happened to the protest and the rage? / What ever happened to the voices of the sane? / What ever happened to the people who gave a damn?"

What did happen to the people who used to give a damn? Amid the lethargy of the mid-1970s, Gil and Brian were among the few performers left who were protesting and raging. It was indeed a challenging time to be a revolutionary artist. The major movements erupting in the 1960s (civil rights, antiwar, and anticapitalist) had ebbed, and radical groups such as the Black Panthers had been weakened by arrests and assassinations. Americans seemed tired of flower children and black militants, and wanted to forget problems of inequality and discrimination, but these problems persisted, gnawing away at the heart of the country. Because Gil "remains to prod the movement consciousness at a time when there are less people taking a stand," in 1976 *Playboy* had declared him one of the most important voices of the decade.

Gil's role as an African American griot, the messenger and prophet of his community, was tested by the national mood in the middle of the decade. He often grew frustrated with the sense of complacency that had developed among those who had traded in their revolutionary fervor for bourgeois aspirations in the wake of the turmoil and violence of the 1960s. "We lost a lot of generals," he later said. "And any time you lose a lot of generals, you do not necessarily lose energy or enthusiasm in terms of your aims, but you will lose direction." In a July 1975 column for *Ebony* magazine, "Lost in the Shuffle," he lashed out at those African Americans who had grown apathetic. "We have allowed ourselves to be transformed, verbally, from the conscience of America and the World, as we projected in the '60s, to 're-invisibles' of the '70s."

Specifically, he demanded that people pay attention to how the government was spending billions in tax money on foreign misadventures such as the war in Vietnam. "We retreat to 'not being involved.' *But we are irrevocably involved!* . . . 'Not being involved' with America is only the dreamer's half of society's struggle. We cannot turn our backs on ourselves." Gil ended the column with a plea to put the past aside and focus on the future. "Do we have enough adults who care enough to tell our young Sisters and Brothers why they shouldn't be killing one another and themselves? . . . We have enough people. We have enough talent. Do we have enough love?"

Among those listening to Gil's music were the Black Panthers, including "Honorary Prime Minister" Stokely Carmichael, who befriended Gil and regularly came to his concerts. When Gil and the band were performing at El Macambo in Toronto shortly before the 1976 Summer Olympics in Montreal, they stayed at a hotel on Charles Street. While Gil was doing a radio interview and joking about how the black athletes would win all the gold medals, Carmichael and his entourage entered the room. They were warmly greeted by Gil, who gave Carmichael a big embrace. When the Black Panther mentioned that he had just had lunch at McDonald's, Gil teased him for making such a non-radical choice: "You can't eat that junk." Carmichael laughed.

Gil was mature enough to understand that change goes through its own evolutionary process, with reformers pushing the envelope a little further than those who came before them, and that it was up to him and other activists to adapt to changing circumstances. "You could only lead people who follow you, and they could only follow you at a certain pace. So you modify your pace in order to encourage them to stay with you and see where you are going." Amid the malaise of the 1970s, Gil saw himself as an important messenger whose role was to keep pushing the revolution forward. He felt that the assassinations of King, Malcolm X, and the Kennedys, along with arrests of prominent black activists, had cut off the path of progress. "The vital info that was being spread and passed along in our community was cut off when a lot of the people responsible were killed or put in prison or otherwise disabled. And it gave people the impression—which is the impression that it was meant to foster—that there was nothing happening."

Some of that nonchalance among the public was due to a general impression that the big struggles (civil rights, the Vietnam War, sexual liberation) had ended in success. On the surface, that might have been the case. But challenges still existed: racial integration may have been the law of the land, but subtle racism still resulted in discrimination against African Americans; the last U.S. troops might have left Saigon in 1975, but the American military was still meddling in other parts of the world such as Central America; and women were more visible in colleges but they were still largely missing from corporate boardrooms. Gil called the new challenges "shadow boxing," because the targets were less obvious and required information sharing among activists.

"There are still heroes in this world," he said. "Someone who would dedicate his time and energy to this is a hero to me. We all have the potential to be heroes but it's still good to see that someone sets out in a certain direction, that people see them overcome certain difficulties, this encourages you to see that you can do it yourself."

Sometimes his optimism in the inevitability of revolution verged on naïveté. He would cite socialist leaders around the world, praising their accomplishments but conveniently ignoring their sins. "Mao Tse Tung was a college graduate and when he said, 'Frog,' 900 million people jumped," Gil once said with admiration, adding that such a magnetic personality could have spurred revolution in the United States.

Back in the studio, the group was caught up in its own debates over the direction of their music. Though Gil felt comfortable with the band's blues-based sound, Brian was pushing to expand its repertoire and to be more musically adventurous. Gil was a simple piano player, and he knew his limitations as a musician. Brian, who was heavily influenced by the jazz-funk rhythms of bands they performed with, such as Herbie Hancock's Headhunters, wanted to explore that improvisatory impulse. Gil agreed, but he feared that his own role would be overshadowed and that he wouldn't be able to keep up with others in the band. It was the first sign of a growing schism between the partners.

The pressure to achieve commercial success in the funk and disco era was intense, which also caused friction. Gil could be defensive in interviews, especially when reporters implied that his music was too serious for the dance floor. "George Clinton [lead singer of Parliament/Funkadelic fame] and them didn't invent funk and they aren't the only ones who can hit on the one," he told *Rolling Stone*. "We don't try to keep black people from dancing. I like to dance myself. I think that it's just as natural as breathing to a whole lotta folks. You don't have to think about it to get up and dance. But I do feel as though there are things that can be provided as food for thought, things that can be used as inspirational tools, things that can help people to feel better about themselves and their potential. I think those things are primarily overlooked in contemporary music. Like when we did 'The Bottle,' we damn near invented disco! And 'Johannesburg' and 'The Bottle' were #1 and #2 in France for almost a year. And I don't think that it had anything to do with anything other than the fact that you can dance to our music. You can also sit down and think about it."

Arista, trying to work with the times, managed to land the band prominent gigs, such as three-night sets at the popular Roxy club in Los Angeles, where plenty of Hollywood movers and shakers boogied down the night. And when Arista was pushing "Johannesburg" as a club-friendly single, Gil was pressured to join a nationwide promotional tour partnered with Donna Summer, the queen of disco, whose hit "Love to Love You, Baby" was burning up the charts. But Gil was unimpressed: "As redundant a lyric to hit the public since 'Amen.'"

Clive truly thought that with his combination of stage presence, musicality, and fierce rhythms, Gil could be a superstar. Despite Clive's best efforts, though, Gil never considered himself one. Even after the initial success of "Johannesburg" and "The Bottle," when he was appearing on network television and the album was being praised in mainstream newspapers, he remained modest. Asked by a reporter for the *Black Panther* newspaper if he was a superstar, Gil retorted, "Oh, no sir—hopefully not. Hopefully not. You see, I'm a part of nine people, you know? Like together we have the potential for being a superstar: but individually we don't have but one ninth of that potential."

To Clive, that logic was backward. As he saw it, as a group, they could never make it big, but individually, Gil had the potential. To capitalize on the success of *From South Africa to South Carolina* and to showcase Gil's captivating live show, Clive encouraged him to record a live album. The timing couldn't have been better: It was 1976, and the country was caught up in the patriotic fervor of the Bicentennial, star-spangled hymns overwhelming any critical voices. Now was the time for Gil to accept his role as the American griot, inspiring the country to fulfill its destiny but also denouncing its sins. He immediately agreed with Clive and made plans to record the album while on tour that summer.

On Independence Day, as the city prepared for the arrival of the tall ships in Boston Harbor, Gil and the Midnight Band performed at Paul's Mall, a basement club on Boylston Street. And churned through hits such as "The Bottle" and "Home Is Where the Hatred Is." They introduced some new songs, including the uplifting "It's Your World," which became the title of the double album; the blues-tinged "Possum Slim;" the salsa-influenced "17th Street;" and the tender "Sharing."

He also introduced "Bicentennial Blues," an eight-minute spoken-word poem he'd written for the occasion that recalled "H_2O Gate Blues." A brilliant and caustic people's history of the country and the blues that it inspired, the track took aim at America's heroes, from slave-owning George Washington to Ronald "Hollyweird" Reagan.

For Gil, the blues was born out of every part of the black experience, from "the beaches where the slave ships docked" to "small-town deprivation" and "big-city isolation." Channeling both the authority of a scholar and the passion of a preacher, Gil declares that "America provided the atmosphere for the blues and the blues was born / The blues was born on the American wilderness."

While revelers across the street from the club donned red-white-and-blue sunglasses and screamed "USA, USA" over six-packs of Budweiser, Gil denounced the commercialization of "the year the symbol transformed into the B-U-Y centennial / Buy a car / Buy a flag / Buy a map." Instead of celebrating America, Gil takes aim at the country's failure to live up to its promise. Calling it a "blues year," he decries:

> Halfway justice
> Halfway liberty
> Halfway equality
> It's a half-ass year

As an African American who experienced segregation, he had fought for his freedom and succeeded on his own terms, fulfilling his own manifest destiny, and cherished the liberties he enjoyed. Looking back on his experience integrating the schools in Jackson and witnessing racism in action, he felt strongly that blacks had struggled the most to achieve the American ideals of liberty and the right to pursue happiness. During an interview that year, he said, "But I think that the black Americans have been the only real die-hard Americans. We are the only ones who carried the process through the process. Everyone else has to sort of skip stages. We are the ones who marched, we're the ones who carried the Bible, carried the flag, went through the courts. Being born American didn't seem to matter. Because we were born American but we still had to fight for what we were looking for and we still had to go through those challenges and those processes."

It's Your World was universally praised by critics, who admired Gil's integrity, intelligence, and ability to make music that paired danceable grooves with lyrics that stung. The album's raw power showed off Gil and the Midnight Band "at their collective peak," wrote Maurice Bottomley, and *U.S. News and World Report* called the album a "masterpiece" for its "heartbreaking sonic portraits . . . seething with indignation and sorrow."

Even amid the swirl of energy surrounding the new album, the hit single "Johannesburg," and the tour, Gil's disappointing reunion with his father still simmered within him six months later. On his first Canadian tour that summer, journalist Norman Richmond was introduced to Gil and asked him about his father. Gil snapped, "The Scotts raised me," insisting that his mother's family was responsible for his upbringing. He criticized Richmond for quoting from the Arista press release in his profile of Gil in the Toronto *Globe and Mail*, which focused on his father and didn't mention his grandmother or mother.

He had fonder feelings for his father's older brother, Uncle Roy, who came to the show at the El Mocambo nightclub, where Gil proudly introduced him from the stage. They shared some of the same politics, and Roy was a legend in Canada for his adventurous life and civil rights activism. During high school in Jamaica, he'd organized labor protests and was a member of the Young Communist League. In 1941 he left Jamaica and joined the crew of a British whaling ship, the HMS *Lancing*, which traversed the icy Antarctic looking for the great beasts. Six months later, he returned with a collection of whale eyes, ears, and giant teeth; out of the teeth, he carved a long knife. A committed socialist, he got involved in Canadian politics and was widely respected for his commitment to social justice and to advancing the cause of black Canadians.

Occasionally, when prodded, Gil would talk about his famous father, but it seemed more out of politeness than pride. When he toured in England and Scotland later in 1976, reporters and fans often asked him about the "Black Arrow." His father's team, Celtic, is a legendary franchise in the United Kingdom, and fans would wear the team colors of green and white to Gil's concerts. He was hounded by Scottish TV shows and newspapers to do interviews, but they didn't want him to sing or discuss politics; they wanted him to talk about soccer. Gil didn't really know the sport and had to give himself a quick primer. On the way to one TV station, he stopped at a store to pick up a green-and-white Celtic scarf, along with a hat from the rival Rangers, and arrived wearing both at the same time, to the amusement of the show's producers. Grudgingly, Gil played the proud son, smiling at the fervor surrounding the team. "There you go again," he once joked. "Once again overshadowed by a parent!"

23.

"DO WE HAVE ENOUGH LOVE?"

Many of Gil's early songs on *Small Talk* and *Pieces of a Man* focused on the oppression that he himself had experienced: racism in America. But by the mid-1970s, he started to expand his outlook, wielding his pen to write lyrics that addressed global issues such as the risks of nuclear power and environmental pollution, because he saw how those problems impacted people in poor neighborhoods. "A good poet feels what his community feels. Like if you stub your toe, the rest of your body hurts."

Depending on his audience, Gil would adjust the tenor and content of his message. Before a huge crowd at the Rose Bowl, for example, he might express the militant revolutionary rhetoric of the late 1960s. Gil gave an illuminating interview in April 1976 to the *Black Panther*, the group's eponymous newspaper, which captured his tendency to adjust his message to fit the audience. His comments were more militant than those he made to the mainstream media. At one point, he discouraged white activists from helping the black community, instead pushing them to raise hell in their own neighborhoods: "We say to white people, 'Go revolutionary in your community 'cause it needs it. Do not come here, to help me deal with my community when your community is in such terrible shape.'" He also referred to the end of the Vietnam War as "how the Vietcong got free," attributing much of that to the demonstrations in America. "And I'm saying that the pressure that was brought on the war mongers over here by the things that were happening domestically at the time they were bringing war down on them people, kept Nixon, at the height of Watergate, from going back in there and bombing those people again when they came down this spring and took their shit back, you see?"

Though Gil's rhetoric could be fiery, he avoided some of the more extreme conspiracy theories that ricocheted around the community. Some in the dwindling ranks of black militants attributed their demise to a government plot to distract young Americans with newer movements, from women's liberation to gay rights. But Gil deeply understood that all those liberation struggles were part of a continuum, that Russell Means's American Indian movement had "a lot in common with Joan Little, who has a lot in common with Inez Garcia [a Hispanic rape victim who was put on trial for killing her assailant], who has a lot in common with the San Quentin Six [prisoners who were put on trial for killing guards during an escape attempt]—in terms of being symbols of how America had to change but did not." They were all part of the same struggle, to make America the land of the free for all its citizens.

Though Gil was inspired by socialism, black nationalism, and pan-Africanism (movements and ideologies that coursed across college campuses and cities in that era), he maintained a certain independence of thought. He realized that even the most progressive organizations could become tyrannical and rigid in their rules. Some of his intellectual maturity was due to his observations of single-issue campus groups that stubbornly refused to engage in debate, but much of it was due to the skepticism he'd inherited from his mother, and to his open-minded reading list, which included books that questioned the tenets of Marxism and exposed the mass executions under Stalin and Mao. For over a decade, he had relished late-night jousting sessions with friends and roommates over the issues of the day. Those lively debates only reinforced his commitment to independence of thought.

"I never joined any of these organizations [Black Panthers, SDS], because like once you join one of the organizations, it made you enemies with somebody else," he told *The Brooklyn Rail*. "You start arguing back and forth and you've wasted your energy that could be using and you're both trying to do something for the community. Which is why I stayed out of most organizations. I wanted to be available to all of them. I played for Shirley

Chisholm, I played for Ken Gibson—I played for anybody who was trying to do something positive for black people, just count me in and I'll be there." He later told *Playboy* in July 1976, "I never was too familiar with the Black Panthers—but a lot of ideas they had come into focus with ideas I had." He seemed to have mixed feelings about the slow demise of the Panthers in the middle of the decade. He couldn't think of a particular misstep that had weakened the once-fearsome group, but he blamed the Panthers, which had a limited appeal, for overreaching: "If you can't get but a certain number of people together, then maybe you shouldn't be having gun battles on Main Street." But he retained his appeal to the remaining members of the Black Panthers. Members of the group often showed up at in-store appearances at record shops, flanking Gil and posing for photographs with him.

When he played for Nation of Islam leader Louis Farrakhan's Family Day celebration, he praised the group's focused determination, saying, "Whenever you see something like that, you've got to say, 'Right on.'" But Gil rebuffed Farrakhan's overtures to get him to convert to Islam and privately mocked the rigid ideology of the group, making fun of the bow ties worn by members. When pushed to join, he pushed back. Gil liked the freedom that came with independence, which allowed him to take shots at everyone, even his allies and kindred spirits. The role of the revolutionary black artist is "to hold up a mirror to the community and to make them confront their own bullshit," says black music scholar Craig Werner. And Gil's role as a skeptic and truth teller was echoed by other provocative artists in the black community. A black nationalist theater in Harlem staged radical productions that mocked civil rights leaders. Black poets at coffeehouses were questioning the motives of Farrakhan and the Black Panthers on college campuses. Angela Davis was denouncing the sexism of some civil-rights leaders.

During Gil's time in DC in the 1970s, the city was the heart of every major protest group, from the antiwar radicals and the black militants to the earth-loving hippies and the anarchists. Not a day went by when he didn't walk by a march or get handed a mimeographed screed by a wild-eyed renegade—or witness the expected police reaction: multiple arrests, occasional tear gas, and swinging batons. Yet all the hue and cry didn't accomplish much. The unpopular war limped on for years, the ghetto continued to suffer, and more hippies were trading in their jeans and dashikis for suits and ties. Gil witnessed the transition from dynamism to disappointment, and he realized the limits of radical violence and protests. In the end, some essential reforms could be accomplished only through political and legislative change. This realization drew him closer to civil rights activist Jesse Jackson, who inspired him with his focus on changing the law to get deepseated reform. "You can burn your community down and somebody else will build it up and all you're doing is burning down some houses," Gil said. "But if you change the law, then you have done a whole lot to change the foundation of society." Other veterans of the radical movements also understood that real change takes a concerted effort. "You can throw your fists in the air and say, 'Revolution,' but if you're not doing the real political work, then you're not doing it. It's the political work that will sustain you past the actual feeling," said Amiri Baraka.

As Gil became more outspoken and more high-profile, with his shows attracting bigger audiences, some members of the band started to fear the risk of violence—that his words might just provoke a white reactionary or racist to lash out at the angry black poet. After a typically explosive show in 1976 featuring Gil's fiery monologues, Ade Knowles pulled him aside and told him that he was concerned about his safety. Gil replied, "I hear what you're saying, man. But we got to keep doing what we're doing. If they take us out, I'm not going to back down." Ade suggested getting some security, much like other high-profile performers, but Gil refused. He felt that black artists inevitably made themselves targets if they spoke up about progress for black people. For his people to survive, the answer was not to retreat but for more people in the community to step forward: "I think the only answer to that kind of thing is more artists doing that sort of thing so that it's not easy to identify which one or which two you can do something to to slow down a movement, or to slow down some sort of progress."

When the Midnight Band played for Farrakhan, members of the Fruit of Islam, the Nation of Islam's security team, were all over the stage, a sight that only reinforced Ade's commitment to getting some protection for the band. Coming out of an activist background and with firsthand experience with FBI surveillance, and given that fellow band member Bilal Sunni-Ali was a member of the Black Panthers, he had every reason to be paranoid.

Though the group was long familiar with concerns about the FBI from their experience at Lincoln and more recent revelations of government surveillance of activists and artists, their new prominence as music stars brought a whole new level of paranoia, and the group started to worry about the pushback to their radical message.

Security concerns weren't limited to public appearances. Brian Jackson used to fear that their home in Virginia was bugged. "You picked up the phone, it clicked once, and then it clicks twice. I mean how many times can that happen?" He added, "We weren't actually saying the things that would make us friends of the state, but we certainly didn't consider ourselves enemies, either." With other outspoken black activists harassed by local police forces, often based on thin evidence—such as Amiri Baraka being arrested in Newark for allegedly carrying an illegal weapon and resisting arrest, and poet Sonia Sanchez's home invaded by Philadelphia police looking for drugs—there was good reason for some paranoia.

But no such threat or violence ever happened. Once during a show at Hunter College, while the band was playing "The Bottle," a fan jumped out of the balcony and onto the stage, injuring his leg. "My first thought was that he's going to do something to Gil," feared Knowles. But he was just an overenthusiastic fan, and he was quickly escorted offstage.

24.

KEEPING IT REAL

Gil's fan base on college campuses always had a special place in his heart, and he often would perform by himself in front of small audiences at student unions and coffeehouses around the country, even amid national tours to promote his latest album. Katherine Sama, a young administrative assistant at UCLA, remembers eagerly anticipating his small shows, many of which were never announced in advance and charged five dollars. "You would just hear, 'Gil's in town,' and we never missed him. Sure, some of the girls had crushes on him. But it was more than that. We were in love with his mind." In those small, intimate settings, Gil would play some songs at the piano and recite some poetry and then talk to the audience about current events and issues. Sama remembers one night, in the wake of the COINTELPRO revelations (in which politically active artists and student leaders were targeted for surveillance by the FBI), she quizzed him about the FBI tapping the band's phone. Gil responded, "Don't even worry about that. America has bigger fish to fry."

Gil was also in demand on college campuses where students were being more assertive about the guest performers and lecturers they wanted to invite, eschewing traditional choices. Several times he was invited by student insurrectionists who had taken over an administration building and had decided to bring in performers with a revolutionary consciousness. When black and Latino students at San Francisco State took over the campus in

1976, one of the first things they did was invite Gil to perform. He came by himself, stayed in student housing, and played "Johannesburg" and "Winter in America" to students packed into McKenna Theater.

Not all the students welcomed Gil's polemics. Sometimes his campus visits and inflammatory monologues stirred up trouble, usually at more traditional schools. When Gil and Brian were invited to perform at the University of Georgia, in Athens, for five thousand dollars in 1976, their songs were interspersed with Gil's fiery monologues condemning the CIA, President Jimmy Carter, and political corruption. At one point, a coalition of black student groups got up onstage to present Gil with a five-hundred-dollar check for "the freedom fighters of South Africa." The response to this was divided along racial lines. "I got a lot of glad-handing from black students," says Bobby Jackson, the only African American member of the school's concert committee. "But some white students were not happy, that this is not going to be just fun and games, but we're going to get a lecture about some of the crap the government is pulling around the world." For months, a racially charged debate over Gil's performance and words dominated the campus newspaper, the *Red and Black*. White students argued that Gil was unpatriotic and dangerous; black students asserted that he was speaking some uncomfortable truths about America. The University of Georgia's student leadership was not ready for such a debate: it was the last time that Jackson was ever asked by the concert committee to suggest a musician to perform on campus.

These smaller gigs were interspersed with concerts at large arenas and nightclubs, which made for a schizophrenic experience. When the band played at a college or Gil did a solo show, they had complete creative freedom. But at the bigger shows, they were pressured by Arista's promotional team to play the hits and run through the most recent album, a complete reversal of their usual impulsive choices. Gil liked to structure very personal sets, starting off with some of the quieter and more reflective songs that didn't get as much airplay, and sometimes letting loose with lengthy individual solos. Through relentless performing (more than two hundred gigs a year) for almost a decade, Gil and the Midnight Band developed a powerful and energetic stage show. "We didn't think about how amazing it was; we loved to play," says Brian. "It's what we did; it was a high to get together and make music and to feel the connection with the audiences. We just knew we didn't want to do anything else."

For the band members, performing became a spiritual experience; they felt that what they were doing was more than just playing music. "It was the word, and the word was the music. Gil was the word, and the music and the band was the music drum helping get the word out," says Ade. "Some nights, there was another spirit there, a strong connection in terms of African roots, the ancestors of the spirits. When people die, in certain African religions, the flesh goes, but the spirit is still there, that force of the ancestors. There were times when Bilal would say, 'Did you see that?,' and I would say, 'Yeah, I saw that.' There was someone else up onstage with us, a reminder that you guys were playing something special."

Gil's onstage banter was legendary—part church sermon, part stand-up comic act, part political speech. Sometimes riffing off the top of his head and other times repeating anecdotes that had long been part of his routine, he extended the reach of the songs and was able to communicate with members of the audience. In a way, this technique came close to the writing so dear to his heart with its focus on the word without the distraction of the music and the rhythm. Clutching the microphone in front of his chest, he paced the stage, expertly leading the audience, guiding them and prodding them.

A revolution is just like a war. There are different fronts and different places. And the front and the focus of the effort will not always be on you but you will always have to be struggling. The fact is that right now the focus is on Southern Africa and it was in Southeast Asia and from time to time it's on the Middle East and for a period of time it was over here and it will be over here again. Because change is inevitable. From the wheel to the automobile.

Gil's humor was an essential component of his performances, and a big attraction to his fans. Though some singers sprinkled their onstage banter with a few jokes, Gil went way beyond that, at times rivaling stand-up comics such as Dick Gregory and Richard Pryor in his delivery and his riffs on current events. A classic bit in his repertoire was the "Jaws" part of his

"Bluesology" monologue from *The First Minute of a New Day*. He kicks it off by saying how when he went to go see *Jaws*, he rooted for the shark because Jaws was "the home team."

I'm saying, now if Jaws was to come in here, I would be with you, grabbing something, trying to beat the son of a bitch back. But Jaws was in the water. This is where sharks are known to be, in the water. You going to the beach, he going to the supermarket.

As a kicker, Gil described why Jaws never attacked any black people— "because we can hear the music. Dun-da, dun-da, dun-a. Here comes that goddamn shark with his band!"

Gil was channeling Langston Hughes's sardonic wit and his mother's bitter sarcasm and filtering it through Pryor's microphone. (He actually coveted any comparison with Hughes, when critics made the reference in their reviews. When he met jazz legend Charles Mingus (who'd known Hughes), at the Joyous Lake concert hall in Woodstock, New York, in 1975, Mingus told him that his work reminded him of Langston Hughes, which Gil considered a "high compliment.")

Maybe it was Gil's sense of humor that was behind his decision to take on his next project: to compose the soundtrack for a blaxploitation movie. Just after the release of *It's Your World* in November 1976, he was approached by *Super Fly* screenwriter Phillip Fenty to score his new movie. *The Baron* is the quirky story of a filmmaker who vainly tries to chronicle the life of legendary European racing car driver Baron Wolfgang von Schultz. The star, Calvin Lockhart, plays a black actor/filmmaker who borrows money from the mob to finance his film about the baron with an all-black cast. That description alone should have given Gil pause. But Fenty was persuasive, and able to convince Gil and Brian to take on the project, which they accepted as a creative challenge, though it would be months before they started recording the soundtrack.

25.

PEACE GO WITH YOU, BROTHER

Gil's personal life was proving to be more complicated than the most intractable of political debates. His relationship with girlfriend Lurma Rackley had grown strained due to his other romantic liaisons with journalist Pat Kelly and his lengthy absences when he was on tour. He was emotionally distant, and misunderstandings and unspoken assumptions often got in the way. Though he was so blunt and clearheaded in his poetry and lyrics, he could be evasive with Rackley. "It was the kind of relationship where I was unsure where we stood, and I would try to pin him down, and he assumed that I understood," says Rackley. "One time I asked him about the definition of our relationship, but he didn't like to be boxed in or defined."

Those mixed signals came to a head when Rackley got pregnant in late August 1976. She had been told that she couldn't conceive a child, so at first, she wasn't sure if she was really pregnant. Previously, she had told Gil that if she did get pregnant, she would keep the baby, and that she could raise it on her own. That message was lost on Gil, who assumed that she was telling him that she didn't need him around. "In hindsight, I realize that he must not have heard what I was saying," she says. In his memoir, Gil describes a different scenario. He says that he knew she wanted a family but that when she got pregnant, she didn't tell him and stopped talking to him. "I was confused at first, and then upset and a little angry. . . . I decided she would have to get in touch with me." They didn't talk again for two years.

Gil claimed that in the next year, he started to hear from mutual friends and acquaintances that Lurma had given birth to a son, Rumal (an anagram of her first name) in February 1977. Gil assumed it was someone else's child because Lurma had never told him about the birth and he gave up trying to get in touch with her.

It wasn't the only time that he became a father that year. In March 1977, just one month after the birth of Rumal, Gil's off-again, on-again girlfriend Pat Kelly gave birth to his daughter Raquiyah Nia. At first, Gil denied that the girl was his and ignored Kelly's demands for child support. "Gil didn't want to see her because he didn't want no kids," says friend Tony Green. "He just ignored her until she came by the house, and she was crying." When he started to get tough letters from family court, he grudgingly made a few payments. Gil's mother knew Kelly, and she was so outraged at Gil for not taking responsibility that she once told Kelly to shoot Gil because he was being so capricious: "Just go and get a gun and kill him." Bobbie ended up providing the DNA sample that proved Nia's paternity, forcing Gil to take responsibility. When he later stopped paying child support, the case went to family court and the government seized $47,000 from Gil's ASCAP (American Society of Composers, Authors, and Publishers) account to pay Kelly. Gil didn't show up to contest the case.

To escape the pressure and the responsibility, Gil turned to music and the recording of the soundtrack for *The Baron*. Though he usually hated being in the studio, it was preferable to dealing with romantic entanglements and being hounded by the mother of his daughter. The music on the movie's soundtrack is recognizable as Gil's sound, with plenty of extra effects and horn sections loaded on top. It includes portions of four original songs and largely instrumentals. He recorded much of the score in New York in the spring of 1977, where he worked with legendary choreographer George Faison on coming up with music for a dance routine. The experience was slightly surreal for Gil, who was used to his simple routine of rehearsing and performing with just Brian Jackson and the band rather than with a whole horn section including avant-garde jazz trumpeter Malachi Thompson.

It was all a little overwhelming, and every day while working on it, he couldn't wait to go back to his hotel room to smoke a joint and write poetry. One day, coming back to the Salisbury Hotel, he walked into his room to voices and the overpowering smell of marijuana smoke—which made him upset, because he knew he had stashed some Colombia reefer in a shoe box under his bed. In the living room sat Bob Marley and three of his buddies rolling joints "as thick as a sausage" on a newspaper on the floor. They had been playing soccer in Central Park and were offered Gil's room to stay in while their rooms were being cleaned. In a moment that is haunting in retrospect, Gil noticed a nasty gash on Marley's toe. The reggae legend had not been taking medicine prescribed for him, explaining, "Jah heal, Jah put t'ing for healin'." Gil responded, "Jah might've put that doctor here for healing. Jah's gotta be mighty busy." Marley just repeated, "Jah heal." Despite the malignant melanoma that had developed under his toenail, Marley had also refused the amputation recommended by his doctor, citing his religious beliefs. Ultimately, this cancer is what killed him.

A few months after Gil's encounter with Marley, *The Baron* was released and quickly bombed, though the soundtrack was praised as "groovy" and got decent reviews. Gil grew dismayed about his connection to the project, telling friends that he felt he'd been suckered into the deal and should have trusted his intuition to avoid Hollywood. It also reinforced his suspicion of show business and his commitment to making music on his own terms.

That fierce independence was more difficult to maintain in his love life, which had always been peripheral to his creative accomplishments. But that year, in almost a karmic act of overcompensation, Cupid made sure that Gil felt the sting of those arrows. He was introduced to his latest lover, a beautiful actress, through his old basketball pal Lew Alcindor, now named Kareem Abdul-Jabbar and dominating the boards for the LA Lakers. Abdul-Jabbar knew that UCLA classmate Brenda Sykes liked to play Gil's albums, especially *Pieces of a Man*, and was impressed by the charismatic poet's powerful voice and lyrics. They had joked for years that if she introduced Abdul-Jabbar to one of her actress friends, he'd introduce her to his old buddy from New York. One night in November 1977, Abdul-Jabbar called Sykes impromptu and invited her to a show at the Roxy on Sunset Boulevard. He brought her backstage to meet Gil and the pair clicked.

Sykes, a stunningly beautiful model and actress, had gained the attention of casting agents when she appeared on *The Dating Game* a few years earlier. Born in Shreveport, Louisiana, the daughter of a postal worker, Sykes started modeling in the early 1970s before catching her big break. Soon she was being cast in movies such as *Cleopatra Jones* and *Mandingo*. She later played Jimmie Walker's girlfriend on the sitcom hit *Good Times*.

She and Gil started dating and the relationship soon turned serious. He was captivated by her beauty and gentle soul, and she was charmed by his charisma and intelligence. He soon told Brenda that he wanted to get married. She told him that she'd consider it if they were still together a year later.

They didn't have much time to enjoy the first flush of love: Gil was due back in the studio. On their next album for Arista, *Bridges*, Gil and Brian looked both forward and backward. Musically, their sound had progressed; Brian was determined to take advantage of new instruments and evolving technology. On most of the tracks, he plays synthesizer bass, which allowed for more range than traditional bass—and within a few years would transform the sound of rhythm and blues. Lyrically, Gil pays homage to civil rights icons, looks back nostalgically at his childhood in Jackson, and addresses new challenges, including the dangers of nuclear power.

The album kicks off with a bang, featuring two up-tempo songs about the joys and struggles of life on the road, "Hello Sunday, Hello Road" and "Racetrack in France." Written on the bus in between shows on endless tours, the tracks seem like bits from Gil's diary, full of stray observations and random thoughts. On "Tuskegee No. 626," Gil educates listeners about the syphilis experiments conducted on unsuspecting blacks by the U.S. government between 1932 and 1972.

Empowered by the limitless sonic possibilities of his Fender Rhodes synthesizer, Brian took some songs such as "Hello Sunday, Hello Road" and "Song of the Wind" and transformed them by using a bass synthesizer rather than a bass guitar. "A bass is a bass. There is only so much you can do with it. But with a synthesizer, you can create all kind of sounds and tunes." He did the same with "We Almost Lost Detroit," adding the electronic sound after the rest of the band had gone home.

While the album seemed to be another smooth collaboration between two great minds, there were signs of a growing split between Gil and Brian, and tensions soon began to build between the musical partners. Brian was the band's music director, but he noticed that Gil was assuming more and more of that role; he "seemed like he was stepping on my toes," says Jackson. "So, there was less and less for me to do. We weren't really writing songs together anymore, and he was using more of his songs on the album." Jackson contributed only one song to *Bridges*, "Vildgolia," and only one to the next two albums.

Again, as with "Johannesburg," Gil was politically prescient with "We Almost Lost Detroit," singing about the dangers of nuclear power three years before the Three Mile Island disaster, a partial meltdown of a nuclear reactor in central Pennsylvania that released radioactive gases into the environment. It was the worst accident of its kind in U.S. history. Typical of his writing method, Gil dashed off the song in a moment of inspiration. One night after a gig at the World club in Chicago in 1977, drummer Tony Duncanson handed Gil a copy of *We Almost Lost Detroit*, John G. Fuller's real account of a partial nuclear meltdown in 1966 at the Fermi power plant. By the next day, Gil had turned that story into a powerful song with the same title, poignantly describing how the event impacted the city. The song endeared him to fans in Detroit, who would invite him back to perform. By capturing a near-disaster, Gil showed "how close the tragedy of nameless destruction lay underneath our breathing and distractions," notes writer Walter Rhett. The song tells the story of a nuclear power station thirty miles from Detroit:

> It ticks each night as the city sleeps,
> Seconds from annihilation.

The song's chorus echoes the ominous title: "And we almost lost Detroit / This time."

Some black fans took Gil to task for writing about an issue that didn't seem to impact his community directly. Gil explained his rationale: "Nuclear power is an equal opportunity destroyer. There's absolutely no racism involved with the threat of nuclear power. I feel that this is something that's happening on Planet Earth and it's not going to behoove me to ignore something that could have a serious effect on my life just because there aren't many black people involved in it yet."

While *Bridges* didn't produce a hit single, it was well received by critics and hit No. 16 on the jazz charts. Even acerbic *Village Voice* music critic Robert Christgau called Gil a "reliable pro, like some old country singer," adding that his lyrics had evolved with the times. He concluded, "As long as his eye stays fresh, I don't believe Scott-Heron can make a bad album." *Wire* magazine called "Delta Man" the record's outstanding achievement: "a Blues slow burning, stretched tight; a tense sonic road movie barely containing its prophecies of the change to come." The *Bay State Banner* called *Bridges* Gil's best album so far by distinguishing it from the dominant disco sound prevalent at the time: "His intelligent music is a buoyant discovery for people who really are sick of the bump business."

The band was at a creative peak when they hit the road to promote the album. Each show followed a familiar rhythm while still seeming fresh: Gil would come out onstage and talk about local issues, then read a spoken-word poem, at which point the percussionists would join in, and then, in time, the full band would propel through a few hits and a few surprises, which they extended into improvisatory jams.

Though the band's live performances won over many fans, the albums sales weren't enough to push them into the top tier of artists. For their next album, *Secret*s, Clive Davis brought in Malcolm Cecil, an eccentric genius of a producer whose TONTO studio system featured a wall of synthesizers. Cecil was already a legend in the business for his production work with Stevie Wonder on the soul singer's acclaimed *Talking Book* and *Innervision* albums, and with Weather Report and Billy Preston. Brian was excited at the opportunity to work with Cecil and to further expand the band's sound: "I had been waiting to do something like this." Gil was less enthusiastic.

The new electrified focus was a musical redirection for the band, and it created some tension between Brian and Gil. Brian was eager to explore jazz and improvisation, and to use synthesizers and electronic instruments to add new layers to their music. Gil considered himself a bluesman, and he wanted to stay true to their original, unplugged sound. By the end of recording, Brian was frustrated that Gil had not used any of his songs and had assumed his role in directing the band's music. "I confronted him about it, and he gave me the indication that he was feeling uncomfortable about where the music was heading, that it was more complex than it needed to be. That he was a simple blues singer more than a jazz singer." Gil accused Brian of trying to showcase himself for the purpose of leaving and starting his own band. "I told him, 'If you feel that way, I should just step aside and let you tell me what to do.'" They continued to work together, but Gil grew more discontented with Brian, and Brian was unhappy about his new role, in which he was just arranging and performing. Though Gil and Brian didn't argue when the other members of the band were around, the tension between them was clear. "[Gil] would hold grudges forever, and once he set his mind, his mind was made up," says saxophonist and Lincoln classmate Carl Cornwell.

Though the music may have been a source of strife, Brian and the other band members fully supported Gil's lyrical vision and the politics of his poetry. One of the more poignant songs on the album was "Three Miles Down," which Gil was inspired to write after he read about some recent mine disasters in West Virginia. He was also haunted by accounts of the Farmington Mine explosion, which killed seventy-eight people in 1968. Troubled by the danger of the job, he composed the song as a paean to coal miners, most of whom were white working-class people in Appalachia, demonstrating his growing awareness of problems and issues beyond those shared by the black community and that poverty, rather than racial inequality, was the real defining challenge of our time.

> *Damn near a legend as old as the mines.*
> *Things that happen in the pits just don't change with the times.*
> *Work till you're exhausted in too little space.*
> *A history of disastrous fears etched on your face.*

The song's clarity and significance could apply to many of Gil's overtly political songs, such as "Johannesburg" and "The Revolution Will Not Be Televised": they express his ability to take a serious issue or message and get listeners to hear the lyrics while tapping their feet to the beat. "It's pretty much impossible to write a song advocating government regulation of the coal mining industry—one that criticizes the Taft-Hartley Act by name—without seeming pedantic, or at least extremely boring. Nevertheless, he did," writes music scholar Joseph Schloss. To pull off that feat, Gil relied on his sense of humor and his understanding of the real world. Once, when he performed the song, an audience member shouted out, "We don't need coal! We need revolution!" To which, according to Schloss, Gil replied, "Yeah, but you still need something to keep you warm while you're revolutin'!"

The song reflected Gil's growth out of black radicalism and into an increasing empathy for suffering in other communities. "The problems that I often define are from the black perspective and experience," he later told the *Washington Post*. "But when I'm describing a situation that all people encounter, should it be disregarded because I'm black? There are a whole lot of white people in the world who are oppressed. It doesn't seem to be to anybody's advantage to just concentrate on areas that affect a narrow part of our community or the community at large."

"Angel Dust" became the album's big hit, hitting No. 15 on the charts, though controversy arose over its frank lyrics—radio stations from Buffalo to Miami felt that it promoted drug use rather than condemning it and refused to play the track, despite the fact that Gil recorded a public service announcement to be played by deejays before they put the song on the air: "This is Gil Scott Heron with an important message for everyone. Angel Dust is bad news. It's a powerful drug and a proven killer. Even trying it could be the mistake of a lifetime. Don't be a fool. Don't play with your life."

Gil slammed his critics, who he believed were not listening to the song, and noted that he'd done research, getting information from the National Institute on Drug Abuse, to make sure that the lyrics were accurate. And he claimed that some older fans were in denial, blithely unaware of the devastating impact the drug was having in their communities. "Folks have the feeling that oftentimes if you don't talk about something it will go away," Gil told *Agit Pop* magazine. "Angel dust won't go away . . . a whole lot of old hardheads who were going around talking about how [the song] was promoting smoking it, they didn't smoke it. They didn't know anybody who did. . . . But it was right there in their churches, in their community, right on their block, and in many instances right in their house. And the young folks appreciated us for speaking on it more than they appreciated them for trying to act like it didn't exist." Some record stores also declined to carry the record. This seemed to personally insult Gil, who had always cherished his free-speech right to get a message to the people.

The song did have its fans, though, especially from some prominent members of the black community: the Reverend Jesse Jackson issued a proclamation to thank the group for releasing the song, and Gil was honored with a CEBA (Communications Excellence to Black Audiences) award for his public service announcement warning of the dangers of angel dust. Later, he said he got a letter from a thirteen-year-old girl who said the song had prompted her to turn down some angel dust she was offered at a party.

On the other tracks on the *Secrets* album Gil is as pointed as ever in his critiques, tackling the phoniness of the entertainment world and consumer culture in "Madison Avenue" and "Show Business," which was designed as a warning letter to young musicians about how the music industry actually operated. The latter song was a particular slap at Arista executives, whose obsession with promotion and marketing and sales had disillusioned Gil about the music business. Even the perks, from meeting stars to riding in limousines, were wearying to him. "Most people come to the conclusion that it's 95% show and 5% business and they are very disappointed when they get into it and find out that there is a whole lot that has to be taken care of business-wise just to ensure the purity of your thoughts and your ideas," Gil later said. "It's a tongue-in-cheek poke at those who are naïve enough to think that in 1980 people are going to be giving you something for nothing, that all you got to do is get up there and sing and you get your bread and everything's cool."

In "Angola, Louisiana," over syncopated rhythms supplied by Brian Jackson, Gil indicts the legal system for sentencing a young black man to life imprisonment based on circumstantial evidence. In the song, he describes how he received a letter from Gary Tyler's mother, begging him to reach out to her son sitting in a jail in Louisiana for a crime he hadn't committed. Tyler, a black student, was on a school bus attempting to leave Destrehan High School in New Orleans on the first Monday of October in

1974 when a mob of two hundred white students, upset about the integration of the schools in the area, surrounded the bus, throwing rocks and bottles. Within minutes, a thirteen-year-old white boy, Timothy Weber, lay bleeding on the ground, dead from a single gunshot wound to the head. Local police quickly identified Tyler as the suspect, and he was soon convicted of murder. Every witness who named Tyler as the suspect later recanted, claiming that they had been forced by the police to give false testimony.

The *Secrets* album received mixed reviews, with some critics chiding Gil for the increasing predictability of his music and themes. "We've been here before," wrote Judith Brackley in the *Boston Globe*, deeming it "mediocre, almost formula" with its panoply of "message" songs. "It's not a bad album, just not what it could be."

The reviews didn't bother Gil. He and the band were too caught up in performing, constantly on the road. On a rare visit back to his home in Alexandria at the end of 1977, he stopped in at Martha's Roadhouse, a favorite R&B club in DC. Up onstage was Carl Cornwell, Gil's old buddy from Lincoln University, tearing through Coltrane's "Equinox" on the saxophone. After watching Carl and his band for a few minutes, Gil said, "Don't stop, don't stop," and started singing some lyrics over the song. It was the first time they'd seen each other since being at school together in 1970. A few months later, at the start of 1978, Brian called Cornwell out of the blue and asked him if he wanted to join the *Secrets* tour. It was an eye-opener for Cornwell, who was used to playing in jazz clubs and small venues. Everything was on a bigger stage now, from the size of the crowds to the number of groupies backstage. "All the stories you hear about the road were true. Girls and drugs, and it was phenomenal, and either you get wrapped up in it or hope for the best."

To reach the large audiences that packed the arenas with the same intensity, the group added new visual elements to their show. On most tours, the lighting designer is a peripheral figure who just shines colored lights onstage or maybe a strobe light for added excitement. When the Midnight Band toured, Gil worked closely with lighting designer Neil Fleitell to come up with ideas. He and Fleitell, a self-described hippie, would end up having three-hour discussions about politics and philosophy when they were supposed to be talking about proper lighting for an upcoming show.

Fleitell's goal was to turn Gil's music into visual images, but these images took on added significance considering the politically charged content of the lyrics. Among the images were giant cooling towers for "We Almost Lost Detroit," miners going down shafts for "Three Miles Down," and cat's eyes for "Angel Dust." For the closing number, "Johannesburg," Fleitell photographed his own forearm, from elbow to clenched fist, acid-etched the resulting negative, and shone lights through it, which resulted in a twenty-foot-tall fist dominating the stage.

That same year, Arista capitalized on the band's success and string of hits by releasing in November 1978 *The Mind of Gil Scott-Heron*, a collection of recorded poetry that recycled some tracks, such as "H_2O Gate Blues" and "Bicentennial Blues." In effect, it is a return to the form of his debut album, with Gil's spoken-word poetry over sparse percussion or light instrumentation. Unlike previous albums, which always included some personal hymns and love songs, this one features songs that focus solely on political and social issues, from Watergate to the Attica prison riot. In "Jose Campo Torres," Gil expresses his outrage at the death of a Hispanic army veteran who was beaten by six Houston police officers in 1978; he wrote the song, just weeks after the murder made headlines, because he wanted to expose the continuing "mistreatment of members of minority communities."

Despite such injustices, by the end of the decade Gil was keenly aware that the outrage was missing in the country. Unlike the first half of the seventies, the second half was characterized by narcissism and self-interest. One of the most powerful tracks on *The Mind of Gil Scott-Heron*, "The New Deal," takes on the middle-class activists who marched in youthful fervor during the 1960s but who had moved on to take jobs and join the bourgeoisie.

Not without some sympathy for those former activists, Gil later wrote in his memoir that "they'd been kidnapped by Exxon" and sacrificed their ideals for the sake of surviving an era in which many of their friends "got killed, betrayed, or put in jail for talking about helping the community." He expressed his despair and his rage at the co-opting of the revolution in the song, decrying "these smiles in three piece suits" who "took our movement off of the streets and took us to the cleaners."

By the end of the *Secrets* tour, tensions and creative differences between Gil and Brian had continued to build, and the group grew aware of the discord. Some of them headed for the exit. After finishing a gig in Texas, drummer Barnett Williams walked off at the airport, promising to see the band soon in DC. But when they got back to Washington, Williams never showed up. Some of the band members complained that they weren't being paid enough. "The animosity around that band always came down to money," remembers Cornwell.

26.

FIRE AND WATER

With Gil's creative differences with Brian making life on tour tense and studio pressure building for a hit song, Gil needed an escape, some safe harbor to retreat to when life became unbearable. And that was Brenda Sykes. After dating for over a year, just before Christmas 1978 she and Gil got married in a simple ceremony in the living room of jazz trumpeter Wayne Shorter's house in Los Angeles. Abdul-Jabbar was Gil's best man. "He couldn't stop smiling," remembers Shorter. "Gil was at a level of elation and awe and happiness that I don't think he had reached before." After a casual party, Gil and Brenda took off for a weeklong honeymoon at a friend's time-share "somewhere in California," gossiped *Jet* magazine.

They were a captivating couple, good-looking and charismatic, going to shows and after-parties in LA. "They were so cool," says filmmaker Esther Anderson. "She was exquisitely beautiful, soft and refined. He was so full of fire, and she was the opposite. She was the water in his life." In early July 1979, Brenda told Gil that she was pregnant.

On tour, Gil was focused and a creative dynamo, largely due to the presence of Sykes. "When Brenda was around, he was on it. When she wasn't there, he had a tendency to revert to self-abusive behavior," says Cornwell, adding that the band's contract rider included a bottle of Hennessy, Gil's favorite brand of high-end cognac. "The tour support people didn't really care if he was getting high or drunk as long as he got onstage."

Brenda would join the tour for five or six gigs at a time and then head back home to L.A. "She was as sweet as can be," remembers Cornwell. "She wasn't flamboyant at all for an actress. I wouldn't say she was humble but she had enough humility." Sykes sometimes invited band members back to the two-bedroom house she and Gil shared at 2260 North Cahuenga Boulevard near the Hollywood Bowl, which kept them fairly close to the home of her mother, Elvira. Gil bonded with the older woman— "one of the most sympathetic, pleasant and direct women I'd ever met"—a quick-witted charmer who once dated comedian Redd Foxx. When Gil had down time, he liked to sit in Elvira's living room, read Steven King thrillers, and talk to her about her childhood in Louisiana. He bonded with the old woman, who reminded him of his grandmother Lillie with her Southern roots, loving touch, and lacerating wit.

Soon, Gil was given an unprecedented opportunity to use his music to advance a cause he believed in—and expose his songs to an audience in the millions. His old Fieldston buddy Danny Goldberg, who had become a powerful music producer, was codirecting and coproducing a film, *No Nukes*, a concert documentary that would chronicle a weeklong series of shows in September 1979 supporting antinuclear efforts on behalf of Musicians United for Safe Energy, or MUSE. He invited Gil to take part in one of the shows, at New York's Madison Square Garden, that featured an all-star lineup of (mostly white) rock stars, including Bruce Springsteen, the Doobie Brothers, James Taylor, Bonnie Raitt, and Graham Nash.

At the show, when Peter Tosh refused to go on, Gil's spot in the lineup was bumped up, and he and the band had to get onstage almost as soon as they pulled up to the Garden, with hardly any time to get prepared. The band was a little rusty, and the audience kept screaming, "Bruce," for Springsteen—the night before, Chaka Khan had refused to perform because she thought those chants for Springsteen were boos—while Gil and the band set up their equipment onstage. Gil calmly reassured the crowd that Springsteen would appear soon, and then the band cruised through its set, a funky "South Carolina," a quieter "We Almost Lost Detroit," and a rousing version of "The Bottle." Gil's set was praised by critic Charles Shaar Murray, who called it the only other performance that night to rival Springsteen's intensity. Gil's song was also included on the documentary's accompanying soundtrack, exposing his music to a wider audience. A few days later, Gil and the band made history by performing with other MUSE members in front of two hundred thousand people in New York's Battery Park City, the largest antinuke rally ever held in the country. The event, along with popular films such as *The China Syndrome*, had a powerful impact—not another nuclear power plant was built in the United States for the next three decades.

Just two weeks after the Battery Park show, another musical event shook the country and would prove to be just as pivotal—not on environmental awareness but on popular culture. Hip-hop, a new music genre coursing through New York's black neighborhoods, made its debut on vinyl and exposed the music to mainstream America. Music producer Sylvia Robinson's newly formed Sugarhill Gang recorded their first single, "Rapper's Delight." The first commercial hip-hop single, the track became an overnight sensation, climbing to the top of the charts and clearing the way for dozens of obscure deejays and rappers to be signed by record labels.

These early hip-hop singles were party rap, light and frothy, full of adolescent braggadocio. The lyrics consisted of boasting, romancing, and more boasting, often in the same line—"Cause I'm the baby-maker, I'm the woman-taker, I'm the cold-crushin lover, the heartbreaker." Even after disco's decline, young rappers were still driven by dance music's imperative: to get more bodies on the dance floor. But some wanted to step it up another notch and use the lyrics to express the more harsh realities on the streets where they were living. Gil's ability to fuse spoken-word poetry over funky beats had paved the way. He gave license to some rappers to get more serious. "He showed the people another route," says DJ Kool Herc. "That they could go more hard-core, something more serious than party lyrics."

One of those hip-hop deejays was Bill Stephney, who grew up listening to "The Bottle" and "Johannesburg," played alongside hits by Aretha Franklin and Brass Construction. By his freshman year at Adelphi University in 1980, Stephney was the program director at the college's radio station, WBAU, where he gained a reputation for being one of the first deejays to play the burgeoning hip-hop music bubbling up out of the South Bronx. When Gil performed on campus after being invited by the black student union, Stephney interviewed him for his show. "He was incredible," remembers Stephney. "All I had was this little cassette player, and he was very courteous, talking about the election and Reagan and politics. Me and my friends were amazed that this brilliant artist whom we had seen on *SNL* was at our college, playing and talking to us." One of Stephney's buddies on campus was Carlton Ridenhour, a graphic arts student who was part of a mobile deejay crew called Spectrum City. Ridenhour was also a big fan of Gil's music, listening to *Small Talk* and *From South Africa to South Carolina* over and over on his turntable while in high school. "We were heavily influenced by Gil," says Stephney. "His music was informed by a social consciousness."

Despite the later efforts of music critics and individual rappers to canonize him as one of the forefathers of rap, Gil initially kept a distance from the brash new genre. He once joked, "I ain't saying I didn't invent rapping. I just cannot recall the circumstances." The origins of the genre are murky, going back to his father's native Jamaica in the 1950s. The island nation is very hilly, and deejays put together mobile sound systems, often in the backs of trucks driven through the countryside, playing the latest R&B and ska records. To entertain the audience and get them to dance, deejays such as Count Machouki often talked over the music, telling jokes and stories, a practice known as toasting. Decades later, when DJ Kool Herc was spinning records at parties in the South Bronx, the Jamaican native encouraged friends to grab the microphone. Soon, young rappers were competing with one another to see who had the funniest and cleverest rhymes. The music thrived underground, beneath the radar of the music industry, until the release of "Rapper's Delight."

While rap was blowing up, the Midnight Band was falling apart. With Gil's elevated drug use, imperious attitude, and musical inertia, Brian had lost patience with his creative brother. "I felt that if I had to play 'The Bottle' one more time, I would shove that flute down someone's throat. I had had it." After a show or in between rehearsals, whenever Brian tried to discuss his feelings with Gil, they would argue, and Gil would walk out, avoiding Brian for days. Brian felt that Gil wasn't prepared to take the music in different directions because it was out of his comfort zone. "He never felt that he was that strong as a singer, even less so as a musician," says Jackson.

"Gil always felt underprepared, and taking any chances made him nervous."

In the fall of 1979, Spike Lee, a senior completing his degree in film studies at Morehouse College, invited Gil and the band to perform on campus. They burned through their hits and did a twenty-minute version of "Madison Avenue" to an adoring audience. "When we finished playing, the people went berserk. It was unbelievable," remembers Brian. But his partner's performance that night validated Brian's ongoing discontent with the band's leader. "All Gil did in those twenty minutes was sing the lead, the first two verses, and a second verse at the end and the outro. For the rest of the time, it was us jamming, and he was off to the side playing tambourine. I knew that I had to move on." It was the last performance of the Midnight Band. That night, Jackson walked away and never looked back, catching a flight to Oakland to live with his girlfriend and figure out his future.

Gil didn't have much time to contemplate his next move or to take in Brian's exodus. The father-to-be had to rush back to Los Angeles to spend time with Brenda, who was just about to give birth to their daughter, Gia Louise, on March 9, 1980. Gil remembers holding the newborn in his arms in Brenda's room at the hospital while watching Lakers games. When they got home, they took turns watching over her, with Brenda taking the morning and afternoon shifts, and Gil on the night shift. Sometimes the guys in the band would stop by and play a slow jam to lull Gia to sleep in her bassinet. A month later, in a profile in *Essence* magazine, Brenda and Gil were photographed standing on the side of a hill in Los Angeles, Gil sporting a black leather jacket and a smooth smile, and Brenda, in a red skirt, looking relaxed with her hand on her hip. They were in a good place, and their affection for each other was clear to friends and family.

But the serenity didn't last long. According to Gil's memoir, when the child was just a few months old, Lurma came by his house in Alexandria with her son, Rumal, in tow. As soon as he saw the boy, Gil said he knew instantly that it was his son. "He looked exactly like pictures I'd seen of myself on the front porch in Jackson at his age." The memoir states that Lurma made him promise not to tell anyone that Rumal was his son, without providing a reason. He kept his word for years, laughing off anyone who mentioned a son in Virginia. He says he never mentioned Rumal to anyone, including Brenda and his own mother. "I rarely went a long time without wondering how Lurma was doing and how my mini-me was coming along, but it would be many years before I found out." (Many of their mutual friends in Washington did not know that her son, Rumal, was Gil's. "I knew Lurma as a single mom," says E. Ethelbert Miller, the board chair for the Institute for Policy Studies. "I had no idea that she was with Gil or in love with him.")

Lurma tells a different story. "In the book, he had it that I just disappeared and he didn't know about the baby and he heard about it through the grapevine," she says. "And I didn't pop up until Rumal was almost three." Lurma says that though she told him in 1977, "If we're not *together* together, then let's just be apart," she insists that Gil knew about her pregnancy and should have known that it was his child. In effect, she says that he abandoned their son even though they might have mutually agreed to split up. In his memoir, Gil says that Lurma only told him that he was Rumal's father when the boy was three. Rackley thinks that Gil skewed the details in the book because he wanted to make it clear how much he loved Rumal. "He wants to make it seem as if he did not know he had the choice to be with us earlier," she says. "He doesn't want it to be perceived that he had a choice to be with me and Rumal before he met Brenda and that he chose Brenda."

Gil fell deeply in love with Brenda and they were a happy couple for several years. They were photographed in glossy magazines and breathlessly described in gossip columns, but the appearances masked a complicated reality. They genuinely adored each other, but Gil's personal demons got in the way of his emotional commitment to Brenda. He had a hard time opening up to anyone about his feelings or making himself emotionally available to their needs. He and Brenda shared two homes on both coasts, but Gil spent most of their marriage on the road, performing and staying at hotels.

For someone who had always guarded his fierce independence of spirit by maintaining a cool emotional detachment from those close to him, it was getting difficult to keep his personal life from overwhelming him. One daughter with his wife; former girlfriends competing for his attention and claiming their own love children. The emotional and financial demands were too much for him. He didn't have a model in his own life—neither his own father nor another male authority figure—whose example could have guided him through this challenging time. And his closest friend and creative partner had just walked out on him.

27.

TURNING CORNERS

In his shattered emotional state, Gil had to face the next chapter in his music career: go in the studio and record his first album in the new decade—and the pressure was more intense than ever. He needed to produce a hit (Arista had been disappointed in the sales of the previous three albums), stay fresh and funky (with the advent of hip-hop and electronic R&B, his blues-influenced music was dated) and stay true to himself (his message music was losing the respect of critics and failing to ignite his audience).

To top it off, most of the band was gone, including Gil's creative partner for over a decade. Before leaving the band, Brian had started work with Gil on *1980*, the band's next album, but now Gil was on his own. He auditioned a few musicians, assembled a new team, and started recording in Malcolm's TONTO studio in Santa Monica, but he soon realized that he needed his brother in arms. He was more annoyed than hurt at Brian's departure, but he knew it would be hard to pull off a decent album without his partner's musicianship. His pride deep in his throat, Gil called up Brian. Not that he was humble—he demanded that Brian come help him out with *1980*. Brian was taken aback by Gil's arrogance and was resistant, but he soon agreed to make the trip, largely because his name was still on the album.

Marking their commitment to the new electronic sound and some of the album's proto-rap songs, Gil and Brian posed for the cover wearing bright jumpsuits while sitting in Malcolm's enormous TONTO synthesizer room. They appeared to be the same duo that had always been united in music and message, but behind the scenes, they were feuding again. When Brian found out that Gil had signed another five-album deal with Arista, he was furious. "I just couldn't believe he would do that behind my back," he says, explaining that he felt disrespected by the move. They also clashed over the label's intentions, which Brian had long suspected were only about sales. Gil still trusted Clive Davis, saying that he offered him a freedom that was unique in the record business.

During the making of the album, Brian had been working on a new piece and it needed lyrics, so he called up Gil as he had done for years. "As was our custom, before he wrote a word, he asked me, 'What's it about?'" recalls Brian. "'It's about turning corners, a new page,' I replied. He knew what I meant. It was over. We had gone to the end of the line as musical partners. 'Corners' was the last song we ever wrote together." The lyrics are all about their rift and how it's perfectly timed to the end of the 1970s:

> Turning of the decade
> Is meant to separate;
> Ten years left to history
> And ten years left to fate.

The duo never recorded together again. The split with Brian was irrevocable in some ways; both were proud and stubborn about never letting things go. Band members recall Gil's imperious side—if one of them was late for the tour bus, Gil would *never* let him forget it. Brian could be prickly and oversensitive to the point where it prevented him from forgiving others for their mistakes.

Gil often claimed that Brian had been drifting in a more independent direction for years and that he encouraged him to explore his musical gifts on his own. Brian agrees that he wanted to move in a more progressive direction with his music, but he says that Gil wouldn't let him take a break. He explained that after a decade of relentless recording and touring—up to two hundred gigs a year—he wanted a six-month break, but that Gil took it personally, as he so often did when friends disagreed with him. This time, his feelings of abandonment were more intense because it was Brian,

his closest friend and collaborator, who was leaving him. "He saw my decision as me saying to him, 'You're on your own now,' which is totally not
what I was saying," says Jackson. "But he could never be convinced of that.
He felt abandoned." When Gil was asked about Brian's departure, he was
characteristically sharp: "[Brian] always wanted to do some other things—
and now he's been afforded that opportunity."

They didn't speak again for fourteen years.

28.

HOTTER THAN JULY

Without Brian and other buddies from Lincoln, the band had been completely made over. The Midnight Band was no more; Gil felt that they had to choose a new name. The group had been reduced to a quintet, including a few female vocalists who had joined Gil on *Secrets*. As a result, he dubbed his new band A Mere Façade. The name caused some confusion among fans and friends. Once the band performed at Washington's Constitution Hall as Gil Scott-Heron and A Mere Façade. At the door that night, one guy tried to get into the show by swearing he was a friend of "Amir." "We were laughing our asses off," remembers Val-Hackett. It also baffled the suits at Arista. The label's West Coast rep once joked with Gil, "Who are these Arab dudes you're playing with. Who's Emir Fasad?"

After just a few performances, Gil realized that they needed another name, though one that retained the same sense of irony and loss. Since the band's sound was so different from that of the Midnight Band, he dubbed it the Amnesia Express. The new group anchored Gil's music for the next decade, with occasional appearances by members of the original band. Though the Amnesia Express played many of the same songs as the Midnight Band, percussionist Larry McDonald says that Gil gave them lots of freedom to perform those tracks with their own energy. As a result, they would play forty-minute performance piece versions of "Angel Dust." McDonald says that he was playing "The Other Side" for years before realizing the root of the song. He told music journalist Andrew Nosnitsky that "one day I went up to my brother and he had a forty-five of 'The Bottle' and he flipped it over, and halfway through the song, I said, "Wait a minute, that sounds familiar." It was 'Home Is Where the Hatred Is.' I had never heard [the studio version of] that song before we started playing it! And we was killing it! He gave us freedom to play."

By that point, drugs were a constant distraction for the band. Gil would skip record store appearances, leaving fans waiting for hours, while he got wasted in his hotel room. What had started as a casual cocaine habit, shared by many in the music world in the 1970s, had evolved into an addiction for Gil. Whereas other members of the band were able to do a few lines and pull back from the ledge, Gil pushed things further. At the end of one gig, he asked his half-brother Denis for a thousand dollars, and he took at least a third of that to go buy an eighth of an ounce of cocaine. Always the one to take chances musically and creatively, and to put all his energy into his art, Gil did the same with cocaine. He did more and more lines. Somehow he was able to keep getting up onstage and going into the studio to record. But over time he started to miss gigs and disappear for days. "We would go and take the mirrors off the walls in the hotel room and dump a few ounces of cocaine on it," says friend Tony Green.

At this creative crossroads, Gil was given the opportunity of a lifetime. In August 1980, Stevie Wonder announced that he would be using his concert tour for his chart-topping *Hotter Than July* album to raise support for making Martin Luther King Jr.'s birthday a national holiday. Civil rights groups had proposed this initiative for several years, but it never attracted enough public support to overcome congressional inertia or the opposition of conservative lawmakers. Stevie was planning a rally on the Mall in Washington, DC, in January to pressure Congress into making the date a holiday. Gil had seen the news on *20/20*, during Barbara Walters's interview with Stevie, and he was looking forward to seeing the tour when it came through DC. Instead, Gil got a phone call from Clive Wasson, a promoter. Wasson said that Stevie wanted Gil to join him on tour briefly to replace Bob Marley, who had a prior commitment to play with the Commodores on the same nights as some of Stevie's concerts.

When Gil joined the tour in Houston, he immediately got a taste of Stevie's infectious spirit. Walking into the cavernous Summit sports arena on a hot day in November, trying not to get lost, he heard someone call out, "Aries," a nickname that only one person used for Gil. There was Stevie in his distinctive cornrows and sunglasses, up in the sound booth. "Come on up here, Aries!" When Gil expressed surprise that Stevie had spotted him, the star smiled. "We felt your vibes, Aries." The blind soul singer's ability to spot Gil became a constant prank on the tour. Once, Gil even tried sneaking up on him in his dressing room, shushing all of Stevie's entourage, but the singer still managed to sense Gil's presence. Whether through his sixth sense or getting advance notice from his headset-wearing brother, Calvin, Stevie always managed to nail Gil.

Gil and Stevie developed a smooth show, with Gil and the band performing at 8:05 for an hour, opening for Stevie and Wonderlove, his backup band. Then Gil would emerge at 11:30 to join Wonder for his finale, "Master Blaster" and "Happy Birthday," Stevie's tribute to Dr. King.

Gil's band wasn't always prepared for the tour's fast pace and sudden changes. They almost missed a show in Baton Rouge when they spent an hour at Houston Airport looking for guitarist Ed Brady. Gil ran from terminal to terminal before finding Brady hunched over a video arcade playing *Space Invaders*. To make up for lost time, producer Malcolm Cecil gunned the car down the highway, until they were pulled over by a Louisiana state patrolman. As they waited for the trooper to approach their car, Malcolm, the only white man in the car, told the band, "Don't say a word, guys." Then, in what Gil calls an "Oscar-winning performance," Cecil rolled down the window, played up his British accent, and complained about all the delays he was having while trying to get the "African boxing team" to the Centroplex in Baton Rouge. The patrolman ended up apologizing to them and escorting the band, with sirens wailing and lights flashing, all the way to the stadium.

Later that night, Gil was summoned to Stevie Wonder's hotel suite, where the singer was sitting in a back bedroom. He told Gil that Bob Marley's cancer had worsened and he had entered New York's Memorial Sloan Kettering clinic. Wonder was concerned—and under pressure from his record company, Motown, to find another big name to join the tour. Stevie wanted Gil, and though Stevie was one of the biggest stars in the music world, he had had to fight his label to get Gil on the tour in the first place. The executives at Motown had wanted a more popular opening group, and had suggested some of their chart-topping stars such as the Commodores and the Dazz Band. Either out of modesty or insecurity, Gil said he agreed with the label, telling Wonder that a bigger name might be better at packing the arena and explaining that his upcoming new album, *Real Eyes*, would probably not fuel enough advertising to promote such a big tour.

But Wonder insisted on Gil and his band. On November 2, 1980, he announced in Dallas that the tour and rally in DC would continue as planned, with Gil and the Amnesia Express along for the ride. Much of Gil's lyrics resonated with Wonder, who had experienced his own growth in political awareness over the previous decades. He felt that Gil was the right person to help him inspire support for honoring Dr. King with a national holiday. Two nights later, the two of them joined many African Americans in reacting with shock—"like a brief contact with an open circuit"—at the news of Reagan's victory over Jimmy Carter. Their campaign for a national holiday had suddenly become much harder.

With Reagan's election and the risk that a decade of progress could be undone by a conservative president, the timing couldn't have been better for Gil's next performance: a night of poetry and music on the campus of Kent State University, the campus that had shifted the peace movement into "overdrive" after the shooting of four demonstrators by the National Guard in 1970. Gil's words that night presaged much of what he later included in his epic song "B Movie," which skewers Reagan and the country that elected him. As always, Gil provided some context that night, explaining Reagan's shift from Democratic liberal during the McCarthy era to conservative Republican during the 1960s and '70s, when "there was very little difference between himself and Attila the Hun." Gil enjoyed the audience: students, professors, and informed locals who appreciated his critiques and his sarcasm. Gil told the audience that he had mixed feelings about Reagan's election— sorry for the state of the country but excited about the prospects for his own career: just as Nixon became the ultimate bête noire for Gil and much of the country, serving as a perfect target in some of his memorable songs, from "H$_2$O Gate Blues" to "Bicentennial Blues," Reagan might have even more potential.

Back on tour with Stevie a few days after the election, Gil was experiencing a mix of emotions about his presence onstage with a real superstar. It was exhilarating for him, but it also brought up old doubts about whether he deserved to join such a talented genius on such a major tour. After arriving two hours late at the show in Montreal on November 7, racing to the Forum with Brenda and Gia in a cab, Gil wrote a poem that described his wonderment at being an "ex-country hick" who made it big.

The next stop was the highlight of the concert tour: Madison Square Garden, where the energy of New York was pumped up higher by the presence of someone who, at the time, was the biggest pop star on the planet, Michael Jackson. Gil had always struggled with the requisites of fame, often preferring to jam in small venues or read poetry to a student union at a small black college. And he obviously wasn't interested in chart success or doing what was necessary to generate sales. In many ways, he felt like the kid who had been invited to the movie premiere, the outsider who had been granted inner access but didn't really belong. Still, like most people, he got a buzz from meeting famous people, such as Langston Hughes and Muhammad Ali.

And though his musical instincts veered in a different direction, he had a keen appreciation for pop talent, from his days in high school humming songs by Smokey Robinson and the Miracles. He was in awe of Stevie's humanity and soul—"the extraordinary became commonplace"—and he admired the songwriter's talent for turning out instant hits. But nothing prepared him for the magic of Michael Jackson. All day long, the crew had been buzzing about Jackson's arrival, and when he came out for "Master Blaster," the Prince of Pop did not disappoint. When Wonder introduced his "special guest," Jackson glided onstage to join him and Gil, like a "trick of the light," while the crowd roared in a frenzy. During the song's chorus, Gil vainly tried to keep up with Jackson, but his voice couldn't get that high. "It felt like reaching for water with a butterfly net," he writes with candor in his memoir. Eventually, Gil handed Jackson the microphone and re-treated to the side of the stage while Wonder jammed with Jackson, who twirled "like a boneless ice skater."

Though Gil felt artistically insecure to be in the presence of such stars, the critics felt the opposite: that Wonder gave a lackluster performance and should have been trying to emulate his opening act. The *New York Times*'s Robert Palmer praised Gil for giving a powerful performance, comparing him to Bob Marley as a pop tunesmith who was politically conscious and "transcends his material as a spokesman, oral historian and moral exemplar." They both "have more important things on their minds, and on their tongues, than the writing and singing of silly love songs."

The tour went to Washington, DC, around Thanksgiving in 1980, and the band was looking forward to seeing old friends and familiar faces. Gil stopped in to see Bruce Little's sister at her house in Landover, Maryland, giving her money for a special catering request: to cook a special Thanksgiving dinner for Stevie and him and their bands. A few nights later, the dinner (turkey and candied yams and greens and dessert) was laid out at the old Maverick Room in DC. When Stevie arrived with his entourage, the boisterous group was doing the Rock, the hot dance at that moment, and Gil joined in, getting into a line and kicking his feet out, a huge smile stretched across his face.

Less than two weeks later, on December 8 in Oakland, Gil and Stevie experienced a poignant moment that seemed to mark the end of the 1960s for once and for all. When Gil arrived at the arena, he saw Stevie at the bottom of the backstage stairs. His voice was so quiet and somber that Gil couldn't hear him at first. "Some psycho, some crazy person, shot John Lennon. And I'm wondering how to handle it." Gil was stunned: "I got that same feeling I'd felt when I heard that Dr. King or someone else was killed; that sense of a certain part of you being drained away, a loss of self."

Wonder was trying to figure out how to tell the audience: in an era before cell phones and Twitter and e-mail, nobody else in the area had heard the news of the 10:30 shooting in New York. Gil told Stevie to wait until the end of the show, "Hell, ain't nothin' they can do about it." When Stevie finally made the announcement, he spoke with a tremor in his voice. The audience fell quiet. "There was stunned silence and then cries of anguish, "Oh no, it can't be," "Oh my God, this can't be," remembers Arista promotions manager Bruce Wheeler, who was right in front of the stage with his wife, Kolleen. In his eulogy, Wonder demonstrated his humanity and compassion, giving the audience a look inside his own heart, "where all the insanity and madness of this world really hurt and enraged you."

The crowd was in mourning. "It sort of deteriorated into mass wailing," says Wheeler. "And Kolleen and I headed immediately for the backstage and went back to Gil's dressing room. Everyone in the room was blown away. We were both crying and we hugged. "This can't be happening," said Gil. The experience also made Gil even more committed to the campaign for King's holiday, lending that quest legitimacy and substance. In fact, a poem included in his memoir explicitly links Lennon's song "Imagine" to King's "I Have a Dream" speech.

It was an emotionally tumultuous month—just weeks after Lennon's killing, Arista released the band's new album, *Real Eyes*. For the album cover, Gil used the most personal image to appear on any of his records: a photo of him leaning his forehead against baby Gia, clearly in love with his adorable daughter. The album features one of his favorite songs, "Your Daddy Loves You," an unabashed display of parental affection. As always, Gil couldn't help being honest, telling a sleeping Gia that "me and your mama had some problems" and assuring her that he loves her.

Along with the title track, the album is more tender and grounded in an R&B sensibility than his previous records. It has its share of political tracks, including "Train from Washington," which takes aim at the government's failure to help the working class, and "Not Needed," a moving look at the empty life of a factory worker forced to retire early.

The character in the song has worked on the railroad his entire life and now, at age fifty-five or sixty-five, he's being told that he's no longer needed. Without that job and that knowledge that he needs to do something, the rust sets in. "The only thing that really kept him going was that he was active and he was doing something, and all of a sudden he's retired, and he has time on his hands and he finds that his life is deteriorating . . . that is particularly painful with our older people, one of the more significant ideas even though it didn't attract the same kind of attention. It was a very important piece to me and I had to do it."

The album stands out as one of the few cases in which Gil opened up about the ups and downs of his love life. Though he loved Brenda, he had a hard time fulfilling his role as the dutiful husband. In addition to "Your Daddy Loves You" and its mention of marital troubles, he skewers his own ego and image as a ladies' man in "Legend in His Own Mind":

> *You know he had had more romances than L.A.'s got stars*
> *He had had more romances than Detroit's got cars*
> *He's a, a legend in his own mind and God's gift to women*
> *On a day God wasn't giving up a thing . . .*

The album got decent reviews, and though it lacked a hit single, sales picked up due to Gil's appearance with Stevie Wonder on the *Hotter Than July* tour and the album hit No. 12 on the jazz charts.

The tour with Stevie culminated on a cold, breezy morning, on January 15, 1981, when the two men stood onstage before fifty thousand people gathered for a Rally for Peace on the National Mall. It was the same spot where Martin Luther King Jr. had delivered his "I Have a Dream" speech eighteen years earlier. They joined the crowd in chanting "Martin Luther King Day, we took a holiday!" and singing Stevie's "Happy Birthday" song. In his remarks, Stevie moved the crowd to tears when he said, "Let our hearts beat to the rhythm of this march for life. But how, in fact, can our hearts beat to the rhythm of our march for life if our soul cannot sing out to the sound of love. How can we sing out love, if our lips do not embrace the taste of peace and harmony and unity? But how can our lips embrace these great feelings, if our hands do not reach out and intermingle into a melting pot of one."

Gil was moved by the rally, seeing tens of thousands of his brothers and sisters put their voices behind an important movement. But in five days, Reagan would be inaugurated at the other end of the Mall. To move forward, the country had to recognize those who before them had fought the brave fight, he wrote in his memoir. "Why would the next one of us feel that he or she should make the effort, marshal the strength, and somehow fortify him or herself against the opposition that always seemed stronger . . .

if even a man who won the Nobel Peace Prize was ignored where those efforts for peace had done the most good?"

It would take another two years before President Reagan finally signed a holiday into law, and it wasn't until 2000 that all fifty states officially recognized the day.

29.

FACING BACKWARD

The experience on the steps of the National Mall that day reinvigorated Gil. He started to reflect on the legacy of the civil rights movement and the challenge that Reagan's election posed to that legacy. Those sentiments are expressed in "B Movie," a spoken-word epic that powerfully indicted the new president and the country that had elected him. In the track, Gil is able to expand on a sentiment felt by many black Americans and progressive activists: that Reagan would roll back many of the gains in the civil rights movement. The song was originally titled "Reel to Real," but Gil felt that it might be too vague a title for some listeners. He toyed with changing it to "Reel to Real to Surreal" and even "From Reagan to Shogun," before opting for "B Movie." In the lyrics, he describes the rationale for the song title, explaining that Americans prefer to dwell in nostalgia rather than to face hard questions about the country's present and future. "Not to face now or tomorrow, but to face backwards. And yesterday was the day of our cinema heroes riding to the rescue at the last possible moment ... especially in 'B' movies." In a time of crisis, Americans longed for celluloid heroes like John Wayne, but since he had died a few years earlier, they went for his B-movie version: Ronald Reagan.

In Ronald Reagan, Gil found a target who perfectly matched his lacerating wit. Ever since Nixon's downfall, a suitable presidential chump had been lacking. Gerald Ford and Jimmy Carter were compelling enough personalities to be caricatured but not enough to become Gil's bêtes noire. He dubbed Ford "Oatmeal Man" because of his anonymity, despite his long tenure in Congress, and Carter "Skippy" for coming from the peanut-producing state of Georgia and for his adolescent smile. Gil targeted Ford in "Don't Just Do Something, Stand There," after his famous ungraceful tumble down the steps of Air Force One.

Soon, in the spring of 1981, Gil was back in Malcolm's studio with an expanded Amnesia Express, including more female vocalists such as identical twins Clydene and Lydene Jackson, recording a new album, *Reflections*. Malcolm's production wizardry on "B Movie" deepened the impact of the potent lyrics with Robbie Gordon's bass groove and turned it into a twelve-minute masterpiece. On "Gun," Gil presciently decries the proliferation of guns in the country and its role in boosting the crime rate and violence. But elsewhere, the album demonstrated both the loss of Brian Jackson's influence and Gil's limitations as a musician. At least four songs "are diminished by the mere serviceability" of his music since Brian left the band, wrote Robert Christgau, adding that they "invoke the power of music that only becomes truly powerful when it's more than serviceable."

Perhaps Gil was aware of his limitations as a musician because he added two covers, which he had never done before. One was Bill Withers's "Grandma's Hands," featured on the soul singer's debut album in 1971; the lyrics reminded Gil of his grandmother, Lillie, when he was a boy back in Tennessee. It was a natural song for him, with his warm baritone and the emotional depth he brought to the lyrics. He also covered Marvin Gaye's "Inner City Blues," which he'd loved from the time he first heard it in 1971. Some of Gaye's lyrics—"Rockets, moon shots / Spend it on the have-nots— reminded Gil of "Whitey on the Moon," and the song's passionate plea appealed to him. Knowing that he lacked Gaye's vocal chops, Gil focused on his strengths, adding a spoken-word monologue to his version, including portions of his 1973 poem "This Evening," which tells the story of Mark Essex, a black Vietnam veteran and sharpshooter who came back to the States unable to find a job and went on a shooting spree beginning on New Year's Eve 1972.

Under pressure from Arista executives to deliver a hit single, which had been missing on the last few albums, Gil knew that "B Movie" had that

potential. Unlike with "The Bottle" and "Johannesburg," this time he welcomed the idea of releasing the song as a twelve-inch single. The promoters
at Arista were astute enough to send a copy to every single member of Congress, many of whom wrote back to Gil with praise for the song's biting wit.

The timing of the release of the single in late 1981 could not have been
better—though Gil had written it a year earlier, many Americans were still
unfamiliar with how the newly elected president would actually govern.
"It's one of the few times we had released an idea that was drawing public
attention at the same time," he told the *Washington Post*, proud of the fact
that his criticism of Reagan was being mirrored in society.

The single won high praise, and was dubbed Gil's "smartest political
rap ever," by Robert Christgau, who had less praise for the rest of the album.
It hit No. 49 on the R&B singles chart, quite an accomplishment considering its length and political content. The album did reasonably well, topping
at No. 6 on the jazz charts and No. 21 on the R&B charts, though it still
didn't break Gil into the mainstream. Gil was determined to ply his own
course, personally and creatively, and didn't seem overly concerned about
hitting the top rungs of success. For others, success was sales. For him, success was about surviving the cutthroat music business with his soul intact,
remaining true to his artistry even after recording almost a dozen albums.

"Everybody has sort of a standardized version of building a career," he
told the *Los Angeles Times* that year. "I see success as still being independent
and an individual eleven years after my recording career started. Even though
I'm not as big as a lot of folks who've shown up in the last eleven months,
I will probably still be here when they've gone." This defensive tone may
have reflected his ongoing battles with the promotional team at Arista—he
kept resisting their requests for in-store appearances, interviews with Top 40
radio personalities, and collaborations with R&B singers.

One of the perennial challenges facing Arista was that though Gil's audience was fanatically loyal, it was harder to reach beyond them to a mass
audience. "When a Gil Scott record came out, you could expect X number
of sales instantaneously, but then the sales dried up pretty fast," says Arista
promotions manager Bruce Wheeler. Not that Gil did much to help the label push his songs and albums, taking part in promotional and marketing
tours only reluctantly. Part of this was due to his mixed feelings about suc-

cess. "Because success is more disruptive to our lives than failure," he wrote. "It calls for more adjustments. . . . Perhaps it is because success is always such a long shot that it brings so much disruptive surprise. . . . No one is prepared for it."

The tour to promote the album exposed Gil to a new audience of hip-hop fans who heard "B Movie" played by their favorite deejays, such as Frankie Crocker on New York's WBLS, who once played the twelve-minute extended jam four times in a row. And the band's subsequent tour revealed that the country was still racially divided. When they played at the University of Mississippi, the campus was rife with tension between the majority white student population and black students, who earlier that year had won a struggle to establish a black studies program at the school. During the performance, which featured Gil's incendiary monologues and songs about racism in the South such as "95 South," several white students started to boo and hiss and taunt the band. Nothing more happened during the show, but afterward, Gil and the band hurriedly made their exit. As their tour bus pulled away, gunshots rang out, bullets nearly hitting the bus. "It was terrifying," remembers drummer Tony Green. "They were clearly aiming at us." Campus police later investigated the incident but failed to make any arrests.

These experiences didn't dissuade Gil, who kept traveling without security to gigs around the country, performing at college campuses and to raise money for small nonprofit groups. Among the college students he influenced was Barack Obama, who had many of Gil's albums in his record collection. Obama and his buddy, Eric Moore, would go to the library at Occidental College in the early 1980s and check out speeches by Malcolm X and records by the Last Poets. At night, they would sit around and play Gil's records and talk about the message of certain songs, such as "H$_2$O Gate Blues," "Home Is Where the Hatred Is," and "The Revolution." "Gil's music made an indelible impression on Obama, as did that of Stevie Wonder and Bob Marley," says Moore. "Gil was very influential on Obama's life view."

Gil's reputation for having a big heart and a conscience could attract an overwhelming response. At almost every gig, "there were local activists from food banks or battered women's shelters asking Gil for help that he was in no position to give," remembers Fred Baron, his pal from Fieldston. Gil intimately felt the pressure to help the community, especially in poor African

American neighborhoods, and he was keenly aware that black entertainers had a particularly complicated relationship with fans and their expectations. "Like when you go back to the community—if you go back into the community—people wonder what you're doing there and if you don't go back, they say, 'See, that nigger didn't come back.' "

But Gil couldn't help but give back to his community, especially during a conservative administration that was shredding the social safety net for poor Americans. He was frustrated at the conservative upswing and the rollback of long-sought reforms, yet he saw the need to take a longer perspective. He used to argue that Americans were used to instant results "and when they heard about revolution and didn't get it instantly, they said, 'There must not going to be one.' " He liked to point out that revolution takes time, noting that blacks in Zimbabwe fought for a century to win their freedom and that it might take them even longer to get a government in that country that looked after their needs.

The endless pressure to help different groups and struggling people could be exhausting. "Gil carried a lot of people, mentally and emotionally, and it's hard to maintain yourself in the middle of all that work," says Roger Jones, who met Gil in Paris in 1981 while interning at the *International Herald Tribune.* "How do you continue to generate your own energy and to continue to make sense out of the world for *you*? It can't be easy for someone who dedicated their life to struggle."

Some band members are certain that the pressure on Gil to be the community's griot and revolutionary prophet intensified his use of drugs. "Gil was a very sensitive person," says friend Tony Green. "When he'd do these interviews about him being an activist—that's a lot of pressure to deal with. There was this enormous weight on his shoulders. You can't put out records like *Winter in America* and not expect that. And then people get disappointed when you don't keep telling them what to do and what to think." That responsibility to inform and educate the community exhausted Gil. "Nobody should have depended on Gil to tell them what was going on," says Brian Jackson. "That is way too much responsibility for anyone. If you were the person that everybody was asking, wouldn't you at some point feel a little contemptuous? Do you really have to ask? It's as clear as the nose on your face. 'What's going on, Gil? What is happening with the war in Iraq?' What the fuck do you *think* is going on? He didn't want to be anybody's spokesman and role model. All he wanted was to write his songs and play his music."

The weight of that responsibility was compounded by his extreme sensitivity to the world around him and to his own personal trauma. "He sees everything. The mind is always going. You can't stop it," says Brian. "I don't wish that on anyone. It can torment you. Put those two together—the responsibility that he tried not to feel and his own fear of abandonment. How many people did he really perceive as being there for him? It didn't take much to convince him that you weren't on his side. And if you went against him, that meant you're not with him. And if you went against him, then you abandoned him."

30.

BLACK WAX

Gil's music might have failed to live up to Arista's expectations when it came to record sales, but it was having a powerful influence on the next big revolution in popular music: cuts such as "The Bottle" and "Johannesburg" were already regularly featured in the deejay sets of influential hip-hop tastemakers such as DJ Kool Herc and Grandmaster Flash. But in those early years of the genre, it was the rhythms and beats of Gil's music that inspired hip-hop artists; his lyrics didn't have much of an influence on young rappers—at least not yet.

In 1981, Grandmaster Flash, who had revolutionized deejaying with adept scratching and cutting, was dominating the charts with his group, the Furious Five. With colorful outfits and choreographed dance routines, they recorded light, up-tempo songs such as "Freedom" and "Birthday Party." One of the group's producers was Ed "Duke Bootee" Fletcher, who was ten years older and more musically experienced. He was attending Dickson College in 1970 when "The Revolution Will Not Be Televised" was released, and he distinctly remembers the first time he heard it.

"I remember thinking, 'This guy ain't got a great voice, but I like his lyrics," says Fletcher. "His lyrics were really something different from what you were hearing, that focus on the reality of the streets and the politics behind it. The only one who approached that was Marvin [Gaye]."

Grandmaster Flash and the Furious Five's single "'The Message' follows a lot of the stylistics of Gil," says Stewart. "It has that melodic dimension, streetwise poetic lyrics, and even the beat was very similar to some of Gil's productions." The single went gold in twenty-one days, was universally praised, and is the first hip-hop recording to be inducted into the Grammy Hall of Fame. In the months that followed, other hip-hop artists started to release songs with lyrics about real life. Rappers told the Furious Five that they all had written their own "Message" songs but were concerned about the songs' commercial potential—until they became instant hits. Gil's influence is all over "The Message," which paved the way for socially conscious hip-hop artists ranging from KRS-One and Rakim to Public Enemy and Mos Def.

The message of Gil's music also attracted the attention of an ambitious new TV network looking for provocative content. In November 1981, documentary filmmaker Robert Mugge was looking for a new project. The thirty-two-year-old native of Virginia had just premiered a documentary film on eccentric jazz genius Sun Ra at the London Film Festival and sold it to the then-new British TV network Channel Four. Sitting in the office of the fledgling network's commissioning director, Andy Park, they were tossing around ideas when Park played Gil's "B Movie" on a little turntable. Then Park uttered words that live only in the fantasies of independent documentary filmmakers: "If somebody could make a film about this guy, I would fund the whole thing."

Park, a mischievous rebel, wanted his upstart channel to shake up the establishment. "Ronald Reagan had just been elected president, and all of us were not happy about that fact, and Andy put on that song about Reagan," remembers Mugge. "He loved the idea of having a film done that would needle and get under the skin of American authorities. I could not have been more excited." Mugge flew to Washington and spent a month trying to track down Gil through various club owners and music promoters. Finally, he reached Gil's half-brother Denis, and eventually talked with Gil in January 1982. When Gil told him that he was going to have a birthday concert in April at the Wax Museum, a nightclub that had been an actual wax museum, Mugge thought the setting was perfect to film Gil in concert.

The director found out that the former museum's wax figures of famous American presidents and political figures were sitting in storage in a back room, and he came up with the idea of cutting away from the concert footage to scenes of Gil riffing and commenting on politics directly to the wax figures in a back room of the museum. The monologues, expanding on Gil's thoughts on Nixon, Reagan, and Black History Month, were interspersed with songs shot over two nights of shows that Gil performed onstage at the club.

Brenda was excited about the project, convincing Gil that it was a great opportunity to expand his audience and explain what inspired his music. It was a good time for the couple: she playfully offered acting tips to Gil and was in the front row for the shows at the Wax Club. "They really seemed to be in love," says Mugge. "And she was really happy for him."

At one point, Gil suggested using a song, "Washington D.C.," from his upcoming album, *Moving Target*, on the film's soundtrack. "I got another idea," said Mugge. "Do you have a boom box? Yeah? Okay, so let's meet on the streets of DC; we'll play the tape, and you can sing against it while we walk around the neighborhood. We'll record it with a simple mic on your shirt." That moment in the film is one of the most striking scenes, capturing Gil in all his charisma and verbal clarity, but he is already a little touched from the ravages of drug use: his gait is slower and more deliberate, he is even thinner than usual, and his eyes look sleepy. Having donned a red-and-white baseball cap and skinny black jeans, he walks around different areas in Washington, from the White House grounds to Howard University, riffing on politics. With a boom box hoisted over his shoulder, Gil walked along the basin of the Potomac River, rapping the song to the amusement of locals sitting on park benches. The scene was captured smoothly on Steadicam, a new camera technology that allowed steady tracking of moving figures.

While walking past the White House, holding the hand of his three-year-old daughter Gia, then a toddler dressed in a white dress, Gil the ghetto griot spoke truth to power at its very beating heart on 1600 Lexington Avenue. Looking over protest posters leaning against the White House fence, Gil notes, "You know the protests that are launched in this country are not launched necessarily against the government. They are launched in terms of the fact that this country has rarely lived up to its advance publicity. This is supposed to be the land of justice, liberty, and equality, and that's what everyone over here is looking for."

Mugge bonded with Gil over long discussions about politics and culture and race, impressed by his charm, wit, and intelligence. "He would keep you on his toes, testing you and challenging your assumptions. And he always did it with a smile and a glint in his eye." When one of the musicians in the band confided to the director that Gil had been freebasing for a few years, Mugge was dumbfounded, finding it impossible to pair Gil's charismatic wit with the image of a drug addict. At the end of shooting, they parted ways—Mugge doing postproduction on the documentary and Gil recording his next album.

Over the next few months, in between shooting scenes for *Black Wax*, as the Mugge documentary was to be called, Gil went back into the studio with Amnesia Express to record *Moving Target*. Among the new band members was Larry McDonald, a dreadlocked Rastafarian percussionist who had been introduced to him by Malcolm Cecil. The band spent two long weekends in March and May of 1982 at Bias Studios in Springfield, Virginia, and two weekends in April at the Townhouse and the Manor in England.

Kicking off with the R&B tracks "Fast Lane" and "Explanations," followed by the reggae-influenced jams "No Exit" and "Ready or Not," the album has a different feel from Gil's earlier albums—more relaxed and less political. "Reggae had a big influence on this album," says McDonald, a longtime drummer who played with reggae legends Lee Perry and Peter Tosh. "Gil heard some of my songs and he wanted to use some of those rhythms in his music." As in *Real Eyes*, some of the lyrics in *Moving Target* are intensely personal, reflecting Gil's struggling with Arista's expectations, his disintegrating marriage, and his cocaine addiction. The band had just completed a long period of touring, and some of the songs express Gil's frustration with that relentless pace. Though he went out on the road to escape Brenda and the pressure of being a husband and father, he was physically exhausted by the end of the tour. In the chorus of "No Exit," which has clear echoes of

Bob Marley's sound, Gil repeats the somber realization "No, you can't get away (No, you can't get away) from you." The lyrics seem like his own late-night dialogue with his inner demons:

> *Why you got that mask on*
> *And who you tryin' to fool?*
> *The only one who matters*
> *Is stuck inside with you*

Gil rarely enjoyed being in the studio for long periods of time and usually made sure to wrap up the recording process as fast as possible. But the *Moving Target* sessions were spread out over the spring and summer of 1982, often delayed due to Gil's failure to show up on time. In addition, he was locked in a battle with Clive Davis and his team at Arista, who kept pushing him to bring in R&B producers and to make his sound more radio-friendly—though this pressure only stiffened Gil's resolve to keep doing things his way. He was struggling and felt besieged—under pressure from the studio, his wife, and his fans, and feeling like a political target in the repressive Reagan years—and the album cover pointedly reflects those feelings. From the perspective of a sharpshooter, the silhouette of a rifle sight captures Gil running down a street. The back cover of the album uses the same rifle sight, but this time Gil defiantly points his index finger at the viewer.

When *Moving Target* was released in September 1982, it landed with a thud. The album sounded anachronistic in a music landscape that had been fully transformed by hip-hop and the dominance of electronic instruments, and it hardly made a dent on the charts. The tour was one of the most extensive ever taken by Gil, with hundreds of concerts in the United States, England, Australia, and Germany. But something was happening to his fan base: though he played to packed houses across the ocean and basked in the praise of his European fans, he could get gigs only in smaller venues back home, and the critics were . . . well, critical. In November, he and the band performed at the Bottom Line in New York. When he made his electrifying debut at the club in 1974, Gil's fiery energy had been applauded by Stevie Wonder and Clive Davis. Much had changed over the last eight years.

This time, the *New York Times* lamented Gil's lackluster energy, noting that the "rigid song forms cramped his style sufficiently to dampen any incendiary passion." Not that he appeared to notice: he was in survival mode and distracted by his problems. He was living day-to-day and seemed to be in his own world, remembers McDonald. "You knew that he wasn't happy in his marriage and was doing too much cocaine. But he never opened up about what was bothering him; he didn't want anyone's help and he hated to be pitied."

The album was tanking and his career was in a slump, but they both got a bump upon the release of Mugge's documentary *Black Wax*, which was released on January 12, 1983. Gil loved the tag line featured on the promotional posters: "The Most Dangerous Musician Alive." The response was enthusiastic, with the *New York Times*'s Janet Maslin lauding Mugge for his adroit direction and reserving most of her praise for Gil's "nonchalant charm and intelligence." She noted that the documentary film format is perfectly suited to encapsulate Gil's work and that the film gives him "a chance to explain his concerns and convictions at length, and he rises to the opportunity."

Little did Maslin, the readers of the *New York Times*, or Gil's fans know that he was battling a serious addiction to cocaine right in front of the camera. Or that his addiction was about to go into free fall. Around this time, Gil started to experiment with freebasing: cooking the cocaine and inhaling the vapors to create a stronger high. The habit represented a dangerous new turn in his cocaine addiction—the effect was more powerful, further isolated him from close friends, and could be hazardous to his health. It has been rumored that he was introduced to this method by Richard Pryor, with whom he had bonded during his appearance on *Saturday Night Live* in 1975. Whenever he was in LA, Gil would party with Pryor, the pair daring each other to snort ever larger amounts of cocaine. At some point in the early 1980s, Pryor apparently showed Gil how to freebase, according to several of Gil's friends. "That's when everything spiraled out of control," says Tony Green. Crossing the line from snorting cocaine to freebasing it means "your life is susceptible to being nothing but chaos and death," says old friend Gary Price. In an incident similar to Richard Pryor's near-fatal accident when he suffered third-degree burns while freebasing cocaine in 1980,

Gil once set his hand on fire while freebasing and had to be hospitalized. The story, providing solid evidence of his addiction, quickly made the rounds among Gil's friends in the tight-knit music world. "He told me about it—it definitely happened, but the story got more and more dramatic every time it was told," recalls Larry McDonald, the band's drummer.

Among the people concerned was Gil's team at Arista, who quietly encouraged him to seek treatment. But he denied having any problem, his standard response to any discussion of his drug use. "I snorted cocaine. Some people shoot dope. Everybody was happy," he once said. Stevie Wonder, Gil's musical guardian angel, was particularly alarmed. He'd always harbored fears that Gil would fall prey to the seductive pull of drugs, as he had seen before with Marvin Gaye and David Ruffin. They were all sensitive songwriters whose politically explosive lyrics moved hearts and minds but who were destroyed by their addictions. At one point in the early 1980s, Wonder offered Gil twenty-five thousand dollars to go to a drug rehab clinic in the Bahamas. Gil turned down the offer, which greatly disappointed Stevie, who kept his distance from Gil after that. "Stevie was hurt," says friend Tony Green. "It was the same thing he went through with Marvin. Stevie expected more out of Gil, expected him not to turn into a drug addict after fighting for a cause and winning that struggle."

His personal demons may have driven his addiction, but Gil also wanted an escape from the pressures of the music industry. The bickering with Arista grew worse in the early 1980s, when the label's acts weren't topping the charts and it was bleeding money. In the fiscal year that ended on June 30, 1982, Arista lost twelve million dollars on sales of fifty-four million. Desperate for cash, Clive Davis agreed to sell a half interest in the company to RCA on March 29, 1983. Though Arista was able to continue operating independently, it was under increasing pressure from RCA shareholders to turn a profit, and Clive tried to squeeze more hits out of its roster of artists.

The increasing corporate pressure to produce profits and sales led to more direct interference in Gil's music—and he pushed back. Davis suggested to Gil possible collaborators, such as one of the Chairmen of the Board, a popular R&B group, and other ways of getting commercial traction. Clive started going over Gil's drafts and offering advice to add another chorus or a bridge here and there. "And he would resist it. He never did it huffily, but he also knew he was resisting," says Clive. "I told him, 'You can go from a few hundred thousand to a million in sales with a radio hit.' He understood it but never really acted on it."

It was a vicious circle: the record labels pushed more popular music, marginalizing independent and original work, and in turn, the audience expected that commercial-friendly sound, losing patience with songs that were different or unique. The change in taste seemed to reflect a larger trend in society: from political engagement to materialistic concerns. "The music of protest and rage has taken a back seat to things and material goods, to basketball players on the court, football players on the field and actors on television," said Abiodun Oyewole of the Last Poets. As radio-friendly records dominated the charts in the 1980s, Gil's music failed to reach black people, says Public Enemy's Chuck D. "Black radio didn't support Gil. The black press moved away from him because they said, 'You know, it's passé.' So Gil makes a profound statement like he did with 'Johannesburg,' and black people don't hear it."

Gil felt out of place at Arista, convinced that the label had a cynical view of artists as expendable. The label's executives and lawyers could smell money "the way farmers can smell rain that's still two days in the distance," wrote Gil in his memoir. And, in one of the few times he mentions his own drug use, he writes that "[e]ven anesthetized by good Colombia weed," he felt uncomfortable. He was a revolutionary artist on a major record label, and people saw the irony in his situation: Henderson used to joke that it was difficult for him to get Gil to be "well-known internationally and promoted by a white man when he was telling a white man to kiss his ass."

The advent of hip-hop only increased the pressure on Gil to adapt his sound to please audiences. In the mid-'80s, as groups such as Run-DMC and Grandmaster Flash started to dominate the charts, Clive began promoting the idea that Gil was the Godfather of Rap, another idea that Gil didn't appreciate, says Henderson. "Gil hated that; it just rubbed him the wrong way, and it seemed to him like just another corporate PR stunt."

That opinion may have been shaped by his experience with the twelve-inch single "Re-Ron," released on January 1, 1984. It was one of the rare instances in which Gil allowed an outside producer to come into the studio. Bill Laswell, a respected bassist and producer known for his work with Brian

Eno and David Byrne, was on the cutting edge of electronic dance music and turned "Re-Ron" into an electro-funk track. The track was most obviously influenced by the beat-heavy sound of hip-hop, with Gil rapping over a minimal synth-driven rhythm.

Gil wasn't happy with the result, privately complaining to friends that the rhythm was too much "noise" that distracted from the lyrics. A classic sarcastic poem in the mold of "H_2O Gate," the song had been written to help defeat Reagan's reelection effort that year. Gil intended it to reach voters, to educate them about the evils of the Reagan administration, from invading Grenada to supporting the repressive regime in El Salvador, concluding that Democratic primary candidates such as Walter "Fritz" Mondale and Jesse Jackson were infinitely preferable. The lyrics were reprinted in progressive publications, from the *Village Voice* to the Socialist Party's *Workers Vanguard*: "We don't need no re-Ron, we've seen all the re-runs before."

The track peaked at No. 89 on the *Billboard* charts, never eclipsing or matching the power of "B Movie." Later in the year, when a frequent collaborator asked him at a party whether he'd ever work with an outside producer again, Gil's reply was quick and to the point: "Never again." Publicly, it was hard to disguise his feelings. He told *Melody Maker* that he'd enjoyed working with Laswell, "but the record turned out more like Bill Laswell than it did me and I'm not prepared for that to happen again."

31.

LONG DARK NIGHT OF THE SOUL

The 1980s were a personal wasteland for Gil and members of the band, "a long, dark night of the soul that matched pace with the deepening collective anxieties of African Americans as they watched the Reagan administration slap down Civil Rights and liberties," wrote Nathan West. During the decade, materialist concerns were being reinforced in the popular culture, as personified by everyone from Madonna to J. R. Ewing on *Dallas*, and people didn't want to hear about revolution. Gil also was bitterly aware of the new black bourgeoisie turning its back on the ghettos, where poor struggling people felt *The Cosby Show* was just as alien to their experience as a Merchant-Ivory production. "We now have a class of black people who have become the new white racists. Because the folks that we were supporting to get into a position to where they could help us, in many instances, have turned their backs on us," Gil said.

He was frustrated by the self-indulgent and materialistic content of many songs that dominated the charts in that era. In the week of September 23, 1982, when *Moving Target* was released, the R&B chart was dominated by the Dazz Band's "Let It Whip" and the Gap Band's "You Dropped a Bomb on Me." Gil simply couldn't understand why more musicians didn't include politically aware lyrics. "Cause we live in a political world and it seems to me very strange that so few artists appear to want to comment on what's happening all around us," he told *Melody Maker* in 1986. "I always maintain that if you've got nothing to say for yourself in your lyrics you should make an instrumental record." It was this environment he blamed for the tepid reaction to "Re-Ron," and he felt increasingly isolated.

Gil also felt beaten down by Arista's focus on profits, which included pressuring the band to include crowd-pleasing tracks at their live shows. "They always got some slick nigger giving me a headache telling me to sing songs from the latest album," he once complained to high school friend Fred Baron. And when Gil refused to work with hip-hop producers suggested by RCA executives, the label didn't cut him off, but it slowly starved him of funds. His defiant attitude didn't win him a reprieve. "Why should I listen to some son of a bitch on West 57th Street tell me what to play for black people?" he told biographer Leslie Goffe. He was not dropped from the label, but from 1983 to 1985 he didn't have the money to properly tour or record. It was the worst possible situation: by not dropping him from the label, Arista made sure that Gil couldn't jump to another one.

Drugs were also taking their toll on him. Clive Davis recalls that the label had had no choice, because it had become increasingly difficult to work with Gil. "His face was getting more hollowed and drawn; there was a real change in his appearance," Davis says. "I saw the freshness of him in his youth and his charisma and his love for his parents and his family. What a brilliant, flashing mind. It was frustrating not to be able to see him break through bigger, and to see him fall prey to an insidious affliction."

Ironically, though, the same industry that was slowly walking away from him was also enabling him. "You never have to slip away to get some drugs if you're in the music industry," says Val-Hackett. "There are always some sycophants who can help supply it, people whose express purpose is to make access to drugs easy." When the Amnesia Express was traveling back from Canada during the "Re-Ron" tour and driving through upstate New York, Gil demanded to be dropped off at funk legend Rick James's upstate property, the Farm. "And Gil disappeared on the Farm while the rest of the band was waiting around for him," says Val-Hackett. "Someone went to get him, and he was getting high with Rick James." They eventually got Gil to leave the Farm and get back on the tour bus, but not before a dangerous friendship was formed.

Gil and James shared an instinct to push their drug use to extremes, supremely nonchalant about the potentially fatal consequences. After initially bonding over music, the pair really connected through their mutual love of freebasing. (When Tony Green, a friend of both men, warned James about his freebasing and crack smoking, the funk legend replied, "What do you mean I'm going too far? There is no such place." Green snapped, "Yes, there is. It's called Forest Lawn Cemetery.") Somehow, in a pattern that would become routine over the next two decades, Gil was able to continue touring and performing amid the depths of his addiction. It was a balancing act that always surprised friends and fans. "He could go from being the most drug-addled brain to being the most brilliant brain," says Green. "All he had to do was set his ass on a stool."

Amid the mayhem of his personal life and his relentless tour schedule, Gil got an interesting invitation from filmmaker Robert Mugge. A year after the release of *Black Wax*, Mugge was invited to direct the concert film for the long-running annual Reggae Sunsplash festival in Montego Bay, Jamaica, from June 29 through July 2, 1983. The festival featured top reggae acts such as Musical Youth, Third World, and Rita Marley. Festival impresario Tony Johnson was a big fan of Gil's music and invited him to appear at the show, dangling before him a chance to star in a concert film. Gil was intrigued, but he insisted that Mugge direct the film. Johnson agreed, and soon the director was on a flight to Jamaica. Charmed by Gil's wit and stage presence during the making of *Black Wax*, Mugge was determined to make Gil the star of the film, *Cool Runnings: The Reggae Movie*, eagerly anticipating his reunion with him.

For Gil and Denis, it was a bit of a family reunion and a chance to get in touch with their Jamaican roots, as they brought along their uncle Roy Heron and they hung out with their uncle Cecil, who lived on the island. They didn't even think about inviting their father, assuming that he wasn't interested. Though Gillie kept in touch with Gil after their awkward family reunion and occasionally came to his son's shows in Detroit, it was a strained relationship. When Gil and Brenda stopped by the house in Detroit after a concert in 1979, Gillie wouldn't even come downstairs to greet them. Though Gil felt that he was a disappointment to his father, Denis and Gayle insist that the old man was proud of him for making a living as a wordsmith, that Gil was well-read and well-versed. Not that he was crazy about his music—Gillie preferred jazz vocalists like Arthur Prysock.

At Reggae Sunsplash, Gil's onstage performances with the band were captivating, especially a fourteen-minute powerful version of "The Bottle," as well as "Shut 'Em Down." Gil mesmerized the audience, many of whom were not familiar with his music. But when it came to the monologues and spoken-word interludes that were so striking in *Black Wax*, a lot had changed in the last year. "Gil was a mess," says Mugge. "He was still friendly and still funny, but he was clearly high all the time. He would slur his words and forget his words . . . he just wasn't himself." Though there were some decent scenes of him talking on the beach to his uncle Roy about their Jamaican heritage, other scenes had to be scrapped.

Working with Gil on this film was much more of a challenge for Mugge. Inspired by scenes in *Black Wax* of Gil riffing during a walk around Washington, Mugge came up with the idea to film him talking and reciting his poetry while standing in front of Jamaica's 180-foot-high waterfall, Ocho Rios, as a way to transition between different concert performances. He prompted Gil by suggesting a few topics, such as Africans coming to the Caribbean on slave ships and the origins of Jamaican music. "But he couldn't get the lines in the right order, and I quickly realized it was not going to happen," says Mugge, referring to the ease with which their collaboration had worked in *Black Wax*. In their personal conversations, in which Gil used to be on top of his game, he was also slipping. "Nobody is going to outdo Gil with the sarcastic remarks, but I was starting to get the better of him. And he was getting frustrated, like somebody in a cutting contest who's not used to losing."

The film premiered at the Rotterdam Film Festival, whose director sent Gil a first-class plane ticket so he could appear. But Gil missed his flight. When *Cool Runnings: The Reggae Movie* was finally released in the States, in 1988, it got mixed reviews from critics, who complained about its poor technical choices. But Gil won acclaim for his captivating show—"one of the film's best performances," said the *New York Times*'s Jon Pareles. Though he couldn't improvise poetry, he could still command a stage and run through his hits.

The audience in Jamaica made Gil and the band feel like stars, but when they returned to the United States, they faced an uncertain future amid Gil's drug problems and Arista's refusal to pay for them to go back in the studio to record. The band started to drift apart, taking other gigs and recording opportunities for over six months, until they hit the road again to promote the international release of "Re-Ron" in January 1984. On the group's European tour that fall, Gil brought his critiques of Reagan to international audiences, many of whom were still coming to terms with the jingoistic American president. And he won acclaim and respect from audiences and critics overseas. Though his political lyrics marginalized him in the United States, they won him new fans in Europe and the rest of the world. "Unlike his peers, he is not afraid to seem a throwback to more outspoken times," wrote critic Len Brown in *NME*. "Although protest songs are no longer in vogue, Scott-Heron remains a committed wave-maker, sweeping out on the beach of public awareness such disturbing matters as drug abuse, poverty, police brutality and international conflict." Again, the lengthy tour represented an escape for Gil, a chance for him to avoid the responsibilities of parenting and marriage and music industry pressures that made him feel trapped. By the mid-1980s, he was living on his own while Brenda raised Gia in Los Angeles. Whenever he came to visit in LA, Gia remembers that her mother "would get me all gussied up, braid my hair and set out my clothes. We were always at our best when we were around Daddy." Brenda tried everything—giving him space, reaching out to him, going on vacations with him—but Gil could not escape his own demons. "Brenda married me. I just showed up," he later told friends. "Gil got tired of that whole life," says friend Tony Green. "It got to the point that he had to go out on the road with the band just to get some rest because all he had to do was play. There were no emotional obligations. Gil wasn't made for married life."

In a pattern that would continue for the next two decades, he became estranged from friends and family. When he was in New York, he occasionally stayed with his mother, Bobbie, who was in an apartment he'd bought for her in Harlem, but he was increasingly embarrassed about his cocaine addiction. She saw the physical change in his features and knew that he was abusing drugs, and confided her worries to close friends. But when she confronted Gil about his problem, he denied it. This dishonesty forever altered their relationship, one that had been built on trust since they first reunited after Lillie's death. Gil couldn't live with his shame, later telling a girlfriend that it broke his heart even to be in Bobbie's presence.

Besides the addiction, he was often just unavailable to help his mother, whose diabetic condition was worsening, because of his touring schedule. On his birthday in 1985, he called her from London, and promised to call again when he landed later that day at Newark Airport. He did, a few times, but all he got was a busy signal. He started to panic, jumped in a cab, and headed to her apartment. When he got to 106th Street, he located a Housing Authority cop and pounded on the door of apartment 19A.

"Who is it?" a voice creaked.

"It's your son! Open the door!"

"My son doesn't live here anymore," she said.

Finally, Bobbie opened the door a bit, revealing a gash on her cheek surrounded by a purple splotch, an injury she'd suffered from falling to the floor. Gil walked her to the kitchen, and they waited for an ambulance to arrive to take her to the hospital. He soon moved her to another apartment in Harlem, kept a closer eye on her, and paid her bills. Though his addiction problems often clouded their relationship, Gil says they bonded because they were independent souls who'd rather fly solo than be stuck in an unhappy relationship. "We were alone because that was preferable to the bullshit we would have to accept to be involved with someone."

Gil also felt musically isolated—he was no longer recording, and was too distracted by drugs and touring to write poems and songs—until another opportunity came along that he couldn't refuse. In the summer of 1985, he was approached about participating in an all-star musical event to raise awareness of South Africa's long-standing apartheid policies. The cast of artists included superstars such as Bruce Springsteen, U2, Keith Richards, Jimmy Cliff, and Run-DMC. Gil was intrigued, and when he found out that one of his musical heroes, Miles Davis, was involved, he "broke records to get to that studio." Gil's spoken-word poetry paired with Davis's searing trumpet dominated "Let Me See Your I.D." (a title borrowed from one of Gil's lyrics on "Johannesburg"), a track that also featured rappers Run-DMC, the Fat Boys, and Melle Mel. Though he was critical of most rap, Gil

Gil Heron and Bobbie Scott, shortly after their marriage in 1948. (*Courtesy of the Scott family*)

Gil "Black Arrow" Heron, playing for the Scottish soccer powerhouse Celtic in 1951. (*Getty Images*)

"Scotty" as a toddler in the early 1950s in Jackson, Tennessee. (*Courtesy of the Scott family*)

Home Paper to 70,000 Readers —and Growing!

★ Final ★
24 Pages

The Jackson Sun

114th. Year, No. 22   Associated Press   JACKSON, TENNESSEE, THURSDAY, JANUARY 25, 1962   AP Wirephoto   Price: FIVE CENTS

JFK Appeals For Support Of Trade Plan

By STERLING GREEN

WASHINGTON (AP) — President Kennedy appealed today for prompt bipartisan endorsement of his five-year plan to dismantle the tariff barriers to a freely trading, trillion-dollar economic partnership with Europe.

"We will move to the world that we believe in peacefully tearing down walls instead of arbitrarily bulking them," the President told Congress.

Tigrett School Enrolls Three Negro Students

By JOHN PARISH

Groups in Plea That Citizens Abide by Ruling

Three Negro students were enrolled this morning in previously all-white Tigrett Junior High School. Jackson's first school desegregation was peaceful and without incident.

The youths, all eighth graders, were accompanied to school by their parents and arrived at 8:15 a.m., some 15 minutes after the start of regular classes.

Burke Testifies On Censoring

ARRIVING—Three Negro students, accompanied by their parents, arrive at Tigrett Junior High this morning for enrollment in the eighth grade. Their requested transfer was approved this week by Jackson's City Commission, acting in its capacity as the city school board. Left to right are: Gillard Glover, 12; Gilbert Heron, 12; his mother, Mrs. Bobby Heron; Madeleine Carol Walker, 13, and her father, Frank Walker.

When Gil (center front) and two classmates integrated the schools in Jackson, Tennessee, on January 25, 1962, it made the front page of the local *Jackson Sun*. (*Jackson Sun*)

Gil in his high-school yearbook
at Fieldston Academy.
(*Fieldston*)

Gil, Nathan Nichols,
and Fred Baron
(bottom), at Fieldston.
(Courtesy of Ira Resnick)

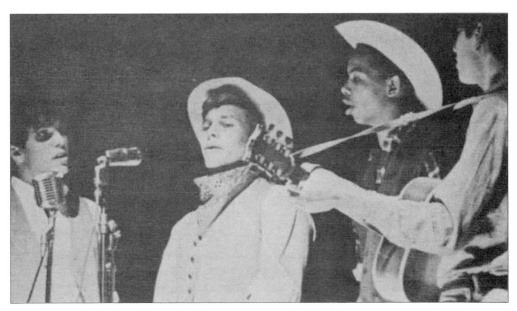

Gil and some classmates at Fieldston performing "Home on the Range" at a class assembly.
(Fieldston)

Gil and Brian hanging out on the lawn at One Logan Circle, Washington, D.C., in 1972. *(Photo courtesy of Gary Price)*

Gil performing in 1974. *(Getty Images)*

Richard Pryor introducing Gil and the Midnight Band before they performed "Johannesburg" on *Saturday Night Live* on December 13, 1975. *(NBC)*

Gil and the Midnight Band performing at the Afro-American (AFRAM) Exposition in Baltimore on August 8, 1976. *(Photo courtesy of the Robert Breck Chapman (RBC) Collection)*

Performing onstage in November 1977. *(Getty Images)*

Gil and wife Brenda Sykes, just weeks after the birth of their daughter, Gia, in 1980. *(Corbis)*

Gil performing with Stevie Wonder on the "Hotter than July" tour in 1980 to help raise support to make Martin Luther King Jr.'s birthday a national holiday. *(BBC)*

Gil, Stevie Wonder, Jesse Jackson, and Gladys Knight at a press conference at Rafu Gallery, in Washington, D.C., on January 15, 1982. *(Afro American Newspapers/Gado/ Getty Images)*

Performing at the Heineken Jazz Festival at Doelen in Rotterdam, the Netherlands, on September 17, 1988. *(Getty Images)*

Gil and Brian reunited to perform in South Africa in 1998. *(Photo courtesy of Monique Delatour)*

Gil and his mother, Bobbie Scott, in her Harlem apartment on his birthday shortly before she died in 1999. *(Photo courtesy of Monique Delatour)*

Gil and longtime girlfriend, Monique Delatour, in 1999. *(Photo courtesy of Monique Delatour)*

Mugshot from his arrest by the New York City Police Department in September 2001. *(NYPD)*

Backstage with rapper Common after performing together at Central Park SummerStage in New York City on June 27, 2010. *(Getty Images)*

GSH mural in downtown New York City, on October 17, 2012. *(Photo courtesy of Marcus Baram)*

liked some of the socially conscious tracks, such as Grandmaster Flash's "The Message," which had been inspired by Gil's work. In the *Sun City* sessions, he bonded with some of the rappers and reunited with Springsteen, whom he had first met at the *No Nukes* concert six years earlier. Getting the respect of his musical peers made him feel less isolated during a low moment in his career.

The song was released at the end of the year, and much like the *No Nukes* tour, it helped Gil garner a whole new audience unfamiliar with his music. But the very reason for the benefit single and album demonstrated how little had changed in South Africa in the ten years since Gil sang "Johannesburg." To him, part of this was because of U.S. apathy and ignorance about apartheid, and global affairs in general, as mentioned in one of the more comedic lines from the song: "The first time I heard there was trouble in the Middle East, I thought they were talking about Pittsburgh." The tribute album demonstrated to Gil the limits of his own activism and polemical lyrics. Even after the Artists United Against Apartheid album made a splash, with videos in heavy rotation on MTV, apartheid was still in full effect. "You know, Botha is a fucking ostrich," Gil told *Melody Maker*, referring to the African country's white prime minister. "He's got his head in the goddamn sand, with his ass sticking up to get kicked."

Aside from the brief glory of taking part in the *Sun City* project, Gil's career had hit a new low. In 1985, after years of frustrating disagreements and ultimatums, his record company finally dropped him, though Gil's pride made it hard for him to acknowledge the situation. In July 1986, during a tour of England and Europe, he must have been joking or misleading reporters when he told them that things "aren't bad between me and Arista" because they hadn't dropped him yet. Armed with a lot of songs, he claimed he was hoping to go back into the studio the next month. But, he warned, he would only record under one condition: if he were given full control of production. "So if you find out I'm no longer in the business, you'll know what happened. It won't be that great a loss—it would be more of a loss if I subjected my material to someone else and let them destroy it." He seemed resigned to a postrecording career—performing, writing books, and going on lecture tours. "I don't exactly feel as though it would buckle my bridge if I had to move on, as I suppose I soon will."

Looking back years later on his rejection by Arista, Gil was either angry or amused. "Where I was coming from irritated some people. I wasn't the standard room-service artist," he told *Los Angeles Times* critic Mike Phillips, acknowledging his own stubborn personality. "But this is what the spirits gave me to work with. They gave me the outrage and the manner, so to make up for it, they gave me a sense of humor."

32.

THE GODFATHER OF RAP

For the first time in almost two decades, Gil's creative life was barren. And his home life was not much better: While Brenda and he were still legally married, they hadn't lived together for years. She thought for years that he would eventually stop using cocaine, "that he would get sick of it or bored with it, that he wouldn't want to be apart from us," she says. "I thought so many things would bring him out of it. And he tried many times to stop, but then he would go back to it."

Without a label, a band, or a family to go home to, he found his days consisted of playing gigs at familiar nightclubs and occasionally touring to fund his drug habit. He shuttled back and forth between friends' apartments in New York City and Washington. Though he occasionally jotted down poems and thoughts in a beat-up notebook, he wasn't writing lyrics or composing music.

In the summer of 1987, Gil made one final effort with Brenda, taking her to Hawaii. He tried to stay away from drugs on the trip. "Toward the end, he started to get edgy and irritable. And I realized that he couldn't stop, that as soon as he came back, he would get some [drugs]." His effort to kick the habit and reunite meant a lot to her, but she recognized the depths of his addiction, and realized that while they still loved each other, she couldn't stay with him. She filed for divorce soon after that trip. "I felt terrible when I finally did it," she said, "but there had come a time when I realized that he wouldn't be able to give up the addiction and I had to move on, to raise my daughter in light and not in darkness." Gia struggled with her feelings. "I was always wondering, 'Why are mom and I not enough? In what way were we deficient that drugs were preferential to us.'"

Brenda and Gia moved out of their apartment and back in with her mom at Elvira's house on Don Miguel Drive. But Brenda still loved Gil for years to come. "I don't think she ever gave up," says friend Gary Price. "Always hoping and wanting. She would still go to his concerts even after she remarried." When the divorce happened in 1987, Gil wasn't even aware of it for a couple of months. Brenda's brother delivered the divorce papers to him during a show at Blues Alley in Washington. "Me and my wife had been separated for about four years," he told *American Visions* magazine, adding that it took him time to realize that Brenda was serious about getting a divorce. "The divorce papers showed up, and I was already divorced. It just shows how disconnected I had been." Years later, Gil blamed himself for the breakup, writing in his notebook that he was incapable of loving. "Love is a difficult thing for me to experience," he wrote, though he doesn't probe any deeper into his own psyche, opting instead for a sociological explanation: "For black men, we have the shortest life expectancy, we work the hardest jobs, live in the most dangerous neighborhoods. And we have a more callous attitude sometimes towards everything because we're just trying to make it."

Without a steady partner in life and love, Gil drifted further into drugs, and paid for his habit through a relentless performing schedule. His shows managed to both test and reward the patience of his fans. Once, he arrived hours late for a show at Toronto's BamBoo nightclub on August 30, 1987. But when they finally took the stage, they moved the crowd. Gil "has become more eloquent, if somewhat less angry," ran a review in the Toronto *Globe and Mail*. "He is no longer young—the beard that frames his long, gaunt face is peppered with grey—but he still performs with an energy and intensity that gives [sic] soul to the polemics of his songs." The reviewer praised Robert Gordon's sharp guitar attacks and Ron Holloway's sax playing for bringing out the "anger that simmers under Gil Scott-Heron's words but never cuts through in his voice."

Around that time, Gil's home was back in New York, near family and old friends. At first he'd stayed with his mother in Harlem, but then re-united with former girlfriend Pat Kelly, who had kept in touch with him over the years and come to his shows in the city. She was still dabbling in journalism and photography, and Gil respected her artistic energy. He moved into her apartment in the Fort Greene neighborhood of Brooklyn, which became his home for several years, and tapped her writing skills to help him with an ongoing project. Since shortly after the *Hotter Than July* tour in 1981, Gil had been crafting in multiple notebooks a new book de-voted to telling the story of Stevie Wonder's campaign to make Martin Lu-ther King Jr.'s birthday a national holiday. Gil asked Pat to read his early draft, then written in the third person and narrated by a character called "The Artist." They would stay up late at night discussing the material while Gil punched out the words during the day on his trusty Brother word pro-cessor. It became an endless project that consumed him for the next two decades, a story with so many false starts and twists and turns that the re-telling of it requires its own book. Gil mentioned the project in so many interviews that for years many friends considered it another of his many unfulfilled promises.

As Gil's output declined and his star dimmed, his influence in the world of hip-hop kept increasing. A new generation of rappers who wanted a tougher sound and harder-edged lyrics, to reflect the reality of life in the ghetto, found inspiration in Gil's music. The first rapper to sample him was Schoolly D, a Philadelphia braggart widely considered to be the first gang-sta rapper, setting the stage for N.W.A. and other groups whose fetishizing of violence and misogyny Gil later condemned. On his second album, *Smoke Some Kill*, in his song "Treacherous," Schoolly D sampled Brian's flute loop in "The Revolution Will Not Be Televised," updating the lyrics for the 1980s, including new cultural references and commentary on the era's materialism:

> *The revolution will not be televised*
> *We cannot have a revolution because there are no revolutionaries,*
>   *brother*
> *We will not be able to get Bill Cosby's black ass off NBC and move his*
>   *black ass back to the ghetto*

We will not be able to convince Kareem that he is America's new nigga
The revolution will not be televised, will not be televised, will not be
     televised.

Carlton Ridenhour, the deejay at Adelphi University who played Gil's music on the air, was full of charisma and blessed with an authoritative baritone. Soon after meeting Bill Stephney and fellow students Hank and Keith Shocklee, he renamed himself Chuck D and they started Public Enemy, one of the most explosive and influential rap groups of all time. The group's politically charged lyrics about racism, blacks in the prison system, and revolution were directly influenced by Gil's songs, and they shaped Chuck D's authoritative delivery. The group's 1988 track "Rebel without a Pause," which includes the line "Impeach the president, pulling out the ray gun / Zap the next one, I could be your Shogun," is a direct homage to "B Movie," says Stephney.

"You can go into Ginsberg and the Beat poets and Dylan, but Gil Scott-Heron is the manifestation of the modern word," said Chuck D. "He and the Last Poets set the stage for everyone else. In what way necessary? Well, if you try to make pancakes, and you ain't got the water or the milk or the eggs, you're trying to do something you can't. In combining music with the word, from the voice on down, you follow the template he laid out. His rapping is rhythmic—some of it's songs, it's punchy—and all those qualities are still used today."

Gil doesn't sound like a rapper—"the lyrics don't rhyme, for starters, and his meter and enunciation bear only a nebulous relationship to the downbeats and backbeats" of his rhythm section, wrote music scholar Jack Hamilton. Yet the very orality of Gil's music (poetry recited in a "spoken" manner rather than in a recitative way) made it important to the emergence of rap. And many of Gil's literary tropes and motifs, "exaggerated language, speech imitation, wit, spontaneity, image making and braggadocio," were later used by most rap artists, says historian Michael Eric Dyson.

Gil clearly influenced Chuck D's politically conscious lyrics, such as those in "Don't Believe the Hype" and "Welcome to the Terrordome," in which the enunciation of the opening couplet ("I've got so much trouble on my mind, Re*fuse* to *lose*") evokes Gil's vocal delivery. When Public Enemy toured Europe for the first time, Chuck D says that audiences had never heard such words by a rapper. "They were like, 'Damn, this is rap? He sounds like Gil Scott-Heron." Chuck D understood that Gil represented an important bridge between the two strongest black movements in the 1960s, between rising black consciousness and challenging music. When he was growing up, he says that Gil "helped me find a voice. He was my single biggest inspiration." For him, Gil "was the link between 'Trane and Malcolm X because his work represented both. He did not bite his tongue about what he said, and he was very eloquent in his poetry and delivery."

In early 1989, militant streetwise rapper KRS-One (born Kris Parker) sampled Gil's "H$_2$O Gate Blues" monologue on his chart-topping track "Why Is That?" Parker's mom used to play "The Revolution Will Not Be Televised" when he was a child growing up in the Flatbush section of Brooklyn in the mid-1970s. He was instantly drawn to Gil's baritone voice before he even understood the lyrics. "There used to be a style of black man in the hood who did not succumb to what the hood offered—he wasn't a Muslim or a Christian, he wasn't in the army, he didn't do sports. He spoke truth to the people," says Parker. "He represented the upright man who was conscious and aware of his times. That was Gil."

"That voice—'You cannot stay at home, brother'—it was that voice that became the first voice of hip-hop," says Parker. "The rhythm of the voice, the way he presented his voice really became Melle Mel's style, Grandmaster Caz's style, even Run-DMC's style."

The burgeoning hip-hop movement in the South Bronx was still primarily spread through hand-selling homemade cassette tapes of live shows, eventually traveling to the other boroughs, New Jersey, and beyond. As a teenager, Parker dreamed about rapping like the MCs he heard on tapes he bought on the street. He left home at sixteen to become a rapper, moving to the heart of hip-hop, the South Bronx. Parker became homeless, lived in a shelter, wrote lyrics in a notebook, and tagged graffiti as KRS-One (Knowledge Reigns Supreme Over Nearly Everyone). By that time, he says he really started listening to Gil's lyrics, "He stands alone and at the top among musicians for his consciousness and always educating and pointing you in the right direction."

Parker linked up with a local deejay, Scott La Rock, to form Boogie

Down Productions, a groundbreaking hip-hop group. They made their name through battle songs aimed at Queens-based rappers and through violence-soaked lyrics on their debut album, *Criminal Minded*. When Scott La Rock was shot and killed while trying to resolve an argument between one of the group's members and a local thug, Parker kept the group alive and focused on a more political message. On the cover of his next album, *By All Means Necessary*, he mimicked the famous photo of civil rights leader Malcolm X brandishing a gun and standing at a window. The lyrics (such as those in "Stop the Violence," which Parker says was directly inspired by Gil's bitter sarcasm and political insight) targeted violence in the black community, government corruption, and police brutality: "They paid missiles, my family's eating gristle / Then they get upset when the press blows the whistle."

33.

REUNITED

The start of 1989 felt like a time of reckoning and new beginnings for Gil. Divorced from Brenda, estranged from friends, apart from his children, rejected by the music industry, yet honored by a younger generation of musicians, he decided it was time to clean up his act. Here he was, almost fifty and all alone, with almost nothing to show for it. Gil needed a family.

In late February, he was doing a Black History Month show at Blues Alley in Washington, DC. In the audience was ex-girlfriend Lurma Rackley, who had come because she heard that he was divorced from Brenda. They hadn't seen each other in years, and they embraced tenderly; they still had feelings for each other. She'd never stopped thinking about him, and Gil had always regretted how their relationship ended. Here was his second chance to make it right. A month after their reunion, Gil was on his way to JFK Airport to fly to Europe, but he told the cab driver to redirect him to a shuttle flight to DC. Soon, he was knocking on Lurma's door at her home in Silver Spring, Maryland.

Soon Gil moved in. When eleven-year-old Rumal came home from a spring break vacation, Gil was living there and the man he'd always known as an old family friend hung out with him for a few days, playing basketball and talking about school. One cold winter afternoon, they sat down with Rumal in the living room and told him that Gil was his real father. Rumal nodded his head and said that was okay.

He was pretty nonchalant about the revelation: "I was never sitting around, longing for something," Rumal later explained, saying that he got plenty of love from his mother. But he understood his mother's desire for the reunion: "She didn't want her child to be disappointed all the time." Gil soon took on the role of a daddy, sometimes stern but always loving. "We connected quickly," said Rumal. "He would just do stuff that only a man would do with his teen son." They bonded over their mutual love of sports, though Rumal was a basketball fan and Gil preferred baseball. And though Gil wasn't a fan of hip-hop, he once took Rumal to a Run-DMC concert at Capital Center. "He was tuning it out, falling asleep, but he was doing it for Rumal," says Lurma. Gil once came to visit Rumal's school, the prestigious Sidwell Friends School. It was Parent-Work Day, and Gil gave a speech to Rumal's seventh-grade class. Rumal slunk into his chair in embarrassment when Gil came in, hair akimbo, followed by the school's principal, and started talking. "But it was actually amazing and inspirational, and all the kids were impressed," says Rumal. "I breathed a huge sigh of relief, and everyone clapped at the end."

At home, Gil used to tell Rumal about his family the Herons, and expressed pride in his father's soccer accomplishments. "He did say he was kind of conservative, and he told me a story about his dad's temper, about how he didn't take any shit on the field. People were intentionally fouling him, and he wouldn't let them get away with it."

The reunited family followed in the footsteps of every good American clan, going to the Hilton Head resort in South Carolina for vacation. Things took on a semblance of normalcy for almost nine months: they ate dinner together, and Gil used to wash the dishes. "What else would I do? I'm not going to have my legs up on the table." He seemed happy, and productive again: he'd continued writing a book about his experiences traveling with Stevie Wonder on the *Hotter Than July* tour. He often discussed the book with Lurma, who helped clear up some of the chronology of events. They were falling back in love, and when he returned home from a European tour, he brought back a beautiful diamond ring for her. Everything seemed good—until the fire.

One morning in December 1989, Lurma was in her office at City Hall, where she worked for Washington's notorious mayor Marion Barry, when she got a call from Gil. "I've got some bad news. We had a little fire in the house." He tried his hardest to be nonchalant and not to alarm her. When she got home that evening, the foyer was dark because Gil had removed the light bulb so she couldn't see the extent of the damage. Soot and ashes were everywhere in the blackened apartment, and some windows had been smashed in when the firefighters broke in that morning.

That morning, while Rumal was at school, Gil said he had been sleeping upstairs in the bedroom when he woke up with a thirst. He headed downstairs to the ground-floor office, and when he opened the door, flames leapt out, singeing his eyebrows. He stumbled back, called 911. The fire department arrived quickly, dousing the house in water. The office, where Gil had worked through the night on his writing, was a mess. The couch was destroyed, many of his papers were singed, and some photographs were lost, but his typewriter was salvageable. Among the items damaged were early drafts of his memoir, which he used to carry around in a green Hefty bag. The family had to spend a few nights in an Extended Stay hotel while the house was repainted and the floors redone.

When the fire marshal investigated the fire, he determined that it wasn't an electrical fire and, without getting into specifics, implied that his team had uncovered something suspicious. "He took pity on me," says Lurma, explaining that the marshal never referred the case to the police. Gil's reaction was consistent: "I just don't know what happened." But it was pretty clear that he was back to his drug habit. When he moved in at the start of the year, Lurma had made him promise not to do drugs or associate with his old drug buddies. "I think I was in denial," she says. "When we reunited, he was trying to get a grip on his addictions. He wasn't walking around with a crack pipe." Soon after they got back together, he explained to her that when he left in 1976, he fell in with a bad crowd of people. He told her that maybe he wasn't good for her now: "When they see us together, they're going to say, 'Why is that pretty lady hanging out with a drug addict?'" Lurma jumped on him: "No, why would they say that? You're not a drug addict. You're somebody who would get a grip on it. Nobody in the world would ever wonder why we're together." But she says now that she didn't realize how serious his addiction was. "I should not have said that," she says. "I was just so damn elated that he was back in my life."

By coincidence, the same struggles Lurma was dealing with at home she was also dealing with at work: cleaning up a mess left by a drug addict. As Mayor Barry's press secretary, she was at the center of the controversial politician's turbulent reign and infamous downfall. Shortly after Barry was captured on national television smoking crack in a hotel room with some prostitutes in January 1990, Lurma was fielding calls from hundreds of pesky reporters and angry constituents. As with Gil, she was compassionate with her boss. She penned an op-ed piece for the *Washington Post* criticizing the condemnation of Barry's drug problem and advocating sympathy for addicts. She said that "booze and cigarettes" are the "cousins" of cocaine, arguing that it was unfair to treat hard drug users more severely than barflies. The next day's paper was full of letters, some of them from drug treatment counselors, who criticized her op-ed as self-serving and naïve. (To this day, Rackley stands by her piece, insisting that society is ill equipped to treat addicts.)

It seems natural to assume that her experience with Gil, and with Mayor Barry, shaped her empathy for drug addicts. But Lurma grew up with an alcoholic father, and she read as much as she could on the illness. But the damage, physical and emotional, was done. It looked more and more likely that Gil might be tempted to do something dangerous or put Lurma and Rumal in a risky situation. He stayed with them for shorter and shorter periods and then, when it became clear that he couldn't get clean, moved back to New York at the end of 1990. "I wanted him to change so that we could live together, but he realized that he couldn't change," Lurma admitted. Whenever they talked about his addiction, Gil's defenses would rise up, his stubbornness would emerge, and he'd resist the pressure. "He would cut off his nose to spite his face if he knew someone was trying to force him to do something," she says. "He'd say, 'Well, *you* drink coffee!'"

34.

DEEP IN EXILE

At the start of the new decade, it had been five years since Gil's last recording and six years since his last album, *Moving Target*. He was deep in the exile that would define the last stage of his life. Lost in addiction, estranged from friends and family, eclipsed by the hip-hop performers he'd inspired, he was a shell of his former self. Physically, his drug use had taken a toll on him: his cheeks sagged, he was missing a few teeth, his once-potent Afro was now scruffy and sparse, and his posture was more stooped and angular than ever. He had always been thin, but now he was gaunt, which made his long neck even more prominent, jutting out from his skeletal frame. And those eyes, which had once glared with intensity, now had a faraway look. The new look lent him an anonymity that deepened his exile. He was often unrecognized, even on the streets of Harlem or in his old neighborhood in Washington, DC.

Gil's absence from the recording studio may have disappointed his fans, but it didn't bother him. He was occasionally requested for projects, sometimes collaborations with rappers, but either he turned them down or he couldn't be located. "I don't know if I will ever put together an album of new material," he said, claiming that he couldn't find a good record label. For a period, he was easier to locate overseas, where his fan base was still strong, than at home. During a tour of England at the start of 1990, Gil was approached by some producers at Castle Records, an independent record label based in London, who wanted to release a new album of his songs. He wasn't interested until he heard how much they were offering him: twenty thousand dollars plus royalties for a twelve-inch single. He jumped at the chance, since he was desperate for cash.

At the time, England was consumed with club culture, spawning new genres such as acid jazz, which added heavy beats to jazz-funk rhythms, and rare groove, which resurrected old hits such as "The Bottle" for younger audiences. For Castle, Gil wanted to record one of his poems, "Space Shuttle," a sarcastic take on the space program that echoed "Whitey on the Moon." For the first time, he didn't have a band or trusted musician friends to accompany him on the track, which mainly was created through studio wizardry. Castle Records brought in keyboardist Paul Waller to add heavy percussion and synthesized bass. Though the music was intended for the dance floor, Gil's lyrics were as incisive as ever. The song "has to do with expending money for weapons of war as opposed to some things that would benefit people," he told the *Los Angeles Times*. Released in February 1990, the single peaked at No. 77 on the UK dance charts, but it never charted in the United States. The single certainly didn't revive his career, though it's not clear if that was his goal. After an appearance by Gil at London's Town and Country Club, critic David Toop snarled, "His regular visits to Britain cannot hide the fact that his music has lost much of its relevance."

That irrelevance was tied to the emergence of socially conscious hip-hop from Public Enemy to Arrested Development, which the critics adored. Though his music had influenced these new artists, it now seemed frozen in the past, and his musical heirs had succeeded him on the world stage. He was frustrated with the constant comparisons of his classic music to hip-hop, even the hip-hop produced by those groups inspired by him, such as Public Enemy. ("It seemed as though they were pretty good," he once told a reporter.) He felt that it wasn't fair to link him to the genre because "the beat in rap seems to be more important than the words. That's not the case in my music."

On February 26, 1990, Gil was scheduled to perform at the Kennel Club in San Francisco. One of the doormen at the gritty club in the city's Mission District was Michael Franti, a six-foot-four dreadlocked gentle giant who had grown up hearing Gil's music; Gil's lyrics had shaped his own progressive politics. Franti made sure that he was working that night so that he could meet Gil. True to his reputation, Gil showed up hours late to the sound check, and high, but he apologized and rehearsed for hours with the band.

Gil could barely make it to the stage for the performance, but he managed to step up and put his heart into his music. "His view of the world was so sad and yet so inspiring," wrote Franti. Franti could tell that Gil was an addict, and he was heartbroken to see his idol in such bad shape. But Gil did inspire him to go into music. "He made me think about the man and musician I wanted to be, and I always left his shows questioning my own beliefs and wanting to go out and change the world." Several months later, Franti started his own hip-hop group, the Disposable Heroes of Hiphoprisy, who, with their politically conscious lyrics, sounded like the most obvious descendants of Gil. The group released several critically acclaimed albums. Though they never topped the charts, they acquired a cult following and often opened for better-known acts, such as U2, the Red Hot Chili Peppers, and Nirvana.

As with his San Francisco show, Gil's performances were becoming increasingly erratic, but his lack of musical vitality was soon to be the least of his concerns. Coming back from London on May 18, 1990, after performing at the World of Music, Arts, and Dance festival, he was arrested at Heathrow Airport with 19 grams of cocaine and was swiftly deported. A few months later, in between shows at Club Lingerie on Sunset Boulevard, he suffered a stroke at the age of forty-two. He remembers standing onstage, enjoying the finale of "The Bottle," introducing band members, and reveling in applause. He walked down some steps at the front of the stage, already planning his next set, when he says he went blind, comparing the experience to being struck by "lightning but without the electrical burns or the flash of light."

Guided to his dressing room, he collapsed into a chair, vaguely listening to people around him referring to him in the third person. The next show was canceled; his manager collected the proceeds and called Brenda, who came rushing from her nearby home to take care of Gil. She packed his bag and escorted him to his room at the Franklin Hotel, where he collapsed facedown on the bed, feeling waves of regret about his life. "I was stunned, feeling extremely naked and exposed," he later wrote in a rare moment of candor about his vulnerability. "Because I was at a loss for words and because the most important questions had not occurred to me."

Gil's sight returned the next morning, and he later attributed the stroke to simple dehydration from wearing a sweat suit onstage. But he was permanently scarred, his right cheek sagging slightly, "like someone prematurely yanking down a venetian blind at an awkward angle," and his speech slurred. Yet he didn't heed this warning, and continued on a downward spiral with his drug use. He also grew even less attentive to his hygiene and dress. When he arrived for a show later that year in Great Neck, Long Island, he was wearing two different sneakers, two different pairs of socks, and a filthy shirt. "I had to buy him a shirt—he'd had that motherfucker on for three days in a row," says Amnesia Express drummer Tony Green. (Green and other members of the band were also using drugs, but they were functioning enough to get themselves dressed. The drummer, who first met Gil in Washington in the early 1970s, also smoked crack and he occasionally joined Gil on excursions to buy rocks in dangerous parts of town. Once, the two of them were robbed of all their money when they tried to buy crack at a spot in Southwest, DC.)

On tour in Europe that year, Gil kept missing gigs and misusing money, infuriating the tour promoter. He avoided the promoter's wrath by changing rooms in hotels at the last minute, making himself hard to find. He became so nonchalant about his drug use that he sometimes took his crack pipe and a propane torch in-flight to get high in the airplane bathroom, only to be occasionally dissuaded by band members who tried to convince him that it was a bad idea.

During another gig at Fat Tuesday's, in New York City, the band arrived and was waiting for the sound check, but Gil never showed up. When show time arrived, still no Gil. The band went over to the apartment of his then-girlfriend, Pat Kelly, but she hadn't seen him. When they returned, they performed one set before the club manager told them to go home. The next day, Tony Duncanson was talking to his cousin, who said that he had seen Gil riding the A train the night before, just sitting there and riding the subway from one end to the other. A few days later, Gil showed up to meet the band at a rehearsal. "It was always something," remembers Tony Green, recalling Gil's generosity of spirit and incredible irresponsibility. "Gil would do some shit and then you would forgive him because he would do something so cool it would cancel the negativity."

When he did show up for gigs on that tour, Gil was rediscovered by music critics, who had lost track of him. Previewing his arrival in San Diego in August to perform at a small nightclub called Elario's, the *Los Angeles Times*'s Dirk Sutro wrote that "it's almost as if Scott-Heron vanished from Earth around 1979," noting the year of the last major magazine interview or profile of the artist. Asked by Sutro about his hiatus from recording, Gil was defensive, stating that his group preferred to do live material and claiming that "the record companies are looking for studio projects."

He was also rediscovered by publishers, which pleased him enormously, since he took writing so seriously. Though he was always writing, occasionally sketching out scenarios for a novel, none of his writing had been published since *The Nigger Factory*, in 1972. His career had veered off in a musical direction since 1970, but many black poets still considered Gil first and foremost a writer. Among them was Haki R. Madhubuti (born Don Luther Lee), a major figure in the Black Arts movement, whom Gil cited in his first poetry collection, *Small Talk at 125th and Lenox*. In 1967, Madhubuti founded Third World Press in a basement in Chicago, turning it into the largest black-owned press in the country, publishing authors such as Gwendolyn Brooks and Sonia Sanchez. The publisher had met Gil in the late 1960s in New York and they had kept in touch through the years. When Madhubuti approached Gil in 1990 about putting together a poetry collection with new and old works ranging from "H_2O Gate Blues" to "On Coming from a Broken Home," he quickly agreed. Published in early 1991, *So Far, So Good* was sold largely at African American bookstores. It revived Gil's reputation as a writer only slightly; the book was ignored by mainstream critics, and occasional book readings were sparsely attended.

Strung out on crack, bouncing from house to house, Gil veered between extremes in the early 1990s. One night, he could enchant an audience with a lopsided grin; on the next night, sulk in the shadows. The second-floor office at Sounds of Brazil in downtown New York became one of his many homes away from home. He would crash on the couch, read the tabloid stories about the latest travails of his favorite hangdog baseball team, the New York Mets, and ask owner Larry Gold for money. He was just doing what he needed to get by and to get high, and was not very hopeful about the future.

His spare existence served as a wake-up call for another drug-addicted musician, Jerry "Groovemaster" Jemmott. A bass guitarist who worked for Gil, Aretha Franklin, and Herbie Mann in the 1970s, Jemmott was at his usual spot one winter day in 1991, a "basehouse" (another name for crack den) in Washington Heights, when someone pointed out a thin, hunched-over man and said, "Hey, you know who that is?"

At first Jemmott didn't recognize Gil, but when he got closer and heard the man speak, he realized who it was. Jemmott was rattled, and left the house in despair. It took a while, but after that encounter with Gil, he cleaned up his act. "Meeting Gil there was a key point in my recovery. He looked bad, and the fact that he was there made me take a long look at my life."

It took a new generation of fans to revive Gil's flagging spirits and resurrect his career—but it did happen. When he performed at Queen's Hall, London, in 1992, graduate student Jamie Byng talked his way backstage to meet him. The long-haired, fast-talking Scotland native handed Gil a Jamaican recording of his 1983 performance at Reggae Sunsplash and asked him to autograph it for him. Gil had never seen that particular album before, and the two hit it off. Later, Gil put Byng on the list for shows, and gradually they became good friends. Byng told Gil about his university thesis (on hip-hop lyrics and the development of the black oral tradition), and they discussed literature. Gil told him about his taste for Chester Himes, Iceberg Slim, Herbert Simmons, and Conan Doyle's Sherlock Holmes stories. Byng had discovered Gil's music as a college student in Edinburgh, when he went through his friend's record collection and first heard "H_2O Gate Blues." "I was just taken aback by the voice, the words, the poetry," he says. "I had been raised on rock, but this was breathtaking. The seasoned voice, the wryness of the delivery, the level of irony and satire in the lyrics—the whole thing just blew me away. Discovering those songs was an epiphanic moment for me."

Gil's endless tour schedule was grueling, and he spent more and more time in Europe at the start of the 1990s. Though he was increasingly drug-ravaged, he was still able to perform and move a crowd. When he did shows in London in May 1993, the *Times* of London's critic noted that his voice had grown rougher and deeper and that his performances verged on the predictable, but that he "compensates by his relaxed and passionate delivery and by the sheer diversity of the choices."

35.

DON'T GIVE UP

Though Gil preferred the energy of performing onstage to the tedium of the studio, by the early 1990s he was itching to record an album. For years, he'd been scribbling lyrics in his notebook and humming new melodies to himself. And though he was still using drugs, he felt that he ultimately had control over his habit and that he could still make new music again—even he was getting tired of recycling his hits at his shows. Most of all, he wanted to get his poems and lyrics out there again, to reach a new audience. He was occasionally approached by record labels that wanted him to collaborate with rappers on albums or to lend his voice to songs, but he always turned them down. He had been spoiled by the independence he enjoyed in the early years at Strata-East and Arista, and he insisted on maintaining full artistic control of the recording process from beginning to end. Most labels weren't comfortable with that arrangement, especially the idea of handing the reins over to a drug addict with a reputation for inflexibility and a problem with deadlines—except for Steven Gottlieb.

A music entrepreneur with a law degree, Long Island native Gottlieb was better known in 1993 for his TV theme song compilations than for the roster of artists he'd signed to his small record label, TVT Records. But he was eager to make a splash in the music world. A longtime fan of Gil's music, Gottlieb kept hearing in the early 1990s that Gil was looking to record, and he finally reached out to him. Gil had a few tracks already written, and

Gottlieb thought they were "amazing. I think he wasn't used to that reaction." Eager to capitalize on Gil's status as the Godfather of Rap, Gottlieb signed Gil, helped him get ownership of his records back from Arista, and partnered him with several prominent producers, including Ali Shaheed Muhammad of the rap group A Tribe Called Quest.

Being back in the studio after a long absence, Gil reached out to his old musical partners for support, making the recording of his new album, *Spirits*, a bit of a family reunion. He brought to New York's Electric Lady Studios most of the members of Amnesia Express who'd been touring the world with him in recent years (Rob Gordon on bass, Ed Brady on guitar, and Larry McDonald on drums). A few members of the last version of the Midnight Band (Tony Duncanson on drums and Ron Holloway on saxophone) also joined in. On a flight from California arrived producer Malcolm Cecil, his white mane a little thinner but his instincts just as sharp as ever. And for the first time in almost fourteen years, Gil reconnected with his old partner, Brian Jackson.

Though they had been estranged for over a decade, Gil asked Brian to sit in with the band for an upcoming gig in New York. Jackson had been hearing about Gil's crack addiction for years, but he was unprepared for how the drug use had transformed his old buddy. "He came up onstage and he looked like my grandfather," Jackson remembers. "I couldn't believe it. Oh my God, the guy is only three years older than me and he didn't have any teeth, his speech was slurred. It kept me up a couple of nights."

It became routine for Gil to disappear for days or weeks at a time, and most of the band became used to these delays, sometimes double-booking their own calendars because they knew that Gil probably wouldn't show up on a given day. Gil didn't have a phone, so Gottlieb had to work through a network of friends, including Larry McDonald, to track him down. "There were times when I thought that the whole thing would just fall apart," remembers Gottlieb. "Gil was just too erratic." Sometimes, he would sleep in TVT's office, and once set off a burglar alarm in a conference room.

Gil did manage to finish *Spirits*, though, and his old friend Gary Price was brought in to direct the video for "Don't Give Up," the second single. Price had kept in touch with Gil and was familiar with his idiosyncrasies, but the video shoot still tested his patience. Price had planned to shoot Gil on the streets of DC, but Gil never showed up. So he was forced to shoot the band and the street scenes without Gil, and to go back to New York City, where Gil was, and film him against a blue screen and then insert him into the scenes. Price had known about Gil's drug problems as well, but his bad state shocked the filmmaker nonetheless: Price had to go buy clothes for him because Gil's shirts were filthy, and Gil's teeth were so bad that one of the few things he could still eat was ice cream. Still Gil was in denial, brushing off his drug problem whenever Price pressed him about it.

Yet, in song Gil revealed much more than he let on: it is in the lyrics to "Don't Give Up" in which Gil admits his worst flaws, his tendency to isolate himself emotionally from people, his penchant for insulting friends and his life "inside a drug-infested cell." He admits that his self-imposed isolation kept him from getting the help he needed. It was a state in which "those who told didn't know and those who knew didn't tell / And I could continue to feel sorry for myself."

The experience was surreal for Price: observing his old friend confess his deepest regrets in song rather than turning to others. After filming a scene in which Gil recites the lyrics for the video, he and Price returned to Gil's hotel room, the floor of which was covered in crack vials. "This is not mine," Gil told Price with a straight face.

The album was headlined by a less personal song, "Message to the Messengers." It is Gil's direct plea to the hip-hop world, asking rappers to think before they speak. In it, he directly criticizes the misogyny and fetishized violence of gangsta rap with a head-on rebuke: "Four-letter words or four-syllable words won't make you a poet / It will only magnify how shallow you are and let everybody know it," and ". . . tell all them gun-totin young brothas / That the 'man' is glad to see us out there killing one another! / We raised too much hell, when they was shooting us down."

Later that year, he explained his rationale for the song by citing his role as a father: "I just wanted to be sure that they understood where I was coming from. Cause I don't write no poems my mother and my daughter can't listen to . . . We're not for calling ladies a bunch of bitches, or for calling them a bunch of hos. We'll call them ladies and treat them that way."

He was especially critical of the hip-hop that focused on bling and Courvoisier and fancy cars. Calling it "flash and dash," he condemned the rank materialism of many hip-hoppers. "We ain't trying to spend it. We're trying to share it . . . if you get a break and hit the numbers, then stand on out there and help everyone else out." As an elder statesman, Gil was telling the hip-hop world not to forget the community they came from and not to exploit its tragedies. Rather, he exhorted rappers "to keep it real but not to celebrate the mess," says black music scholar Craig Werner. Gil held his own poetic lyrics apart from the simplistic rhymes that pervaded hip-hop. As critic Mike Phillips noted, Gil's lyrics were the direct opposite of rap's lyrics. "His lyrics clutch at ideas, the imagery flowing out of a more traditional poetic diction. Rap is street language—a narrative of concrete events and attitudes and its imagery uses violent and obscene expletives to create grotesque and shocking descriptions."

One of his criticisms of hip-hop was that most rappers did not seem aware of their history, knowledge that would have helped inform their lyrics. "And without that knowledge, there's a kind of emptiness: you're just a parasite if you're just hanging out and not contributing." Some critics have found his ambivalence about hip-hop difficult to understand, viewing it as either excessive modesty over being called the godfather of the genre or envy at its success in light of his own career struggles. But it may just have to do with a middle-aged man's musical taste: how many fifty-year-olds who were raised on R&B and doo-wop are hip-hop fans?

"It seems to me the equivalent of Chubby Checker and Little Richard records I used to dance to when I was young," he once said. "It's music for young people and when I was young, I didn't expect my favorite records to say very much either." In his house, Gil refused to listen to rap. "It's hard for them tunes to get in my house, so I'm not really that hip to them," he told *Ebony* magazine. "Like I know the easiest way to get rid of that shit is to turn it off. That works every time: the on and off button on your box."

Released in April 1994, *Spirits* pleased critics: Mike Boehm, who called it "a strong comeback, notable for the warm open-hearted stance he maintains while struggling with inner torments." But it was a bumpy revival. TVT released two compilations and rereleased most of Gil's albums, but sales of the reissues were weak. Though the album won critical acclaim, it was another commercial disappointment, though this didn't seem to bother Gil. "He never wanted to be popular," says Gottlieb. "You could tell that he knew he could do it. He knew what it would take to hit it big, and he just didn't want that."

Gil might have made it through the recording process, but he hardly survived the tour. It had been almost a decade since his last album, with its round of promotional appearances and breakneck schedule of shows, and he was a changed man. He was much weaker, more irresponsible, and even more erratic. Once, he crashed the tour van while doing an errand and then lived out of it on the side of the road for a few days. When Gottlieb arranged to get Gil to perform live on the *Arsenio Hall Show* on May 18, 1994, he put together an entourage of five people to stay with Gil on the trip to Los Angeles and not let him out of their sights, to guarantee that he would actually show up. It was a nerve-wracking few days, but Gil made it, performing "Don't Give Up" to an audience of millions. At some shows in London that spring, he slurred his words and seemed catatonic, shocking even longtime fans used to his recent travails. Questioned about his health and his drug use, Gil was as evasive and deceptive as ever. He blamed his slurred speech on not taking the right medicine for his diabetic condition. As for the drugs, he calmly replied, "Now I say that the only problem I have with drugs is that I can't afford them."

While Gil was mired in his addiction, other members of the band cleaned up their acts. The wife of drummer Tony Green, who used to score crack cocaine with Gil, gave Tony an ultimatum in 1994: "You're either going to leave that or leave me"; he went into rehab. "Part of the reason I did that was to show [Gil] that he could whip it," says Green. But it didn't help, and in some ways it only reinforced Gil's isolation and stubborn determination to defy everyone.

Occasionally, band members would confront him about his drug use, but it never ended well. "Sometimes he didn't want me to talk to him about his inner demons," saxophonist Ron Holloway told journalist Patrice Gaines. "As a friend I thought I had to tell him the truth. He didn't always want to hear the truth. He wanted those people who told him what he wanted to hear."

Holloway, who was overweight around that time, remembers betting Gil that he could lose thirty to fifty pounds before Gil stopped abusing drugs. "I did. I kept my word. I lost a great deal of weight when we went on

tour in England. He didn't keep his end of the deal." Though he loved playing with Gil, Holloway got tired of chasing him down to get paid for gigs,
a perennial problem in the 1990s, and quit the band.

Producer Malcolm Cecil has asserted that Gil's use of hard drugs such
as crack cocaine was an experiment that got out of hand. He says that Gil
took the approach of Method actors: how can he write about situations such
as drug addiction unless he's experienced them himself? But it took Cecil
some time to come to that realization—when Gil made that claim one time
in 1994, Malcolm challenged him: "You talk about homeless people, but
you, as far as I know, have never actually been homeless?"

The next night, Gil called Malcolm and asked him to come meet him in
Greenwich Village. When the producer made it down to the corner of Sixth
Avenue and Fourth Street, he waited for almost an hour, expecting Gil to
pull up in a cab. Out of curiosity, he went down to the subway station to
take a look. There, slumped on the floor near the turnstiles, was a dishev-
eled homeless guy, who appeared to be asleep in front of a hat holding some
quarters and sitting in what seemed to be a pool of his own urine. Just as
Malcolm turned to leave, the man opened one eye and quipped, "Took your
time, didn't you?" Gil later explained to him, "Well, I figured I'd find out
what it was like to be a homeless person." Later that night, Malcolm and
Gil went to the recording studio and laid down the vocals about the junkie
for "The Other Side," the reworking of "Home Is Where the Hatred Is"
that appears on the *Spirits* album.

The clear signs of addiction shocked poets and writers who had seen
Gil explode on the scene in the late 1960s. "When I heard that Gil had suc-
cumbed to that, it was really a horrible message," said Amiri Baraka. "I
kept thinking that he would kick that. People would tell me that he was
spending so much money on that. I saw him from time to time and it was
clear that he was bombed out—it wasn't even clear that he could even recognize you. He was getting busted regularly, in and out of prison, it was a
relentless thing." Baraka remembered going with his wife to see Gil perform
at the Blue Note in the last decade of his life. "He didn't look as well. I had
heard that he got busted again and I thought, 'He's still doing that?' I
thought he would have cleaned up."

When Gil returned to England in July, his shows were met with mixed

results. Performing in Clapham, he ran through his older hits and performed only one song, "Work for Peace," off the new album. But the
Guardian wrote that he sang requests "with an integrity so soulful it was
mesmerizing" and that though he was a little frayed around the edges, his
music was imbued with a "subtle, inward-looking strength." Other critics
weren't so kind: Two weeks later, critic David Toop noted that Gil's live reputation "had plummeted from inspiring to depressing" and he expressed
concern that Gil would become "another rock casualty before too long." But
he praised Gil's "nakedly honest" performance, stressing his self-examination
and redemption.

Soon after releasing *Spirits*, Gil did a series of shows to raise awareness
of the plight of Gary Graham, who was on death row in Texas. In 1981,
Graham, a seventeen-year-old African American, was charged with robbing
and shooting to death Bobby Lambert outside a supermarket in Houston.
Graham insisted he was innocent, and the case was flawed from the start,
with faulty eyewitness testimony and changing accounts of what happened.

To Gil, it wasn't about convicting an innocent man—Gil was not totally
convinced that Graham was innocent—he was demanding a new trial because of all the problems that dogged the case. "I don't believe there is any
justice in the Gary Graham trial," he told Houston civil rights activist and
journalist Larvester Gaither. "You know there are a lot of different ways to
trick up evidence, to rig circumstances to put brothers in a jam. We're not saying this is what happened, we're saying that we're aware of those possibilities.
We see them happening all over the country." Gil used the tour to raise
awareness about the many African Americans on death row, such as Graham.
Despite those efforts, Graham languished on death row for years and was
executed by lethal injection in June 2000.

Though he raised plenty of money for Graham's legal defense fund and
other causes, Gil was having his own financial difficulties. Despite the
modest success of *Spirits*, his money troubles continued, as did his drug addiction. To make some fast cash, he sold the rights of his most famous and
incendiary track to Nike to use in a commercial. In 1994 the sneaker giant
hired Spike Lee to create an ad featuring NBA stars playing basketball, to
the tune of Gil's signature song, "The Revolution Will Not Be Televised."
Over the instrumental, rapper KRS-One transformed the lyrics into an ode

to basketball, name-dropping players Jason Kidd and Kevin Garnett and ending on the line "The revolution is about basketball and basketball is the truth." The commercial was widely criticized by music purists, who claimed that Spike Lee and the rapper had flipped the polemic on its head, transforming it from an anticapitalist protest song warning of the dangers of consumerism into an endorsement of an exploitative company trying to sell overpriced sneakers to underpaid black consumers. The irony was thick for an artist who had always denounced consumerism. Fifteen years before the Nike ad, Gil sang in "Madison Avenue":

> *Make it all commercial*
> *there ain't nothin' folks won't buy*
> *New fuel to fire up the monsters of Free Enterprise*
> *Gizmos and gadgets, batteries to make them run*
> *Just give your check up at the first of every month*

Gil's persistent money problems drove him back out on the road, where he could pocket cash from concert promoters and club owners. Life on tour had changed for him since the days when he and the band partied with groupies—now he performed, signed some autographs, maybe scored some drugs, and went to bed. But on a trip to Australia at the start of 1995, he also fell in love. Monique Delatour, a thirty-one-year-old artist and former juvenile delinquent in New Zealand (who later served time in jail for gang activity and robbery in the 1980s before cleaning up her act), was a huge fan of Gil's music; she even had designed some textiles inspired by his lyrics. When she heard that Gil was coming to town in February 1995, she decided to take some of her designs to give to him. Delatour, a striking brunette with fierce, intelligent eyes, talked her way backstage and handed her artwork to Gil. He looked it over and was impressed. "We need to talk," he said. "I want you to design my book covers. Come back to the hotel."

It was one in the morning and she brought along her friend, Stephanie. When they got to Gil's hotel room, he went in the bathroom for a long time, emerging in nothing but a towel and casually lighting up a crack pipe in front of them. Delatour was shocked at his audacity. "You're smoking crack!" Gil told her, "No, it's ginseng." She snapped, "I know what crack is, and that's crack. You're an idiot. I was wondering why you looked like shit." Gil took the pipe back into the bathroom, admiring her take-no-shit demeanor.

After a few hours of conversation about music and poetry, he was captivated. He begged Monique to stay with him for the rest of the tour in Australia. Almost more out of curiosity than out of attraction, she agreed, but over those few weeks, she developed a real affection for him. Once, he took her outside the hotel for a walk, bought her ice cream, and they sat under a tree. He started singing, "Been a long time since I've seen the sunshine." The band was in the lobby, staring at the scene in disbelief. Delatour says that members of the band pulled her aside and told her, "You can't leave. We've never seen him like this."

Gil himself eventually left, returning to New York, but he and Delatour kept in touch by phone and letter. The next time he arrived in Australia (in Brisbane on April 11, 1996), to perform at the East Coast Blues and Roots Festival, he did not have as good a time: after arriving on a Malaysian Airlines flight, he was arrested for possessing four grams of cocaine, a bong, and twelve thousand dollars in cash. In court, his lawyer admitted that it was a "stupid act" but claimed that Gil had been weakened by diabetes, scoliosis, and his poor state of health. He was fined four thousand dollars and released.

36.

HANGING ON TO HOPE

Back in the States that summer of 1996, Gil veered between the abandon of addiction and renewed purpose. He dove back into finishing his book on the *Hotter Than July* tour, telling his publisher friend Jamie Byng about the book. In a letter to Byng that year, Gil described his frustration at the writing process, familiar to anyone who's tried to compose a poem or story: "Not as good as I used to be at throwing words at things and having them stick to the sense of it. I think I've been working on this f'n book too long and prose doesn't demand the same syllable-for-syllable metric discipline that song writing and poetry does. What the hell? You pick up a nickel, but you dropped five cents."

On his next visit to New York, Byng came to see him at the Chelsea Hotel, home to many writers and musicians, from Bob Dylan and Janis Joplin to Leonard Cohen and Dylan Thomas, where Gil was living at the time. Arriving downstairs about two hours after their appointed time, Gil was carrying a sheaf of chapters, one of which recounted the night that Stevie Wonder announced onstage that John Lennon had been shot and killed. The chapters were well crafted, says Byng, but Gil was so determined to make the Stevie Wonder tour the focus of the book that initially he wrote the book in the third person, referring to himself only as "The Artist." Byng and Lurma Rackley, as well as other friends, objected, telling him that it would be a lot clearer and more compelling if he used first person and added material about his own life.

Along with the book, Gil was also energized by his love life. In June 1997, two years after their first meeting, Monique moved to New York with her two kids and found an apartment near Gil's in Harlem. When he was evicted, she had him move in with her, always naïvely hoping that she could help him beat crack. Sometimes when he got high, he would break down in tears and tell her, "I wish you had known me before this. This is not me." There were lighter moments, too, signs of the true bond that connected them to each other, when Monique would bathe him in her bathtub and they would watch Gil's favorite classic movies together. But it was a constant struggle to live with Gil: "That's all I ever thought was, as long as he's still alive," she said, "there's still some hope. . . . You just keep hanging on to hope." When she tried to get him into drug treatment programs to overcome addiction, she says he dismissed her efforts, citing failed attempts by celebrity friends: "Muhammad Ali tried, Kareem tried, Spike Lee tried. You think you're going to get anywhere?"

Once in the late 1990s, she says Gil went into rehab at St. Luke's Hospital, a facility that had treated other celebrity addicts such as Liza Minnelli. But he lasted only a few days and was kicked out for smoking crack. Monique claims that she tried to get an intervention going, but Gil's half-brother Denis was the only person who was interested in participating. "Every band member said, 'No, Gil will hate me.' And he did. Anybody who tried." She claims that she started talking to old friends, telling them, "Let's kidnap him off the street and take him down South and put him on a farm somewhere." She even contacted MusiCares, a nonprofit that helps fund treatment for ailing musicians, but they also couldn't provide an intervention without more people to support him. Monique gave up trying after getting some advice from Abdul-Jabbar, who she claims told her, "Gil is not thinking about you right now. You need to get on with your life. I tried to help him a long time ago. And he doesn't want help."

Gil's isolation from longtime friends left him emotionally vulnerable in a way that only drugs could assuage. Monique reached out to old buddies from Lincoln and musical collaborators, many of whom had been burned by Gil over the years, to try to repair those broken relationships. Her hope was that surrounding him with close friends would give him the strength to help overcome his addiction.

The first call she made, in the summer of 1998, was to Brian Jackson. From her apartment in Harlem, she put him on the phone with Gil, who told his old partner about an opportunity to perform in South Africa; he invited Brian to join him. The chance to travel to the postapartheid country had a special meaning for the two of them, who had dreamed about playing there since they first penned "Johannesburg" in 1976. More than twenty years after the release of that song, the country had been transformed and Nelson Mandela was president. When they landed at the airport in Johannesburg, Gil and Brian both kneeled down and kissed the ground.

The crowd at Johannesburg's FNB Stadium was huge. When they played "Johannesburg" in concert that first night, they were expecting a dramatic outpouring from the crowd, naturally. But when they started the chorus, a ritual at every live show for years, no one responded. "We thought to ourselves, this is the pinnacle, the crowning point." It turned out that no one in South Africa knew the song because it had been banned by the apartheid regime. They were hearing it for the first time.

Although the old friends played well together onstage, their offstage relationship continued to be problematic. "It was great when we were onstage," says Brian. "The magic was still there. That part never faded. But he was a completely different cat." Gil's addiction had changed his personality in fundamental ways: the honest and warmhearted soul of the 1970s had turned into a desperate crack addict who would cheat and lie to get high. When they landed in Johannesburg, Gil realized that he had left his crack hidden in a Tylenol bottle in the back pocket of the seat on the plane, prompting him to hire a car to drive through the seediest streets of the city that night trying to score drugs. "He would take half of the deposit for a gig and spend it on drugs, skip the flight to the show, and leave the rest of the band hanging," says Brian. "His attitude was 'Fuck everybody else,' and I realized that he was not very kind to some of the band members. He was telling them one thing and not following through. They did it because they loved him and they loved the music." But when Brian approached Gil, expressing concern about his health, Gil snapped, "Yeah, man, I'm doing better than you."

Fans still showed up despite knowing Gil's predilection for missing gigs. "Half the thrill of turning up to a concert has always been finding out whether the man actually remembered to get on the plane," noted the *Independent* at one show in England later in the fall of 1998. Looking "several centuries older than his 49 years, hair tumbling in grizzled waves from a black leather cap, bones jutting out from a too-big grey suit, cheeks cadaverously gaunt," Gil still was able to delight the crowd. "He is all angles but his voice still slides smooth as sex."

In retrospect, Brian realized that Gil had started to change in the late 1970s, just around the time of their split. "The person I knew I didn't seem to know anymore; drugs could have been the cause of that."

Some of the original members of the Midnight Band feel that Gil was not surrounded by the right people. "We were like family and we had a love for Gil that was unconditional," says Ade, adding that they used to call Gil "el Jefe." "We really embraced and surrounded Gil, and once that group unraveled, that level of concern and protection was not there." He adds, "Gil's demise had a lot to do with the fact that a lot of people who were there in the early years were no longer there." At times, Ade used to talk to fellow band member Bilal Sunni-Ali about doing an intervention of their own: "'We ought to kidnap Gil and take him somewhere and let him get cleaned up.' Bilal was trying; he called me and said, 'If you think we can do this, let's do it. There's a number of us. He's really alone. He's not with people who are family.'"

Central to his new circle of friends was Monique; their rocky relationship almost destroyed both of them. Delatour says that she once gave Gil mouth-to-mouth resuscitation after he stopped breathing, and once came home to find him high and "buck naked with a bunch of two-dollar crack whores." He was prone to paranoid moments. Once, believing that the light bulbs in the apartment were secret cameras watching him, he ripped them all out. Occasionally he would knock holes in the wall, looking for hidden cameras and microphones. Other times, he would turn off the TV, convinced that "they were looking" at him through the television. But it was when he threw a drafting table at Monique during a fight that she kicked him out of the apartment, sued him for personal injury, and obtained a restraining order.

He didn't have many choices, so he moved in with his mother, where he would secretly smoke crack in the spare room, all while his mother got sicker and sicker in her bedroom. Finally, he moved out, drifting from cheap hotel to hotel, smoking and sleeping. During this time, he would rack up a string of arrests, sometimes for trespassing and sometimes for possession.

Meanwhile, Bobbie had essentially gone blind and was deeply aware that her life was ending. In the summer of 1998, Rev. Bill Shillady, the pastor of Park Avenue United Methodist Church, started visiting her at her apartment, where she had a piano in the living room and had lined the walls with pictures of Gil and some of his albums. She confided in Shillady, sharing with him her pain about Gil's addiction. "We would pray for him," he remembers. "She was so proud of him but also so worried." Because she could not rely on Gil, the church was her emergency contact.

On the morning of April 18, 1999, Gil was supposed to take Bobbie for a doctor's appointment. But he never showed up at her apartment, because he had been picked up for possession the day before and spent the night in jail.

So no one was there with Bobbie the next morning to answer the door when Meals on Wheels tried delivering her breakfast. Out of concern, the organization called the church. Rev. Shillady and his secretary grabbed the key and went over to the apartment, but the chain was on the door. While they waited for the police to arrive, Shillady broke the door open to find Bobbie in bed, dead of a heart attack brought on by a diabetic seizure. The only saving grace to the story is that she didn't know that her son had been arrested yet again. Gil was released the next morning, still unaware of his mother's death.

Then the search was on to find Gil, to tell him that his mother had died. McDonald and other friends fanned out across Harlem, checking his usual spots and hotels. McDonald headed for Gil's latest haunt, the Ebony Hotel. When he got to Gil's room, he heard loud music and laughing. McDonald knocked, and the room became silent. No answer. He knocked again, saying, "Hey, man. It's Larry." The music went back on and the laughing started, and Gil answered the door. He smiled his big toothy grin at his longtime friend. McDonald pulled him into the hallway. "Man, I got some bad news. I don't know how else to break it to you. Bobbie is dead."

Gil collapsed into McDonald's arms and then started pacing the hall-way, moaning in shock and horror.

"I thought that he would kill himself," says Monique, who explains that Gil was angry at her in those weeks, blaming her for everything wrong in his life. The night before the funeral, Monique was coming home from a studio where she'd been printing out funeral programs featuring photos of Bobbie. She was walking home along Amsterdam Avenue in Harlem when she bumped into Gil on the corner of 145th Street. "He was in a zombie state, just speechless. He looked bad," she recalls. "I hugged him, and he said, 'Come with me,' and I stayed with him."

The next morning, they went to Bobbie's funeral service at the church in the same clothes; Gil was wearing a raggedy shirt and a pair of jeans—and he was in no shape to say any words. At the viewing, he just sat in the front pew, nodding off and refusing to look at Bobbie's open casket, while Brenda and Lurma sat a few rows behind. Gil was in shock. "We just sat there like two zombies," says Monique. Shillady talked about his friendship with Bobbie, the stories she had told him about coming up from Tennessee, her love of Gil and of music, and how important the church was in her life. "Jesus welcomes her into the kingdom, and she is now fully restored in a new way in God's kingdom." The only person who spoke about Bobbie was one of her friends from the choir.

Later, a stunned Gil returned to his mother's apartment to go through her things, "ugly drops of salt and rage twisting their way down my cheeks." In her small bedroom, he went through her drawers and reflected on his own selfishness, blaming his "lifelong insistence on fucking isolation" on his concern that he would end up hurting those who grew close to him, he wrote in his memoir. In some of his most personal words, he poignantly describes the joy of his youth when he'd get close to a lover, "squeezing shoulder to shoulder, giggling, sharing warmth deliberately." But those days of abandon were over for him—"life has taught me that I have to avoid that kind of close. There was no one I could be close to now."

Frozen with grief, Gil sank into guilt and started imagining different objects in the room that had been a part of Bobbie's life starting to stir and move around the room, blaming him for her death. For months after the funeral, Gil was almost suicidal, taking even more risks, smoking even more crack, and avoiding friends. He was fond of quoting Robert Louis Stevenson to sum up the recent decades: "There is so much good in the worst of us and so much bad in the best of us, that it behooves all of us not to talk about the rest of us."

It was painful for friends who had known Gil in his prime to see him as a full-blown addict. They struggled to understand why someone so intelligent and talented could not fight his addiction or at least have the self-awareness to go into recovery. What had happened? That was the question on everyone's mind. Former girlfriend Sumchai, a doctor for thirty-two years, is certain that Gil was self-medicating for some underlying mood issues brought on by childhood trauma. "He was able to fuel a lot of that into creative expression, and there are some valid links between mood disorders and intelligence and creativity and madness," she says.

Gil himself wrote about that connection, with references to Poe and Freud, in a note that his daughter Gia found in the pocket of one of his old leather jackets. "He made some reference to needing to do [drugs] because of the thin line between genius and madness, thinking about other people who had also gone through that shit," says Gia.

But he also relied on drugs to soothe his anxiety to such an extent that it damaged his physical appearance. Except for the basic skeletal features, he was unrecognizable to some friends. Sumchai wonders if, during their relationship, she missed some clues that he was in trouble: "If you look back at his earliest songs, there is always this theme where he talks about being a junkie. Was that a clue that he may have needed help? He kept telling us. Could all of us have done more?"

In February 2000, after a show in Emeryville, California, Gil hung out with friend and musician Michael Franti. He seemed in good spirits and hopeful about the future, telling Franti that "rap is poetry put to music and the role of the poet in our society is to make difficult things easy to understand." He put his arm around the young rapper and said, "It's on you and your generation now."

The next morning, Monique called Franti to tell him that Gil had missed his flight and could he check on him at his hotel. When he got there, there was no answer at Gil's door; Franti begged the hotel manager to let him in the room. When he barged in, Gil was passed out on the bed next to a pile of cash, drugs, and candy wrappers. Franti took Gil to an IHOP, fed him breakfast and coffee. He teased his mentor, saying that Gil's nickname was "Pills Pot-Heroin," which Gil appreciated with a big laugh. Franti escorted him to the airport for his flight to Toronto, but Gil had lost his ticket. Franti shelled out three thousand dollars for a first-class ticket. The next morning, Franti got a call from Monique. Gil never made his connecting flight in Chicago. He went missing for three months and ended up back in New York, refusing to talk to anyone about where he'd been.

Soon after he returned to Brooklyn, he got into an altercation with former girlfriend Pat Kelly, who wouldn't let him see his daughter, Raquiyah. He was arrested for disorderly conduct and thrown in the back of a squad car. While wearing handcuffs, he tried in vain to hide a little bag of cocaine in between the seats. But his stash was quickly discovered, and he was soon back in jail, serving three days, until he was bailed out. Gil later repeatedly denied that he possessed drugs in that incident, claiming that the police probably planted the drugs, even mimicking their hand gestures for a reporter.

When Gil was released, he was desperate for cash and soon took voice-over work, which paid well. Though he'd been approached for years to use his authoritative baritone in commercials, he'd always rejected such offers. But by 2000, he really needed the money. It was something his 1975 self would have hated to do—lending his voice for such commercial gain—but there was enough discretion that his participation was not *too* obvious to his fans. Gil lent his distinctive voice to Tango soda in countless ads ("You Know You've Been Tango'd"), and he did a voice-over for Goodyear tires in 2000, in an ad that touted the company's focus on global exploration. When confronted on how he squared his environmentalism with advertising for Goodyear, he explained that he was told it was a "green thing" that helps the car use less fuel. And he explained that he would never advertise anything for the military or the National Rifle Association.

By the summer of 2000, Gil's shows had become a high-wire circus act fraught with tension. But somehow he always managed to make it safely across the tightrope. When he performed in Edinburgh at the end of June, his trademark drawl "rendered chunks of his stories inaudible," and he just managed to "stay on the right side of rambling without the correct footwear," wrote David Prater. Though he was nonchalant about his legacy, he was all too aware that he was becoming an anachronism, known to a rapidly dwindling audience. He told the *Rocky Mountain News* with a laugh later that summer, "A lot of our stuff, people remembered the song but didn't remember who did it." He knew that times were passing him by, but he couldn't make the personal changes to revive his career or his life.

37.

"DOING TIME IN PLACES
I DON'T WANT TO BE"

On a rainy Sunday night in November 2000, two undercover New York City Police detectives, William Velasquez and Michael Pardo, were watching the streets of Harlem from an unmarked green Ford Windstar van. While driving down Amsterdam Avenue at 147th Street, just a mile from the corner of 125th and Lenox, they saw an older black man approach a young black man and "do a little handshake thing." The older man put something shiny in his pocket. The officers stopped him to search his pockets.

In Gil's pockets, Velasquez found 1.2 grams of powder cocaine and two crack pipes. After being processed at a northern Manhattan precinct, Gil was ordered to appear in court. He skipped that hearing and spent ten days in the Tombs, the spare jail near the New York City Criminal Court in downtown Manhattan. When he walked out of the courthouse at 100 Centre Street, he smoked a Kool cigarette, a smile stretched across his haggard face. "It's no fun being in jail," he told a reporter. "No fun. There's some people that you believe shouldn't be there, and then there's some people that you believe should *always* be there."

Later, Gil claimed that he'd missed the court appearance due to dental problems, that he lost some caps and his gums got infected, requiring antibiotics, which made him sick.

He later told a reporter that, at the time of his arrest, he was just walking home and that the police officers shouldn't have been on the street "because it was raining like a son of a bitch and it seemed like they shoulda been home, you know? Taking care of whatever it is they do when they go home." And he was dismissive of the rationale for his arrest. "I had a gram of cocaine on me on Amsterdam Avenue," he told NPR. "Everybody who has had a gram of cocaine, raise your hand. They could have arrested everybody on the block that night. They got me."

Gil didn't have money to hire his own lawyer, so he was appointed a public defender. Robert Kitson, a rumpled bear with a big heart who was working at the nonprofit Legal Aid Society, happened to be a big fan of Gil's music. The young lawyer picked up the case by chance from a colleague. "He was a quick wit," Kitson says of Gil. "We discussed legal strategy together." On July 2, 2001, he pleaded guilty to a felony charge of possession of a controlled substance, accepting a plea deal of eighteen to twenty-four months in an inpatient drug rehabilitation program. He continued to deflect responsibility. Gil was due to be sentenced on September 11, 2001. That date was postponed because of the terrorist attacks, but he didn't show up for his later sentencing date and was arrested and sent back to the Tombs. When Kitson went to visit Gil in jail, he found him in bad shape, depressed and complaining about his teeth, a perennial problem over his final two decades. Some fellow inmates knew who he was, but most of the young offenders didn't recognize him from any other fifty-year-old crackhead. "He was not cut out for it," Kitson said of the Tombs. "The food is terrible, the living conditions are horrible. The loss of freedom is complete. It's a soul-killing place."

Kitson fought the case, arguing that the arrest was an instance of racial profiling. Indeed, the police initiative in the part of Manhattan where Gil had been snared was known for low-quality arrests routinely tossed out by prosecutors. In interviews, Gil blamed the justice system, arguing that he should have received community service, and he lashed out at prosecutors. "Motherfuckers so crooked—when they die, they're going to get screwed to the ground."

On the last day of the hearing, Monique called the district attorney's office and faxed a letter to Judge Carol Berkman, begging her to spare him from jail. "If he could be put in a drug program in a place where he *cannot* leave for at least a year or more, this may save his life." She added that Gil spent about two thousand dollars a week on cocaine, had been living in a crack house for a year, and owed twenty thousand dollars for his mother's funeral. "Nobody really sort of demonstrated a real appreciation for how much of a thinker he really was," says Kitson. "Except for Judge Berkman, a very hard-nosed judge, but she was very fair." The judge knew who Gil was and gave him another chance, telling him while he stood there in hand-cuffs in her courtroom, "I'm told that you're an extremely smart individual and you've had a lot to offer the world and I hope you get back to that." She added, "You've had all these opportunities to help yourself and you just don't seem to care."

In return for leaving jail, Gil agreed to enter a residential drug treat-ment program in September. Still, the judge allowed him to leave for a Eu-ropean tour that was already under way, and he was soon performing in Germany and Holland. When he returned to New York, he was typically indifferent about seeking out drug rehabilitation treatment. Soon after his return in 2001, he shared a beer with Fred Baron, his old Fieldston buddy, and joked about the legal system's skewed priorities. "He thought that with all the crime that police had to worry about, they wouldn't bother coming for him," Baron said.

A few nights after his beer with Baron, police broke into Gil's apart-ment at four in the morning, handcuffed him, and dragged him off to jail for not fulfilling his agreement to go into a drug treatment program. Though he was depressed to be locked up, the experience wasn't bad for him. He lifted weights, ate three square meals a day, and "looked more re-laxed and fit than I'd seen him in years," says Jamie Byng. But when he was released, he seemed bitter about the experience. "I've been in America all my life. I'm used to doing time in places I don't want to be. Fuck white people and the way they treat you sometimes. That's how I dealt with it."

In October 2003 he was arrested again for possession, this time at New York's La Guardia Airport, on his way to Chicago. He was shipped off to Riker's Island for a few days. At the time, Monique was writing a story about an AIDS research clinic in Brooklyn run by Dr. Beny Primm, who kept a "Wall of Shame" of photographs of famous people who'd died of drugs. When she mentioned that Gil was imprisoned at Riker's and that she was worried about his health, Primm made a call to a doctor he knew who ran the jail hospital. While he was on the phone, Monique heard him get quiet. Primm came back into the room and asked Monique, "How well do you know Gil?" When she told him that they had been lovers, he told her to sit down. "Gil has been diagnosed with HIV." Though she had not slept with Gil for four years, Monique was shocked; she later tested negative for the virus. Gil, for his part, simmered with rage; when he was asked how he'd contracted the virus, he seemed to implicate Monique, saying that it was an "old girlfriend." Afterward, when she wrote letters or called the counselors at the facility, they told her, "Mr. Heron doesn't want anything to do with you." He was sent to an inpatient drug treatment program, but walked out.

Consistent with his denial of his drug problems, Gil also seemed to dismiss the severity of his health problems, especially the HIV diagnosis. Instead of taking antiretroviral medication, he often self-medicated with painkillers such as Motrin. He shared his concern about his ailments with Rumal, telling him about his scoliosis and other back problems. "He didn't feel like the doctors were doing anything to help him; I think he was probably hurting much of the time." Gil also had Ronald Jones, a doctor friend and old pal from Lincoln University, come over to the apartment to inject him with "vitamins." In 2000, Jones had been arrested by federal agents and charged with taking part in a conspiracy to illegally distribute painkillers such as Dilaudid, avoiding jail by successfully claiming that he was insane. But that fact didn't bother Gil.

On July 5, 2006, Gil was sentenced to two to four years for violating his plea deal by leaving drug treatment. He was soon remanded to Collins Correctional Facility, a New York State jail near the Canadian border. Though a medium-security prison, Collins was a difficult place to serve time. Because he was a well-known performer, Gil was placed in the segregated unit, which included sex offenders, pedophiles, Wall Street fraudsters—and actress Lindsay Lohan's father, Michael Lohan, who remembered Gil and his dental problems. It was a tough place: fellow prisoners used to spice up Lohan's food with broken glass on the chow line. Of the segregated unit where Gil served, Lohan says, "It was not an easy place for an older guy, and they didn't have a medical facility."

Monique says that she grew desperate when Gil was in jail, writing letters to some of his acquaintances from over the years including Oprah Winfrey, Dick Gregory, H. Rap Brown, and even Darryl Strawberry (Gil was a big fan of the former Mets slugger) for assistance in getting Gil help. Oprah's staff wrote back that they were "more focused on positive subject matter." Gregory never wrote back. Brown, who was doing time in federal prison in Colorado, wrote back to tell Monique that correspondence between inmates is illegal and that he was concerned about his letter being intercepted but to tell Gil to stay strong. Strawberry was the only one who wrote to Gil, telling him to keep positive and that he could make it. As for family, Gil dissuaded them from visiting him. Rumal didn't visit him in prison. "I don't think he would have wanted me to go," Gil's son says.

Friends tried to help Gil in whatever way they could. His high school buddy Fred Baron was concerned that the rail-thin Gil would freeze at Collins, so he asked if he could send him some silk pajamas. Prison officials told him that gang colors (red, blue, gold and black, and green) were forbidden. "So that left white, so I sent him these off-white pajamas." While at Collins, Gil kept writing poems and lyrics in his notebook, but he seemed to be dispirited. "He was depressed and sick a lot of the time," says Stanley Bethune, a fellow inmate. "And he was concerned about his kids." Gil took small jobs in prison, such as handing out sports equipment in the prison gym and volunteering in the library. Occasionally, he joined the dozen or so other prisoners who sang in the choir, pacing himself through gospel classics like "Rock of Ages" and "What a Friend We Have in Jesus," songs he had memorized from his days as a young boy in Jackson, Tennessee, when he played them for his grandmother's sewing circle. "He'd close his eyes and just sing, seemed to be lost in his thoughts," says a fellow convict who was doing time for murder. When other inmates asked him what he was doing in prison, Gil maintained his sense of humor, quipping, "Time."

Byng and his future wife, Elizabeth, visited Gil in jail, and when they saw him in his orange jumpsuit, it was a bit of a shock. "He actually looked like he put on some weight," remembers Byng. "His hair was normally longer than it was. He was teaching other inmates to read and writing letters for people. Like everywhere, he tried to change things for the better."

Another prison visitor was Richard Russell, a hip-hop deejay who had become a talented British music producer and later started his own label,

XL Recordings. He had an ear for catchy and innovative electronic music, specializing in the genres that dominated the 2000s, from dubstep to grime. The label found success with artists such as Radiohead, the White Stripes, and Vampire Weekend. And he was a big fan of Gil's music. Russell recorded a diary with impressions of that prison visit, describing what it was like to go through body searches and the endless waiting in holding areas while guards confiscated your possessions. When a guard at Collins read the name of the prisoner whom Russell had come to see, the guard added, "Don't tell me it's *the* Gil Scott-Heron."

Russell introduced himself, told Gil he liked his music, and asked him why he wasn't putting out records. "The contrast of Gil's spirit—intact and inspiring—with the bleakness of his surroundings was inspirational," says Russell. "It's hard to appreciate something as fundamental as freedom when you have it. Gil was peaceful, while surrounded by misery and tension." The two bonded, and agreed to work together when Gil was released from jail.

While he was sitting in a cold cell at Collins, Gil's old classmates at Fieldston were getting ready to celebrate their fortieth reunion. A greater study in contrasts is hard to imagine. Danny Goldberg, Ira Resnick, Fred Baron, and some other pals all wrote letters to the parole board, pleading with them to release Gil. "He wrote me this handwritten note, very emotional, about how he appreciated our efforts and how he learned to write and express himself at Fieldston," Goldberg says of Gil. His only request of his Fieldston buddy: a reference for a good dentist. Gil said that he had broken a cap from a front tooth and he was "reluctant to get it done here." He added that it had been over two years "since I had a thorough physical exam."

The letter helped, and Gil was released in March 2007, the first time he was up for parole. Goldberg invited him to a reunion party, but he didn't show up. He came back to the city and prepared for the next chapter in his life. He worked on his memoir, *The Last Holiday*, talked about a new record, and performed to adoring fans at his old haunt SOB's, on September 13 and 14. He seemed relaxed and openhearted, playing classics such as "Home Is Where the Hatred Is" and "The Bottle" and joking in between songs about his time in prison.

That first show attracted plenty of old friends, including Brian Jackson, who had come to say good-bye to his old friend out of years of frustration at Gil's addictive personality and concern that the end was near. "Sometimes you have to let people go," says Brian. "I went backstage and told him 'I love you and have a nice life' and that was it. He was like, 'Okay, cool.'"

38.

ME AND THE DEVIL

Gil's new freedom didn't last long. On October 10, just a day before a second scheduled performance at SOB's, he was arrested again for possession of cocaine. He was sentenced to probation, and by New Year's Day, he was out of prison. When his friend Malik Nasir went to a commemorative concert at Radio City Music Hall to mark Martin Luther King Jr. Day in January 2008, he met Stevie Wonder, who asked him, "Is Gil out of prison? Well, bring him here now." Nasir phoned Gil, picked him up in Harlem, and brought him to Wonder's dressing room that same night. When Gil walked in, Wonder stood up and said, "Gil Scott-Heron y'all," and the whole room broke into applause. Gil beamed and told the room of admirers that he was working on a new album, his first in over a decade.

It wasn't an empty promise. Soon after getting out of Collins in the spring of 2007, Gil met with XL Recordings' Richard Russell. They discussed ideas for an album, and Gil soon signed a contract to finish his thirteenth album. He didn't have to write too many new songs—most of them he had been holding on to for years, written down in one of his many notebooks.

Completely different from his previous work, the album, titled *I'm New Here*, seats Gil at the beating heart of the new electronic music world, way beyond the Fender Rhodes or Malcolm Cecil's TONTO studio innovations. But the new throbbing sounds and electronic bleeps did not detract from Gil's ability to tell stories. "The words just seem to flow through him," says Russell, calling it one of the easiest albums he's done. That's despite the fact that they were operating on Gil time—he would turn up late or skip some days, not answering his phone. Once he'd recorded his lyrics (over a two-year period), Russell took the tracks back to England, where he added a lot on the back end, bringing in overdubs by filmmaker Chris Cunningham and production work by Blur's Damon Albarn. For an artist who always considered himself a writer first, Gil's work on *I'm New Here* most adheres to that assumption. He wrote some of his frankest lyrics about his regrets, his troubles, and his despair but was not involved in the music, modern tracks with spare and fuzzy beats.

He did add a few covers, providing his own twist to them, including Robert Johnson's "Me and the Devil Blues," Bobby Bland's "I'll Take Care of You," and Bill Callahan's "I'm New Here." In Robert Johnson's classic version, the main character is a violent thug beyond repentance. Gil portrays him differently, "as boastful, lunatic, and malignant—proud to be acknowledged by someone capable of appreciating the trust cast of his soul," wrote Alec Wilkinson. And what had made him a target for the devil? Because he beat his woman, Gil believed: "In my family, back at least four generations, guys don't hit women or children." Gil had found the Robert Johnson track in a blues archive along with another song, "Jackson, Tennessee" by John Lee Hooker, which seemed fitting. But he said the Hooker song was too dark and needed an up-and-down feel to it, so he wrote "New York Is Killing Me." Just taking that title, he kept repeating it to himself, improvising lyrics around it from his memories and feelings. The song reflects Gil's instinct for putting emotions in a song or a poem, rather than expressing them to friends and family.

The recording sessions at New York's Clinton Recording Studios were pretty impromptu. One day, guitarist Pat Sullivan came by and hit it off with Gil. He played acoustic guitar on the title track. Russell and Gil hit it off so well that the producer recorded their conversations in between takes, and many of those were included on the album and an accompanying CD. "It was profound when he spoke to you," Russell says of Gil. "Like he might have been talking to one of the great Greek philosophers, who also liked to get off their heads, no?"

One deeply personal track was based on a poem that Gil had written thirty years earlier, called "On Coming from a Broken Home," on which he says, "Womenfolk raised me and I was full grown before I knew I came from a broken home." He also makes a pointed critique of a racial assumption about the term *broken home*, which tends to be used in reference to poor African American households and not to the wives of "firemen, policemen, construction workers, seamen, railroad men, truckers, pilots who lost their lives."

In addition to Russell, friends in the hip-hop world also supported Gil, lending him money and paying him for appearances during 2008 and 2009. Rapper Mos Def always had a special place in his heart for Gil. For him, Gil embodied "the elder statesman and the man on the corner at the same time," the rapper used to say; he viewed Gil as a mentor and a peer. In July 2008, a time when Gil's bank account was particularly low, Mos Def invited him to join him during a concert at Carnegie Hall, an event that put money in Gil's pocket and introduced him to a whole new audience of hip New Yorkers born after his star had faded from view.

As hip-hop matured and rappers such as Mos Def, Common, and Aesop Rock introduced more conscious poetry into their lyrics, Gil softened his edge and had an easier time acknowledging his role in influencing the genre. "I think we came along at a time where there was a transition going on in terms of poetry and music and we were one of the first groups to combine the two . . . and for that reason I think a lot of people picked up and decided we were the ones who had originated it." He had mixed feelings about sampling, however. His music has been sampled by dozens of hip-hop artists, including Black Star, Dr. Dre, Grand Puba, and MF Doom. His seminal track, "The Revolution Will Not Be Televised," has alone been sampled more than thirty times. "You can see how profound his influence was in the sampling by Common, by Kanye," says Clive Davis. Though Gil decried the lack of originality of some of the hip-hop artists who sampled him, he was also sincerely flattered by the imitations. "You have to be good to be ripped off," he once told NPR. "You have to have done something that was important for people to rip off in order that people recognize it."

The fact that drug addiction consumed the life of the musician who wrote such chart-topping cautionary tales about the danger of substance abuse as "The Bottle" and "Angel Dust" is a paradox noted in most profiles of Gil written over the last three decades. It would be just another music cliché if it weren't so bitterly ironic. He remained deeply conscious of that irony to the end of his days, expressing his inner despair in lyrics and to a few lovers. But to live with himself in public as well as with close friends, he ended up having to give up his reputation as a truth teller. In almost every interview about his drug addiction, his denials and disingenuous explanations became variations on a theme. On the rare occasions that he acknowledged the irony, he claimed that several of the songs cited most often, such as "The Bottle" and "Home Is Where the Hatred Is," weren't true antidrug polemics. That analysis may make Gil's addiction less ironic but it doesn't make it any less poignant. When viewed as cautionary tales expressed with compassion, his songs are even more powerful, heartbreakingly describing the "catastrophic situations from which addiction might arise or the hell of coping with a drug habit," writes Maycock.

After years of observing Gil's decline, friends and family were stumped: how could someone so self-aware and intelligent fall prey to this wicked addiction? Speculation ranged from conspiracy theories that Gil's addiction was a government plot to claims that he had become addicted deliberately in order to learn about drug addiction from the inside, to aid in his song writing. Gil understood all too well how drugs had destroyed the lives of musicians and artists. His early days in the industry were shadowed by the infamous drug-fueled deaths of Jim Morrison, Jimi Hendrix, Janis Joplin, and others. On tour back then, he witnessed musicians overdosing or being hospitalized for their overindulgence. And while he liked to smoke a joint back in the day, he was dismissive of those who abused harder drugs.

Many of his longtime friends say that Gil, like many musicians, was surrounded by people who enabled his addiction. Hangers-on who could make money by plying him with drugs, or whose paychecks depended on their not confronting him about his addiction. He himself hinted at this, telling the *New York Times* in 2001, "The people who have the most access to me, people who I've played music with for 20 years—the fact that they're still around, either they have the I.Q. of a plant or I don't have a problem."

It was difficult for friends and family to see the decline, especially since they were powerless to stop him. "It was a real sad thing for me to see someone I admire musically and politically and who I considered a mentor to go so far off," says Michael Franti. "I think he felt that he had a lot more control over his addiction than he obviously had," says Carl Cornwell. "I remember one night in San Francisco in the mid-nineties, where I stayed in the hotel room with him while he was trying to [quit] cold turkey. He'd say, 'I can stop anytime I want.' As soon as I left town for a gig, he stole the car keys from the drummer and went down and popped." Gil's amazing perseverance in the face of clear health problems and a stubborn crack addiction also made it more difficult for him to get treatment. "I guess we were hoping he would hit bottom, and we could jump in," said his half-brother Denis Heron. "But he's a survivor. He's learned how to hover right above crashing." Denis admits that he lost interest in helping Gil, explaining that he saw nothing to do "short of grabbing him and throwing him in a room and saying, 'One of us isn't walking out until we're both sober.'"

Other artists recognized that the pressures of the music industry and the expectations placed on his shoulders by political activists could lead Gil to seek solace in drugs. "The mantle he had to carry was enormous," says Ed "Duke Bootee" Fletcher. "When I was a minor celebrity, I would get drunk and go to the White Castle, and people would say, 'What are you doing?' I can't imagine how hard it must have been for him."

Others were more supportive of him. Jamie Byng, publisher and friend, was frustrated at how Gil was treated like a criminal for his addiction problems. "He is a victim of our lunatic, hypocritical drug laws that continue to maximize the damages that drugs laws have on society," he wrote in 2001. Gil's old partner, Brian Jackson, though often estranged from Gil over the last few decades, sympathized with his drug problems. "There's a little bit of an addict in all of us," he says. "Like in the last line of 'The Bottle,' where he says, 'Everybody needs something.'"

Gwendolyn Brooks, the award-winning poet, asked by Byng to comment on Gil's oeuvre, wrote a poem in which she highlighted Gil's many personas, from "chance-taker," to "emotion-voyager," to "street-strutter."

At the time and in retrospect, her comments seem like an obituary, and this encapsulates the difficulty faced by fans of his work during the last two decades: because he wasn't active and releasing new work, he was frozen in time, stuck during the era of his peak creative output. Aside from the ongoing tribulations of his drug addiction, there was nothing else to talk about with Gil except the golden years.

In the canon of rock royalty, drug addiction is almost a mark of pride, and the stories of overdoses, near overdoses, and drug-fueled orgies have become clichés. For every ritual casualty, from Jimi Hendrix and Janis Joplin to Kurt Cobain and Amy Winehouse, there are also plenty of rehabbed rockers such as Iggy Pop, Ozzy Osbourne, and Keith Richards. And the jazz world worshipped Charlie Parker and John Coltrane, insisting that their heroin use fueled their creative fervor: "Bird" even inspired dozens of future jazz-playing drug addicts who were convinced that smack was a muse.

But Gil wasn't given that honorable dishonor: he was exiled to the edge and made to suffer the worst fate, obsolescence. Some of this seems due to his unfortunate choice of poison: crack cocaine. Cocaine seems glamorous, heroin scandalous, but crack just seems sad and pitiful. Rock fantasies are built on stories of guitar gods literally using thousand-dollar bills to snort lines of coke off a groupie's ass in the finest hotel suite on the Sunset Strip. But you never read about toothless crackheads holed up in the basement of a building in the South Bronx, or huddling around a garbage can fire to stay warm.

On those rare occasions when he opened up about his addiction, Gil often explained that he used drugs to soothe his chronic scoliosis and back pain, because crack was a more effective painkiller than the pills he was prescribed, which made him feel "like a piece of furniture." Lurma says that Gil suffered from chronic dental problems, scoliosis, high blood pressure, and diabetes, among other ailments. Throughout the 1990s and 2000s, he was taking prescription drugs and self-medicating to soothe some of this pain.

In July 2008 he was living in a bedroom in a friend's apartment on 138th Street in Harlem. It was a busy block, with old men playing dominos on overturned milk crates, a radio blasting hip-hop station Hot 97, and kids chasing one another up the street. In Gil's room, which faced a courtyard, a white cat named Paris walked across the windowsill, Miles Davis's album *Kind of Blue* played on the stereo, and a giant Muhammad Ali poster dominated the wall. Gil smoked Marlboro Reds while punching out his memoir on an old Brother typewriter.

In between *The Last Holiday*, setting up recording sessions for a new album, trying to get the band out on the road again, and dealing with his health issues, Gil wasn't sure he had the stamina to do it all. "It's like a one-legged man in an ass-kicking contest. He may get in a shot or two but . . ." And his perennial fear of death haunted him, waking him up in bed from dark nightmares of despair that often ended in his demise.

That fear was tested on November 27, when his eighty-six-year-old father died of a massive heart attack at a nursing home in Detroit. He had been ailing for years and his obituary appeared in newspapers throughout the United Kingdom, which paid tribute to the passing of the "Black Arrow." Though they had kept in touch over the years and had developed a cordial relationship, Gil couldn't bring himself to go to the funeral. "It was too much for him," remembers Monique. "He thought he was doomed if he went, that death would catch up with him too."

39.

BACK FROM THE DEAD

After almost three years of discussions, itinerant recording sessions, and drug-fueled absences, *I'm New Here* was finally released, on February 8, 2010. The album was critically acclaimed—though Gil's voice had gotten rusty, the integrity of his lyrics was unmistakable to his fans. "Implausible as it seems, Gil Scott-Heron's new album is a total triumph: his voice sounds powerful and booming, the lyrics—which tend to autobiography—are fantastic, while the music is amazing," wrote *Guardian* music critic Alexis Petridis. He concluded that it was "maybe the best, certainly the most improbable, musical lap of honour in recent memory." The *Guardian*'s Jude Rodgers called it one of the next decade's best records.

Other critics took note of Gil's somber tone and simmering rage, attributing it to his time in prison. As usual, Gil dismissed these criticisms, during a monologue at a concert later that spring. "I learned that those things we did on our new CD were written because I was so angry when I got out of jail. Let me tell you something. When you get out of jail, you are not angry. I may not have been too happy when I was in that son of a bitch. But when I got out, I was happy!"

On the album, Gil seems to be trying to make amends for mistakes and to honor those who helped him in life, some former colleagues say. "You had to really know the man to understand what he was trying to do: he was trying to clean up some mess in his life," says former manager Henderson.

"There are references [in the lyrics] to his grandmother and mother. He didn't show his mother the respect when she was alive that he could have. He was living in New York and she was there in Chelsea, and he was not attentive at all."

The poignancy of the nostalgia for his old hometown of Jackson in "On Coming from a Broken Home" is intense, as that sleepy town from the 1950s has long been replaced by a busy area crisscrossed by interstate highways and strip malls. "That Jackson doesn't exist anymore," says Gil's childhood friend Pedro Newburn. "Those were simpler times, and I knew what he was saying, that he wanted a simple life. He wanted something else. It was breaking my heart to hear the song; it was all moving too fast for him."

On the track "Where Did the Night Go?" he seems to refer to the passing of time since his peak years with the Midnight Band:

Long ago, the clock washed midnight away, bringing the dawn,
Oh God, I must be dreaming,
Time to get up again, time to start up again,
Pulling on my socks again
Where did the night go?

In an interview with Gladys Palmera, Gil's sentiments seemed to match the title of the album: "When I finally get out of prison for something that I shouldn't have done, I go back in the studio and I make a statement, I'm a new person. I was an old person but I'm another person now. You have chances to remake yourself. In times of silence and times of quiet and times of real introspection, you have time to change. And in many ways, I believe that I have changed. That if you stand up and you do something, you can become something."

Even after all the ravages of his life in recent years, Gil seemed hopeful and was optimistic about the future. "I feel older/younger, older on the outside but younger because I know more things. I have a daughter who is 12—I see a new world with her. I've seen things that I never believed would happen. Not just Obama but the things that happen in terms of our international connections, understanding among young people who are interested in changing the world. I see it in Africa, I see it in Asia. Those who want to see a new world."

Gil was an extremely sensitive person, acutely observant and aware of others' pain and suffering. But he often was uncomfortable discussing personal topics or disclosing that side of him. Though *I'm New Here* seems like one of his most personal albums, with tracks that detail his despair and abandonment by his parents, Gil shot down an interviewer who asked him if the album was cathartic, a natural question: "Cathartic? No man, I don't have no catharsis and shit like that. Don't expect no motherfuckin' psychoanalysis or personal introspection on wax. We were just talking." Later he added, "I don't put my pain on records."

One of the highlights of the tour was performing at the legendary Blue Note jazz club in downtown New York, where Miles and Dizzy and other greats had played for years. Gil's cousin Carenna Ransom, who often came to Gil's shows, brought along her eighty-four-year-old father, Max. But like many in the family, she was concerned about Gil's propensity for showing up late. Before the show, she pulled him aside and warned him, "Listen, Negro, my father does not have the time to piss off like you. I would strongly suggest that you come onstage at the appointed time and don't fuck around." Gil got the message, coming out onstage at exactly 8:00 p.m., grabbing the microphone, and calling out, "Uncle Max, are you out there?"

Occasionally he could get his act together for a show, but the breakneck pace of an international tour and his refusal to take antiretroviral medicine for his HIV started to take a toll on his health. (On the European tour that spring to promote *I'm New Here*, he suffered from arthritis and sometimes had to be pushed around in a wheelchair by members of the band.) Maybe sensing that his time was limited, he reached out to Brenda and Gia. He and Brenda had kept in touch over the decades, occasionally seeing each other in LA, but Gil had only recently begun to reunite with his daughter. "I don't know if he knew that his time was drawing close or that bridges needed to be fixed and mended, but when I saw him he said all the things that I wanted to hear or needed to hear," she says.

With his return to the spotlight—multiple interviews with international media and the intense tour schedule—Gil was kept busy, sometimes too busy to indulge his addiction. But he couldn't stay clean. In the summer of

2010, Last Poets member Abiodun Oyewole got a phone call from longtime New York radio deejay Gary Byrd telling him, "Brother Gil is smoking crack on One hundred and twelfth street," and urging him to do an intervention. For a few minutes after putting down the phone, Oyewole debated whether going to Gil would have the opposite effect: prompting him to retreat deeper into his addiction. But Oyewole, who was sixty, went to the old Ebony Hotel in Harlem, where half a dozen crackheads stood outside guarding the entrance. When he told them what he was doing there, one of them barked, "What do you want to see Gil for?"

Oyewole talked his way past the addicts and went up to Gil's room, where he knocked on the door. Gil opened it up and came out to meet the Last Poet in the hallway. "He looked emaciated, to the point where his vertebra was [sic] coming out of his chest," remembers Oyewole. "It frightened me so much."

He asked Gil, "What's up with you? I'm a little concerned about you, brother." Gil waved him off, telling Oyewole, "I'm cool, I'm all right," before going back into his room. Oyewole walked back down the hallway, shaking his head in despair. Later that day, he called his friend in the Last Poets, Umar Bin Hassan, who had overcome his own heroin addiction in the 1980s. He told him, "I don't know what can be done. You've been in that world. Maybe you can check him out."

Hassan went to the hotel the next day and spent time with Gil, who had received a royalty check that morning. "Let's go to the bank and cash this check and we'll get some lunch," said Gil. The two walked over to Gil's bank, the Chase at 106th Street and Second Avenue, where his mother used to bank. Then they headed to a store, where Gil picked up lunch: an Entenmann's coconut cake and a six-pack of Coke. "If that's not a crack lunch, I don't know what is," says Oyewole. "Sugar on top of sugar. Then he bought some rocks and went back up in the hotel."

When they got back to his room, Gil lit up an industrial acetylene torch; the flame started shooting up to the ceiling. Hassan shouted, "You're going to burn this place down!" Gil turned down the flame and started smoking the rocks. That was it for his old friend, who left the room and never turned back. When he met Oyewole later that afternoon, Hassan told him, "Dude, I'm not going back there. Gil is gone, man."

Many longtime fans of Gil's music were first exposed to the depths of his addiction by reading a profile of him by writer Alec Wilkinson that ran in the *New Yorker* in August 2010. The piece was shocking in its graphic portrayal of Gil's drug use. The writer spent weeks hanging out with Gil in the spring and summer of 2010, to the point where Gil felt comfortable enough to be himself in front of him: lighting up a torch to smoke crack. The experience haunted Wilkinson, and he went to his editor to talk about whether to include it in the published story. "He felt that he didn't want to describe it but that he *had* to say what he saw," says Monique. She claims that Wilkinson later told Gil, "I told the truth and I wrote about you smoking crack."

Gil was not happy, though he seemed resigned to the fact that Wilkinson was just calling it like he saw it. But he grew upset when he read the lengthy piece upon its publication. "I believe that it almost gave him license to keep smoking crack because it was out in the open," says Monique. "Before that, he could at least pretend that not everyone knew about his problem."

Other friends, who had long avoided confronting Gil about his addiction, felt compelled to take action. His old friend and former cocaine buddy Tony Green sat down with Gil and tried to impart some of the self-knowledge he'd learned in recovery: "that any problems are due to my own arrogance or my own neglect." But Gil didn't listen to him. Green believes that part of Gil's refusal to deal with his addiction was due to his inability to deal with the trauma of his childhood and his abandonment fears. "What he went through—you need therapy for it," Green explains. "He blamed his father, but he became the same motherfucker" by abandoning his own children and being emotionally distant. Gil may not have expressed much contrition for his sins, but he was honest enough to admit that he had a dark side. In "I've Been Me," an interlude on his last album, he embraces his demons as an indispensable part of his personality:

> *I don't know who else I could have been.*
> *I don't know who else I'd want to be.*
> *If I hadn't been as eccentric, as obnoxious, as arrogant, as aggressive, as*
> *   introspective, as selfish as I am—I wouldn't be me.*

40.

HITTING A WALL

Gil was hospitalized in November 2010 (for rheumatoid arthritis), which forced him to cancel a British tour, and again in December. "He didn't want to talk," remembers Carl Cornwell, who called Gil in the hospital after Thanksgiving. "He was like that when he was sick." For the next few weeks, his despair overtook him and he morbidly told friends, "I'm doomed."

Due to his health problems such as rheumatoid arthritis, tours for the spring were canceled. Gil talked to Rumal on his birthday, on April 1, 2011, just before he was admitted to the hospital again. Rumal was struck by how the usual casual tone of their conversation turned serious. "It wasn't a conversation when you're feeling I wish I had said something—things that you always know but you don't always say, like 'I'm here for you.'" Gil told Rumal to "look out for the girls," referring to Chegianna, his daughter by a girlfriend in London, and Gia, and to take responsibility for a lot of things that were not in order.

That day, Gil also talked to Lurma. "He wasn't feeling well for that stretch of time and he talked about how he loved the children," she said. About a month later, the record label executive Richard Russell got a call from Gil that gave him pause. Gil sounded different, philosophical about life. "One of the things he told me was not to become someone different just because you can," he recalls.

Just a few weeks later, on April 30, Gil woke up and couldn't get out of bed. His vision was blurry and his back ached. When he tried to get up, he collapsed. He fell to the floor, smashing his elbow and breaking his glasses. With the help of a friend, he checked himself into St. Luke's–Roosevelt, where doctors did tests and kept him overnight because he was suffering from dehydration and a rapid heartbeat. Due to his weak health, he ended up staying for a few weeks, which frustrated him. "He was raising hell with the nurses, pulling out the IVs," says daughter Gia.

On May 25, 2011, Rumal got a call from a tour manager that Gil's condition had worsened, and he quickly booked a flight to New York. The next day, he called the hospital and a nurse told him, "It's not that big a deal"— but Gil couldn't come to the phone. Two days later, on his lunch break, when Rumal called to follow up and find out what floor his father's room was on, a doctor got on the line and broke the news: "Sorry to tell you this, but he passed." Gil had died that morning of congestive heart failure. Rumal was driving in suburban Atlanta when he got the news, and he almost crashed the car into the side of the road. "It was like hitting a wall, it was so quick."

On that day, the only ones with Gil in the hospital were longtime aide JT and assistant Mimi Jones. When Gia called the hospital that morning to check on Gil's condition, a doctor broke the news to her, telling her that when Gil was admitted, the staff was told that he didn't have any next of kin. Gia was shocked but later realized that it was just like Gil. "Sometimes a man just wants the dignity of dying alone. Maybe he didn't want people to see him in that weak and vulnerable position."

To Gil's friends and former band members, it wasn't clear what had actually happened. Rumors were rampant that he was bitten by a bedbug, that the wound got infected, and because his immune system was already compromised by HIV, he didn't have the strength to survive. Byng suggests that he may have picked up an infection on his European tour that was too overpowering for his vulnerable immune system. Some questioned whether he even had HIV and Gil's claim that he was taking a cocktail of drugs; no such medications were evident when he was on tour. "There were a lot of contradictions," says Cornwell. In the end, even the ultimate survivor couldn't outlast his mounting health problems and the ravages of a thirty-year addiction.

As soon as the news spread via social media on May 25, a flood of musicians, artists, fans, and friends expressed their tributes and condolences. Old fans called each other up both in shock and resignation at a fate that had seemed inevitable for years—that their griot had rejoined the spirits.

Gil's obituary made the front page of the *New York Times* and the *Washington Post* and tributes poured in from around the world. "He was always challenging and exciting. Even at the darkest and most difficult stage of his four-decades-long career, Scott-Heron could reach heights—intellectual and musical—that few artists have even imagined," wrote John Nichols in the *Nation*. The *Socialist Worker* lauded "one of the more brilliant minds and powerful voices for freedom . . . Gil Scott-Heron, too, will live on. His contributions to art and radical politics will not be forgotten, and his legacy will far outlive his too-short life."

"He felt layers of the world that most people toss aside or are smothered by. He took these forces and dived undaunted into their rhythms and found their music and poetry and gave it as a gift to the people," said Walter Rhett, a writer in Charleston, South Carolina, who once gave Gil a ride home when he spotted him at a bus stop in DC. "Gil made music and poetry about what mattered: Joy, love, economic forces, hidden secrets, creation and creative people, struggle at every level, personal to neo-colonial, inner demons and happiness." Soul music deejay Cosmo Baker called Gil "our American hero," noting, "He is the voice of the city, he is the voice of the everyman, the voice of struggle and desperation, he is the voice of my youth, the voice of the tragedy of the game. He was our flawed, fragile Superman (although the brother himself would say there ain't no such thing)."

A flood of other musicians and artists expressed their tributes and condolences. Public Enemy's Chuck D posted a response on Twitter: "RIP GSH . . . and we do what we do and how we do because of you." Eminem stated that he "influenced all of hip-hop." Lupe Fiasco wrote a poem, "The Television Will Not Be Revolutionized," which he posted on his Web site. One of Gil's close friends in the hip-hop world, Common, was heartbroken. "The soul of his music touched my heart and spirit. His voice and his words and his songs were like the revolution being told in the freshest way. He is a true father of hip-hop and he will always be cherished and loved." Michael Franti says that Gil was like the Johnny Cash of rap: "He's like that guy who was always there, speaking on behalf of the voiceless. Like Johnny, he had his own personal demons, drugs took a hold of him but he was also that warm-hearted guy who wanted to connect with you." His old friend Henry Letcher says that Gil was brave to stick his neck out every day and say the things he did because "this country has a way of eating people like that up."

In the New York State legislature, Senator Bill Perkins introduced a resolution to honor Gil's legacy a month after he died: "Armed with a humanistic spirit, imbued with a sense of compassion, Gilbert Scott-Heron leaves behind a legacy which will long endure the passage of time and will remain as a comforting memory to all he served and befriended." In a fiery speech delivered to the South African parliament, lawmaker Phillip Dexter dedicated his words to Gil's memory, "a friend to Africa and a fearless anti-apartheid activist." He riffed on "The Revolution Will Not Be Televised" to condemn mine owners in the country, where recent worker fatalities and injuries had prompted outrage: "If the government of the day has its way . . . we will not hear about mine deaths, silicosis, about profits before worker safety . . . the death of the revolution will not be publicized."

Some fans touched on the humanizing impact of Gil's addiction. Kalamu ya Salaam posted a touching tribute online: "Ultimately, Gil is uplifting not because he is perfect, but rather because he is honest about his flaws, and in being so honest about being so fucked up, he encourages us who are less fucked up than he is to be honest about our own contradictions." Mark Tuggle, who met Gil after his performance at Central Park SummerStage in 1994, says that he's never been the same since. "Also, I understand addiction intimately: clean and serene now over 10 years. My compassion is endless for his talent & trauma. The brother remains a spiritual mentor." And poet Dream Hampton: I grew up poor & w hiphop my gen began to strip shame from poverty. Before us, Gil reminded us that poor ppl are human. . . . Gil sang about health care, police brutality, nuclear proliferation, racism, marriage, hunger and hurt. . . . Gil seemed sensitive to the point of being skinless. Yet he was strong."

The day of the funeral, long-simmering disputes over the true paternity of Gil's children broke into the open. At the wake at the Frank E. Campbell funeral home to view the body, Gia took a few locks of hair from Gil's head and a fingernail while he lay in the coffin, as part of her attempt to prove that Rumal is not really Gil's son. That lock of hair was later ruled inadmissible by a family court judge because Gil was dead when it was removed. Instead, Rumal's DNA was later compared with that of Gil's brother Denis by a lab in August 2011.

Those results show that Rumal was a biological "stranger" to Gil, according to court documents filed by Raquiyah in New York Supreme Court in August 2013 that challenged Rumal's petition to continue as the administrator of the estate. Raquiyah also claims in the filing that Rumal "defrauded" Gil into thinking he was his child later in Gil's life. That petition is still being litigated but Rumal questions the accuracy of what that DNA test can prove about his paternity since the sample came from Gil's half-brother. And he insists that the "overwhelming" evidence that Gil treated him as his son and considered him his son trumps the value of a DNA test.

The estate, which is estimated to be worth about $1 million, has sidelined Gil's siblings, Denis and Gayle, though they were the only family members with whom he regularly communicated, more so than his own children, whom he often kept at a distance. "It hurts to be sidelined like this—he was my brother," says Gayle.

At the funeral home that day, there was a misunderstanding and the minister didn't show up, forcing Denis to conduct the final rites. Some members of the band helped out, Bilal Sunni-Ali playing saxophone and Kim Jordan at the piano, while Denis read a Kahlil Gibran poem and some lines from the book of Revelation, after which friends and family got to give short testimonials. Denis thanked his brother for changing his life: "Without him, I wouldn't even be standing here. I'd probably be working in a factory in Detroit if he didn't come and get me."

The children—Gia, Raquiyah, Rumal, and Chegianna Newton, a teenage daughter whose mother had met Gil while he was on tour in England—agreed to cremate Gil and split up the ashes four ways, with each child taking home a small container. That decision poignantly echoes the lyrics of "Pieces of a Man" when Gil described his grandmother sweeping up "jagged jigsaw pieces / Tossed about the room," not knowing that she was "really sweeping up / Pieces of a man." That arrangement went against Gil's wishes, say some including former girlfriend Monique Delatour. "If they had known Gil, they would have buried him with his grandmother," she says. Gil's headstone sits in Kensico Cemetery in Westchester, alongside his mother and his uncle, William.

In the immediate aftermath of his death, Gil's family split apart, with his heirs fighting for control of his estate and legacy. Gil did not leave a will because he was afraid of tempting death, and that lack of clarity has spawned an endless series of feuds. When Brenda Sykes and her daughter, Gia, tried to organize a funeral ceremony at New York's Riverside Church, Lurma Rackley and Rumal hired a lawyer to try to stop it because they didn't want it to compete for guests with their own memorial service. The event took place, attended by many friends and band members, though family members like Denis and Gayle declined to attend.

At the ceremony in the mammoth cathedral, Sykes recalled how Kareem Abdul-Jabbar introduced her to Gil in 1977. Friends offered their own memories, including Gil's old buddy, Gary Price, who showed a clip from a movie he directed of Gil and the band performing in March 1980 at the Roxy in LA. Tony Green joked about how nobody ever saw Gil eat and people could never understand how he survived without food. Gil's daughter, Gia, a spoken-word poet in LA, read three poems. And hip-hop king Kanye West performed "Lost in the World" and "Who Will Survive in America," which was cowritten by Gil, fittingly sampling from a poem, "Comment #1," on Gil's first album. West quietly confided in Sykes that Gil had shared with him the words he used to propose to her back in 1979, saying that he would borrow some of those phrases for when he meets his future wife. Gil's longtime mentor and guardian angel, Stevie Wonder, was listed as an honorary pallbearer on the program but never showed up to the service.

Though he had been sidelined by the music industry for the last two decades of his life, at the 2012 Grammy Awards, Gil was recognized with a Lifetime Achievement Award and cited for his social commentary and influential role in the development of hip-hop. His award was accepted by all four children, including Raquiyah, who in an oblique reference to her father's most famous song said about that part of the ceremony, which was not included as part of the CBS telecast, "I'm kind of glad it's not televised. He would have probably said something and gotten CBS fined."

Though they were all smiles at the award ceremony, Gil's heirs launched the vicious legal battle over his estate just a few weeks later. On February 23, 2012, Rumal sued Gil's ex-wife, Brenda Sykes, and her elderly mother, Elvira Sykes, and Gil and Brenda's daughter, Gia. In explosive allegations, Rumal claimed that the elder Sykes had fraudulently claimed that Gil was still alive in 2012 and forged his signature on two of his Chase savings accounts to withdraw two hundred thousand dollars. The Sykeses vehemently denied the claims, and the case was dismissed in 2013.

In addition to the legal battle over the estate, there have been skirmishes over an effort to do a tribute tour. Several months after his death, Gil's former girlfriend Pat Kelly contacted members of the Midnight Band, including Ade and Bilal, about getting back together to play in different cities as a tribute to their friend. But the estate has declined to participate, and Rumal is trying to organize his own tribute events.

41.

THE LAST HOLIDAY

For years, Gil had been mailing Byng bits and pieces of his memoir, *The Last Holiday*, written on all types of old typewriters and archaic computers and scattered all over his office and home. "It wasn't even [Microsoft] Word; they were just text files," says Byng. After Gil died, Byng compiled as many as he could find. When he was looking for more chapters on the Stevie Wonder tour, Gil's assistant, Mimi Jones, printed out more material found on Gil's archaic computer and sent it to him. The complete draft ended in 1981, at the end of the tour, with a brief mention of the tour's successful result in 1986, when Martin Luther King Jr. Day was finally made a legal holiday. Since the book was Gil's tribute to Stevie Wonder, he had wanted the star's blessing for it. He was obsessed with trying to get Wonder a braille version of the book. But he never heard back from his old friend over the last few years of his life, despite several efforts to reach him.

The book was published on Martin Luther King Jr. Day in 2012, and most of the reviews were overwhelmingly positive. "Much of this book's beauty derives from its bedrock humility," noted the *New York Times*'s Dwight Garner, who praised it as an "elegiac culmination to his musical and literary career." The *Guardian* called it "a riveting read that is, like its author, unpredictable and eccentric and funny and always compassionate."

42.

SPIRITS

Back in Jackson, sitting under the dogwood trees, you can sometimes hear voices in the howl of the winds. Even in the quiet breeze of the afternoon, whispers ricochet off the branches and up into the sky. Old-timers say that it's the spirits just trying to talk to us. Spirits of the ancestors.

Sitting on the porch of Lillie's home in the 1950s, Gil would hear his grandmother talk about her late husband, Bob, and other family members and friends who had passed away, as if they were still alive. She always used the present tense and would talk about their opinions on current events. Around the corner from the house, Gil would visit his aunt Emmeline, his grandfather's younger sister, whom everybody called Aunt Sissy. He would often run errands for Aunt Sissy, who was tall, with African cheekbones and sad eyes. She would hug him tightly, run her fingers up his spine, and call him her only blood relative. She told Gil that they shared royal African blood. Sissy was on another level from other people, inventing words for imaginary ailments and calling on the spirits.

The spirits followed Gil, up to New York and over to Lincoln University and through Washington, DC, and around the world. For the rest of his life, even in college, he attributed his accomplishments and tribulations to the spirits. "I try to take a minute every day to thank the Spirits for blessing me with my children being healthy and my friends being alright and that keeps me going."

Through to the end of his life, Gil always maintained a positive outlook in interviews, often referring to the spirits. And he seemed genuinely happy that he had survived so long, though bruised and battered, to live another day. "I've always been blessed. Blessings don't stop because you run into obstacles, they just become more profound."

Among those who witnessed the impact of the spirits on young Gil was childhood friend John Odom. He remembers Lillie talking to him and Gil in the backyard of the house on South Street in Jackson about his ancestors and his legacy. Soon after Gil died, Odom penned a thoughtful tribute to him:

> *I've read articles about his successes and failures, about the downward spiraling of his health and his career. I've seen the pictures of a man who looked closer to 92 than he did to 62 and I concluded that there was nothing some childhood friend could do to help an international star.*
>
> *Instead, I've pulled out my GSH 33 rpms and I'm listening, learning, reminiscing, and reflecting.*
>
> *We've all heard so many conflicting words abt life whether wrong or right*
>
> *How you gotta be working hard and it ain't no easy job*
>
> *Tryin' to survive, just staying alive . . .*
>
> *What my life really means is that the songs that I sing*
>
> *Are just pieces of a dream that I've been building . . .*
>
> *Willing*
>
> *I pray rest for his soul*

ACKNOWLEDGMENTS

It all began back in the early 1990s, when I first saw Gil live in concert. After years of listening to his music in college, where I was first exposed to and inspired by "Liberation Song" and "The Bottle," I finally saw him perform at New York City's Sounds of Brazil nightclub at one of his legendary annual gigs on the Sunday before Martin Luther King Day. Gil looked tired as he walked up onstage, but as soon as he sat down in front of his trusty Rhodes keyboard, he charged the room with his rhythms and his energy, later pacing the stage and mesmerizing all of us with his wit and passion. It transformed the music for me—adding layers of depth to songs that already captivated me.

It was a revelation—I had grown up on great folk music and protest anthems by Bob Dylan, Victor Jara, Merle Haggard, and Gordon Bok, and I was a big fan of Public Enemy and the Native Tongues collective of hip-hop artists—but this was something different. Gil's music moved my mind and my feet, its rhythm and blues amplified his lyrics and empowered them in a way that I had never heard before.

At the time, I was a teacher at an elementary school on 129th Street and journalism only seemed like one of many potential career paths. But at that concert and at many others to come, I remember thinking that Gil's story needed to be told, that there were plenty of books out there about Dylan and Woody Guthrie and the pantheon of protest singers, but there was nothing on this amazing talent. And it sounds melodramatic, but I remember thinking, "I'm going to write a book about Gil," and knowing deep down that I would fulfill that promise one day.

Years later, after innumerable shows, I finally met Gil backstage and then interviewed him for a profile in *New York* magazine, still harboring my dream of a biography. In 2009, I started reaching out to some of his band members and friends, just wanting to lay the groundwork for a book. When Gil passed away, I was working at the *Huffington Post* and I asked then books editor Amy Hertz how to undertake such a project and how to attract the interest of a publisher willing to take on an untested book writer. She filled my head with ideas. Then I approached Liza Ghorbani, a good friend and music journalist, who will always have my gratitude for introducing me to my agent, Sarah Lazin, who fought hard to get me a book deal and has guided me through this experience with such care and wisdom.

And thank you to my first editor at St. Martin's Press, Kathy Huck, who stunned me when she offered me a deal based on a three-page proposal, overturning all of my pessimistic assumptions about the publishing world. She did a wonderful job encouraging me and steering me in the right direction when my first draft was just a mess of notes with clumsy transitions. The editors who followed her, Yaniv Soha and Tim Bartlett, as well as editorial assistant Claire Lampen, pushed me past the finish line.

To complete this project, I interviewed almost two hundred of Gil's friends, family members, and fellow musicians over two years and I thank them for giving me their valuable time, answering my annoying questions, and giving me such thoughtful responses. Gil's musical partner, Brian Jackson, was an invaluable participant in the process and I thank him for his insight and honesty. The rest of the band—Eddie "Ade" Knowles, Victor Brown, David Barnes, Carl Cornwell, Tony Duncanson, Larry McDonald, Bilal Sunni Ali, Charlie Saunders, Tony Green, and Jerry Jemmott—were extremely generous with their memories.

I thank Gil's ex-wife, Brenda Sykes, and his daughter, Gia Scott-Heron, for their insights and anecdotes. Gil's family from New York to Detroit and beyond was also extremely helpful, including Denis Heron, Gayle Heron, Melissa Heron, Richard Mitchell, Anona Savage, and Cookie Savage.

I thank former girlfriend Lurma Rackley and her son, Rumal Rackley, for their generosity and memories. I thank Gil's friends from childhood and school—John Odom, Gillard Glover, Portia Hegmon, Pedro Walter Newbern, Howard Ramsby, Albert J. Porter, Danny Goldberg, Fred Baron, Brenda Monroe-Moses, and Ira Resnick, and Ron Welburn. Thank you also to personal and family friends like Jamie Byng, Miss Mimi, Jill Newman, Pat Kelly, Ahimsa Porter Sumchai, Rev. Bill Shilady, Esther Anderson, Gary Price, Ivan C. Brandon, Henry Letcher, Eric Moore, Karen Olden, Marie Gangemi, Leon Collins and Jane Woodside.

Former girlfriend Monique Delatour was extremely generous with her remembrances and insights. Musicians KRS-One, Michael Franti, Chuck D, Talib Kweli, Kool Herc, Wayne Shorter, Abiodun Oyewole, Scorpio, Ed "Duke Bootee" Fletcher, and Johnny Pate were very kind to offer me their thoughts and reflections.

I also thank poets Amiri Baraka and Nikki Giovanni for their observations as well as music critics and writers Alan Light, Bill Stephney, Nat Hentoff, Rodger Kamenetz, David Rigsbee, Aldon Nielsen, Craig Werner, Cornel West, E. Ethelbert Miller, David Nicholson, Larvester Gaither, Bill Adler, Haki Madhubuti, James B. Stewart, Norman Otis Richmond, and Betty Medsger.

Some invaluable resources were Gil's own memoir, *The Last Holiday,* including thousands of pages of unpublished chapters that publisher Jamie Byng shared with me; dozens of Gil's interviews for radio, TV, and print over the last four decades; Leslie G. Goffe's excellent biography, *Gil Scott-Heron: A Father and Son Story;* and several excellent scholarly studies.

I thank Jennie Thomas and Lauren Onkey at the Rock and Roll Hall of Fame, James Stimpert at the Eisenhower Library at Johns Hopkins University, Jack Wood and Evelyn Keele at the Jackson–Madison County Library, Lan Wang at the Lane College Library, Toby Himmell at Fieldston, and Jesse Steinbach, Harry Hantel, and Jenna LaSpina for their research assistance.

I thank my parents, Michael and Heide Baram, who exposed me to so much great music and encouraged my writing instincts as a child.

Most of all, I thank my wife, Liza, who inspires me every day with her creativity, passion, artistic integrity, and honesty and our wonderful son, Roscoe, who brings me joy and makes me cherish every moment of my life.

SELECTED BIBLIOGRAPHY

Abbey, John. "Gil Scott-Heron: Good Evening, Here Is the News." *Blues & Soul*, February 1976.

Abdullah, Luqman Muhammad. "The Sounds of Liberation: Resistance, Cultural Retention, and Progressive Traditions for Social Justice in African American Music" (graduate thesis). Cornell University, May 2009.

Agovino, Michael J. "Living with Music: Michael J. Agovino." *New York Times*, November 19, 2008.

Ajanaku, Mzee. "Newsmaker: Gil Scott-Heron." *Jackson Sun*, June 3, 1979.

Anderson, Stacey. "Rebooting Gil Scott-Heron's Untelevised Revolution." *Village Voice*, February 9, 2010.

"'Angel Dust Is Bad News,' Singer Warns." Associated Press, December 31, 1978.

Anthony, Gwenda. "Still Learning." *Jackson Sun*. February 9, 2004.

"Babe Ruth of Soccer." *Ebony*, July 1947.

Baram, Marcus. "The Weary Blues." *New York*, June 30, 2008.

Baron, Zach. "Remembering a Young Gil Scott-Heron and an Unlikely Family Connection." *The Daily* (News Corporation) January 15, 2012.

Bennett, Jon. "Gil Gets on The 'Trane" *Mojo*, May 2003.

Bolden, Tony. "Kalamu's Blues: Decolonizing the Mind in 'My Story, My

Song.'" *Obsidian III: Literature in the African Diaspora* (Fall 2001/Winter 2002).

Bordowitz, Hank. "Gil Scott-Heron." *American Visions* (June/July 1998).

Boyd, Gail. "Scott-Heron Uses Voice of Conviction." *Jackson Sun*, December 21, 1980.

Boyd, Herb. "Gil, the Man I Knew." *New York Amsterdam News*, June 2, 2011.

"Brian Jackson: Still Breathing." FlyGlobalMusic.com, January 28, 2008.

Brown, Len. "The Passing of a Prophet." *Sabotage Times*, December 27, 2011.

Burroughs, Todd Steven. "Between Baby Boomers and Russell Simmons." *ColorLines: Race, Culture, Action* (Winter 2002–2003).

Chuck D. "First Groove." *Bikini*, August 1998.

Click, Carolyn. "Orangeburg Civil Rights Icon, Educator Dies." *The State*, December 10, 2010.

Cook, Dennis. "Brian Jackson: The Revolution Is Alive." JamBase.com, June 23, 2005.

Detrick, Ben. "Hell of a Life." *XXL*, July–August 2011.

"Drugs Matter" (editorial). *Washington Post*, August 12, 1990.

Ellison, Mary. "Songs of Resistance: Gil Scott-Heron." *Marxism Today*, January 1983.

Eneh, Akunna, Khury Petersen-Smith, and Alan Maass. "The Sunshine of His Accomplishment." SocialistWorker.org, June 2, 2011.

Fitzpatrick, Rob. "Gil Scott-Heron Interview." *Telegraph* (London), February 17, 2010.

Fletcher, Bill Jr. "Saying Good-bye to Gil Scott-Heron." *Pambazuka News*, June 9, 2011.

Fonville, Althea. "Gil Scott-Heron Creates the Collage." *Pittsburgh Courier*, November 23, 1974.

Gaines, Patrice. "Gil Scott-Heron Remembered as Tortured Genius." BlackAmericaWeb.com, May 31, 2011.

Gaither, Larvester. "Giving Back to the Community!" Interview with Gil Scott-Heron." *Gaither Reporter*, February 28, 1996.

Garner, Dwight. "His Story: A Writer of Words and Music." *New York Times*, January 9, 2012.

Geesling, Don. "An American Griot: Gil Scott-Heron." *Brooklyn Rail*, November 4, 2007.

Gensler, Andy. "Gil Scott-Heron: The Revolution Will Not Be Blogged." *The Daily Swarm*, March 10, 2010.

Gibbs, Vernon. "The Fire This Time." *Playboy*, July 1976.

"Gil Scott-Heron: Black Music for a New Day." *Black Panther*, November 15, 1975.

"Gil Scott-Heron Faces Issues." *Los Angeles Sentinel*, August 23, 1984.

"Gil Scott-Heron, His Music Feels the 'Black Experience.'" *Atlanta Daily World*, October 10, 1976.

"Gil Scott-Heron, Midnight on Interface." *Los Angeles Sentinel*, March 12, 1975.

"Gil Scott-Heron: Pieces of a Man." *The Wire*, February 1993.

"Gil Scott-Heron Receives First Omega Writing Award." *Lincolnian*, May 15, 1968.

"Gil Scott-Heron 'Turned It Out' at Morehouse College." *Atlanta Daily World*, April 5, 1979.

Goffe, Leslie Gordon. *Gil Scott-Heron: A Father and Son Story* (Kingston, Jamaica: LMH Publishing, 2012).

Goldberg, Danny. "Gil Scott-Heron in High School." Blog.dannygold berg.com, June 12, 2011.

Gray, Geoffrey. "Gil Scott-Heron's Rap." *Village Voice*, July 17, 2001.

Gray, Geoffrey. "An Interview with Gil Scott-Heron." *Village Voice*, July 17, 2001.

Hamilton, Jack. "Pieces of a Man: The Meaning of Gil Scott-Heron." *Transition*, November 2011.

Harold, Claudrena N. "Deep in the Cane: The Southern Soul of Gil Scott-Heron." *Southern Spaces*, July 12, 2011.

Harrington, Richard. "Black Wax." *Washington Post*, June 14, 1983.

Harrington, Richard. "Scott-Heron Perspective." *Washington Post*, April 1, 1982.

Heron, Gil. *I Shall Wish For You*. Detroit, MI: Aaron Peal Publishing, 1992.

Hutchinson, Earl Ofari. "Gil Scott-Heron Was More Than the 'God-father of Rap.'" *The Grio*, May 29, 2011.

Jenkins, Mark. "Gil Scott-Heron Remembered in Multimedia Tribute at Bohemian Caverns." *Washington Post*, May 31, 2011.

Kahn, Ashley. "The Impulse! Records Story: The House That 'Trane Built." *Jazz Times*, September 2002.

Johnson, Wanda. "Spiderman Raps." *Lincolnian*, May 15, 1970.

Kelly, Pat. "What 'Last Holiday'?" *Safari Lady Speaks*, June 15, 2012.

Kirk, Kris. "Master of the Arts." *Melody Maker*, July 19, 1986.

Kopano, Baruti N. "Black Radio Announcers and Rappers: The Historical and Rhetorical Links." *International Journal of Africana Studies* (Spring 2004).

Kot, Greg. "Rare Appearance Disappoints." *Chicago Tribune*, October 14, 1998.

Kot, Greg. "Song Poet." *Chicago Tribune*, October 9, 1998.

Lawrence, Stephen. "Gil Scott-Heron Is on Parole." *Overland* (Summer 2010).

Lee, Byron. "Gil Scott-Heron: Poet and Prophet." *RiverCity Examiner*, June 2011.

Lee, Felicia R. "Artists Remember Gil Scott-Heron." *New York Times*, May 30, 2011.

Litwack, Leon F. "Fight the Power! The Legacy of the Civil Rights Movement." *Journal of Southern History* (February 2009).

Lynskey, Dorian. "Gil Scott-Heron: Tribute to the Man." *Guardian*, November 14, 2001.

Martin, George. "Gilbert, The Broth of a Boy from Detroit." *Daily Record* (Glasgow), August 22, 1951.

Maslin, Janet. "Musician's Portrait." *New York Times*, January 12, 1983.

Maycock, James. "Gil Scott-Heron and Brian Jackson: Brothers in Arms." *Mojo*, December 2003.

Maycock, James. "Rap's Fallen Godfather." *Times* (London), July 16, 2004.

McKeithan, Larry. "Gil Scott-Heron: Slow Burn to Gold." *New York Amsterdam News*, October 28, 1978.

Melton, R. H., and Rene Sanchez. "Rackley Letter on Addicts Causes Stir." *Washington Post*, August 9, 1990.

"The Messenger . . . Gil Scott-Heron." *Los Angeles Sentinel*, October 26, 1978.

"Midnite Special: Successful, Despite Rude Crowd." *Pittsburgh Courier*, August 31, 1974.

Mike the Poet (Mike Sonksen). "Gil Scott-Heron and Words from His Daughter Gia." KCET, September 7, 2012.

Milloy, Courtland. "It's Good to Hear Gil Scott-Heron's Voice Again." *Washington Post*, August 26, 2009.

Minister of Information JR. "The Mind of Gil Scott-Heron: An Interview wit' the Legendary Musician." *San Francisco Bay View*, October 1, 2009.

Mitchell, Richard. *A Heron Family Forest Grew in Manchester*. Self-published ebook, 2011.

Moore, Marie. "Gil Scott-Heron: Today's Musical Prophet." *New York Amsterdam News*, October 25, 1980.

Murphy, Tom. "Q&A with Gil Scott-Heron." *Denver Westword*, May 1, 2009.

Nichols, John. "Gil Scott-Heron's Revolution." *The Nation*, May 29, 2011.

Nosnitsky, Andrew. "Gil Scott-Heron: More Than a Revolution." *Pitchfork*, January 18, 2012.

Odom, John. "A Requiem for Scotty." *Madison Times*, June 17, 2011.

O'Hagan, Sean. "Gil Scott-Heron: The Godfather of Rap Comes Back." *Observer* (London), February 6, 2010.

Orth, Maureen. "Midnight News." *Newsweek*, February 10, 1975.

Powers, Mike. "The Revolution Will Be Funky." *The Squall*, June 15, 2005.

Prater, David. "Gil Scott-Heron: Ego, Edinburgh." *The Herald* (Edinburgh), June 30, 2000.

Preston, Rohan B. "Scott-Heron's Jazz Poetry Rich in Soul." *Chicago Tribune*, September 20, 1994.

Prince, Diedra. "Gil Scott-Heron: An Electrifying Artist." *Los Angeles Sentinel*, June 5, 1975.

Reel, Penny. "Gil Scott-Heron / John Cooper Clarke: Brixton Academy, London." *NME*, March 24, 1984.

Revolution Will Not Be Televised, The (video). Dir. Don Letts, BBC, 2003.

Richmond, Norman. "Gil Heron, 81, Father of Gil Scott-Heron, Joins the Ancestors." *Pan-African News Wire*, December 26, 2008.

Richmond, Norman. "Norman Richmond Reflects on Gil Scott-Heron." UhuruNews.com, June 12, 2011.

Salaam, Mtume ya. "Gil Scott-Heron: Beginnings." *Breath of Life*, January 1, 2006.

Salaam, Mtume ya, and Kalamu ya Salaam. "Gil Scott-Heron: 'Blue Collar.'" *Breath of Life*, October 21, 2007.

Salaam, Mtume ya. "Gil Scott-Heron & Brian Jackson 'Rivers of My Fathers.'" *Breath of Life*, September 18, 2005.

Sarig, Roni. *The Secret History of Rock*. New York: Billboard Books/Random House, 1998.

Schloss, Joseph. "The Man and the Music." *New Black Magazine*, June 19, 2011.

Schnabel, Tom. "A Tribute to Gil Scott-Heron." KCRW, June 5, 2011.

Schwachter, Jeff. "Gil Scott-Heron: 1949–2011." *Atlantic City Weekly*, May 29, 2011.

Schwachter, Jeff. "Worth the Ride: Gil Scott-Heron Returns." *Atlantic City Weekly*, February 3, 2010.

Scott, Malcolm. "The Revolution Will Not Be Televised: Exploring Contemporary Social Justice Issues in the United States." *Black History Bulletin* (Winter 2005).

Scott-Heron, Gil. "Black Judas." *Lincolnian*, May 15, 1969.

Scott-Heron, Gil. "Circle of Stone" (master's thesis). Johns Hopkins University, Baltimore, MD, 1972.

Scott-Heron, Gil. *The Last Holiday: A Memoir*. New York: Grove Press, 2012.

Scott-Heron, Gil. "Lost in the Shuffle." *Ebony*, July 1975.

Scott-Heron, Gil. *The Nigger Factory*. New York: Dial Press, 1972.

Scott-Heron, Gil. *Now and Then: The Poems of Gil Scott-Heron*. Edinburgh: Canongate Books, 2000.

Scott-Heron, Gil. *So Far, So Good*. Chicago: Third World Press, 1990.

Scott-Heron, Gil. "The Voice of Lincoln Poets." *Lincolnian*, November 15, 1968, and December 20, 1968.

Scott-Heron, Gil. *The Vulture*. Cleveland: World Publishing Company, 1970.

Scott-Heron, Gil. "WLIU Newsmen Need Help." *Lincolnian*, December 20, 1968.

Simmons, Daniel. "His Revolution Is Continued: Gil Scott-Heron's Relationship to Rap Music." *The Griot* (Spring 2007).

Sisario, Ben. "Gil Scott-Heron, Voice of Black Protest Culture, Dies at 62." *New York Times*, May 28, 2011.

Sisson, Patrick. "The Last Poet: Gil Scott-Heron Is Still the First Name on the Rhyme Scene." *Wax Poetics*, August 6, 2010.

Snowden, Don. "Gil Scott-Heron Has Staying Power." *Los Angeles Times*, April 11, 1981.

Stewart, James B. "Message in the Music: Political Commentary in Black Popular Music from Rhythm and Blues to Early Hip-Hop." *Journal of African American History* (Summer 2005).

Stovall, TaRessa. "Gil Scott-Heron at His Peak, in His Prime: Unedited, Uncensored, after the Show." *Ebony*, November 1979.

Tate, Greg. "Gil Scott-Heron, R.I.P." *Village Voice*, May 31, 2011.

"The Tired Revolutionary." *Economist*, June 6, 2011.

Townley, Ray. "El Jefe's Manifesto: An Interview with Gil Scott-Heron." *Down Beat*, April 24, 1975.

Trescott, Jacqueline. "A Voice Tempered by the Times." *Washington Post*, November 6, 1977.

Turner-Collins, Richelle. "Front Line of Change." *Jackson Sun*, August 4, 1997.

Tyer, Brad, Joe Hon, and Jim Sherman. "The Preacher Returns." *Houston Press*, February 2, 1995.

Vasquez, Perry. "'But the Truth Is . . .': A Gil Scott-Heron Interview." *Agitprop*, May 2011.

Waldman, Amy. "A Ravaged Musical Prodigy at a Crossroads with Drugs." *New York Times*, July 10, 2001.

Webber, Brad. "Gil Scott-Heron: Spirits." *Chicago Tribune*, September 29, 1994.

Weller, Sheila. "Gil Scott-Heron: Survival Kits on Wax." *Rolling Stone*, January 2, 1975.

Wilkinson, Alec. "New York Is Killing Me." *The New Yorker*, August 9, 2010.

Williams, Carla. "Hank Willis Thomas: Winter in America." *Journal of Contemporary African Art* (Fall 2007).

Wilson, Brian. "Gil Heron." *Guardian*, December 18, 2008.

INDEX